Never More Alive:

Inside the Spanish Republic

by

Kate Mangan

With a Preface by Paul Preston
and an Afterword by Charlotte Kurzke

The Clapton Press

First published November 2020 by:
THE CLAPTON PRESS LTD,
38 Thistlewaite Road, London E5

ISBN: 978-1-913693-03-9

Contents

Portrait of Kate by Jan Kurzke

List of Illustrations

All illustrations courtesy of Charlotte Kurzke

Dedication

To the memory of William (Bill) McGuire (1917-2009).
Without him this book would never have seen the light of day.[1]

Letters from Kate Mangan to her ex-husband, Sherry Mangan: Extracts.

13 October 1936

Dear Sherry . . .

I was working for a writer (Left) called Ralph Bates, I don't know if you ever heard of him. He knows Spain very well and just went back there; he is quite intelligent; a renegade Catholic and a big fat man like you, only ugly . . .

I thought it would make me feel better to work for the cause. I must go to the Spanish Embassy tomorrow and try to fix about going to fetch Cristina out . . .[2]

I would like to go to Spain and die too – all the people will die because they haven't got any guns or aeroplanes . . .

30 October 1936

This is just to say that I went to Barcelona to fetch Tina and am now back in Paris with her. But I couldn't resist the war atmosphere of excitement and *alegría* and am returning there tomorrow as I have joined up . . .

Preface by Paul Preston

No one knows with absolute certainty how many books have been written about the various aspects of the Spanish Civil War but there is little doubt that they number somewhere in the region of thirty thousand. It goes without saying that the range of quality could not be wider. Academic works abound, of course. There exist many works of unashamed propaganda, a majority of which have emanated from the Francoist side in the conflict, but there is also a substantial minority of partisan works defending Communist, anarchist or other left-wing groups. Then there are the thousands of memoirs, many by politicians and senior military figures who grind their respective axes with varying degrees of honesty and many others by people who experienced the war in some way or other without being a celebrity or wielding power.

It is among these latter 'non-celebrity' memoirs that Kate Mangan's wonderful book is to be found. I will come right out and say that, ever since I first read the manuscript about fifteen years ago, I have longed to see it in print. I regarded it when I first read it, and ever more so with each subsequent reading, as one of the most valuable and, incidentally, purely enjoyable books about the war. My admiration is a response to the sheer wealth of fascinating information and insight provided in brutally honest yet beautiful prose.

At its core, this is a moving story of the travails of love in wartime but it is so much more. Born in 1904 as Katherine Prideaux Foster, Kate was an attractive artist, who had studied at the Slade School of Art in University College, London and also worked for a couturier as a mannequin. She was unreservedly left-wing without having a specific party allegiance. In 1931, she had married the Irish-American Marxist novelist Sherry Mangan whom she had met in Paris in 1924 when they were both aged twenty. Partly because of money difficulties but also Sherry's jealousy of her ability as a writer, they separated in 1934 and divorced the following year. In 1935, she fell in love with Jan

Kurzke, a German who had come to London on the run from the Nazis. In late 1935 and the spring of 1936, they spent several idyllic months in Spain and Portugal. In these memoirs, she provides a colourful account of their boat journey to Lisbon and about the poverty and the ubiquitous police presence in Salazar's Portugal. In the plush resorts of Cascaes and Estoril, she describes the Spanish reactionaries in their gilded exile from the Popular Front: 'They were fat and well dressed with big motor cars and numerous polite, befrilled children, servants and foreign governesses . . . the Spanish colony of Portugal is not dead, but flourishes like the green bay tree in all its parasitical uselessness and vulgarity.'

Briefly back in London, she approved of Jan's precipitate decision to volunteer to fight in the International Brigades despite feeling great concern and trepidation. Eventually, eaten up with worry, she had gone to Spain in October 1936 in the hope of being with him. At first, she picked up casual jobs as an interpreter in Barcelona and then went to Madrid where she acted as secretary to an old friend from London, Humphrey Slater, with whom she had studied at the Slade. Through Slater, she met Tom Wintringham, the senior British Communist who would soon be the commander of the British battalion in the International Brigades, although officially he had come to Spain as a correspondent of the CPGB's newspaper, the *Daily Worker*. Through Humphrey and Tom, she met a 'petite and vivacious American girl' called Katherine 'Kitty' Bowler. Kate would eventually find herself sharing a hotel room with her and 'swept into the whirl of Kitty's life'.

Having located Jan, she could meet him only sporadically. When he was seriously wounded, she threw herself into a desperate search to find where he had been taken, then devoted herself to caring for him and finally to the complex task of getting him released and back to England. In between, thanks to Kitty Bowler, she got a job in the Republic's press office in Valencia, which had become the capital when the government had left Madrid on 6 November 1936. There, she worked as an interpreter and translator. As a result of her experiences, her perceptions of the political context in which she existed are fascinating.

What she went through to trace Jan and later care for him provides the basis for unique insights into the experiences of an International Brigader both in the front line and behind the lines. Her account of hospital conditions – the lack of drugs and of trained staff, poor hygiene – provides real understanding of the appalling difficulties faced by the Republican medical services. Kate's is not the only account of the privations suffered by the volunteers – not allowed to go on leave, given poor food, without mail from home, inadequately clad. However, her account sparkles with revealing detail such as how those fighting in the Philosophy and Arts building in Madrid's University City built barricades of books to protect their machine gun emplacements, then settled down to wait for action: 'The scholars read old books in Greek and Latin, for several of the English were from Oxford and Cambridge.'

In fact, the entire book teems with insights into the Spanish Civil War. Her account of her time in the besieged Madrid could hardly be more vivid. As the highest capital city in Europe, winter in Madrid is always bitterly cold. In November 1936, it was worse than usual since coal from the Asturian mines could not reach Madrid. There was almost no central heating or hot water in the hotels.

Kate describes *madrileños* eschewing their habitually late dinners and eating at 7.30 or 8 pm, 'since bed was about the only warm place in any home, most residents were there by 9'. 'The cold got into my bones. Nowhere was there any heating and, though I gave up washing and went to bed in most of my clothes, I was never warm and ached and shivered at night so that I could not sleep.' It was so cold that her fingers sometimes froze to her typewriter keys. She recounts having to queue for everything, coal, food, even matches. Yet she never loses her ability to see the funny side of things: 'I do not know what went into the bread, possibly rice flour, but it was only just possible to eat it when fresh; within a few hours it became stone-like and would have made a dangerous missile or a solid barricade.' Of the one bar where you could get whisky, she writes wryly: 'Here one found journalists, commercial aviators and whores still clean and fairly smart, though the ones with bleach-blond hair were becoming piebald for lack of peroxide. It was all at the hospitals and plenty of nurses had blond hair.'

In late 1936, she moved to the very different atmosphere of Valencia where the weather was warmer and food relatively abundant. Every bit as compelling as the recollections of Madrid are her recollections of working in the press office. There she came into contact with a gamut of literary celebrities, politicians, secret agents and war reporters – contacts that she describes vividly and often with a wicked sense of humour. Indeed, her memoirs could be plundered by literary biographers for her unique descriptions of the famous literary figures that she met. These include a sneeringly arrogant Claud Cockburn and a painfully shy W.H. Auden whose literary skills are wasted by the press office other than allowing him to make a superb translation of a speech by the Republican President, Manuel Azaña. Kate liked Stephen Spender for his humility and eagerness to help: 'He was a very tall, thin young man, with open collar and a leather jacket. He had a rather bony, Viking face and wildly straying hair. He looked red and wind-blown and rather distrait.' She depicted the then world-famous American novelist John Dos Passos as 'yellow, small and bespectacled'. He was staying at the Hotel Colón which had been renamed the *Casa de Cultura* and reserved for visiting intellectuals, artists and writers. Locally, it was known as the *Casa de los Sabios* (the house of the wise men) although Kate regarded it as 'a kind of zoo for intellectuals'.

Utterly memorable and rather less reverential than conventional views are Kate's portraits of two celebrity couples, the photographers Robert Capa and Gerda Taro and Ernest Hemingway and Martha Gellhorn. Of Capa and Taro, she wrote: 'They were a striking-looking couple. He was tall and thin with dead black eyes. She was a ripe beauty, with a tanned face and bright orange hair cropped like a boy's. The natural tint of her hair was copper, she had the warm brown eyes that go with it, but the sun had bleached it orange and the effect was startling. She was full-bosomed, very handsome but for her head being a bit too large for her height. She wore a little, round, Swiss cap on the back of the astonishing hair. She had small feet and was a model of

Parisian *sportif chic*. She radiated sex-appeal . . . Capa and Gerda talked about Spain and the beautiful sunshine quite as if they were on holiday, which I thought very frivolous, but they did not neglect their work. They were always ready to leap from the car to take significantly grim pictures and were merely personally detached from their subjects.'

She captures precisely the insecurity that underlay the bravado of Hemingway who 'always came with a large entourage and always wanted to go to Madrid at once. He was a huge, red man, in hairy speckled tweeds, with a crushing handshake. He looked like a successful businessman which, I suppose, was the impression he wished to make. The first time I saw him, he came with Sidney Franklin, a former bullfighter, and two Dutch cameramen, to make the film *Spanish Earth*. One always had the feeling that there were several shadowy, unidentifiable, obsequious figures in the background while Hemingway, the great man, was in the foreground.' Martha Gellhorn 'was handsome in a rather predatory way, with a beaky nose and brilliant eyes. She had an elegant coiffure, a linen dress and a perfectly even sun tan. She wore her skirt rather short, and sat on the table swinging her long, slim legs in a provocative manner. The Spaniards disapproved of this. They believed that sexuality should be directed only at one person at a time, preferably in private.'

Her pages are replete with striking vignettes. Of the two customs men who tried to impede her entry into Barcelona, she writes: 'One was small, desiccated, with beady black eyes, lively as a flea; he wore a little forage cap, half red and half black, that made him look as if he came out of a circus. The other one was very pale with a scar, a high-necked jersey and a beret rammed down like a skull-cap; he was much more reminiscent of the French Revolution *à la lanterne* and as though determined nothing should betray him into a smile.' With equal perceptiveness, she comments of 'Valencian farmers who were holding an orange-growers convention. The orange-growers, plump, rosy and steaming, loud-voiced, with big dripping umbrellas, who clustered thickest after lunch, had apparently no consciousness of the war at all. They were only concerned with the difficulties of marketing their produce that year.'

This fits in with her acute comments on the insouciant lack of awareness of the war that she noted in Catalunya both when she first arrived: 'At that time in Barcelona, the general public was no more aware of what was going on in Madrid than on the moon.' By the time that she was en route out of Spain with the disabled Jan, in the late summer of 1937, there was little sense of a war going on and one that was likely to be lost: 'Very few wounded were about and Jan was regarded with astonishment and asked about the war as if it had nothing to do with Catalunya. Cafés and restaurants were crowded with young men of military age and smart girls.'

Kate's job brought her into contact with politicians as well as literary figures. Juan García Oliver, the one-time anarchist gunman who was now the Republic's Minister of Justice, 'lived in our hotel and was a small, high-coloured, youngish man with bright blue eyes.' The Socialist Prime Minister, Francisco Largo Caballero 'was an old, wrinkled man with pale, shifty blue eyes.' The President Manuel Azaña is accurately depicted as 'a short, fat man with a bald head, receding forehead, wire-rimmed spectacles and a large mole on his chin' and perceptively analysed as being '. . . afraid of doing the wrong thing . . . and did not really want to go on with the war. He was a liberal and would have given up sooner if he had dared.' The attempts of Franz Borkenau, the celebrated Austrian sociologist, to have a sexual liaison with a twenty year-old university student are behind the portrait of 'a dirty old man', 'the professor who was personally greasy and unattractive.' In contrast, Kate pays tribute to the smooth talk of the Comintern's brilliant propagandist, Otto Katz, the real brains behind the Spanish Press Agency in Paris, the Agence Espagne. His flattery put stiff and rather grand English ladies, the Duchess of Atholl, Eleanor Rathbone and Ellen Wilkinson, entirely at their ease.

Kate did not spend all of her time either in the press office or seeking Jan. She also travelled with *Times* correspondent Lawrence Fernsworth and other journalists to investigate the plight of the thousands of refugees fleeing the repression in Málaga along the coast road to Almería. Her grim account of meeting the bedraggled fugitives there is a valuable addition to the important accounts of the tragedy written by Dr Norman Bethune and T.C. Worsley. Contacts with diplomats yield considerable insight into the anti-Republican attitude of London's foreign policy. A shocking revelation came from a conversation with the British Vice-Consul in Almería: 'We asked him if it was true that British warships were taking supplies into Málaga now that it had fallen to Franco and he said it was. We then asked if any of them were coming up here with food and he said not.' Even more shocking, if hardly surprising, was the remark of another British diplomat about International Brigade volunteers: 'I do not see why we should stand in the way of these fellows who come and get killed in Spain. We shall get rid of a lot of undesirables this way.'

Kate's views on the difficulties of the Republic add to what can be learned from academic studies: 'the Spanish Republic was sinking under the weight of the refugees and the problem of feeding so many people. There was little sustaining food to be had. Most of the wheat was grown on the other side of Spain. We had a little rice and, in Catalunya, some potatoes. The fishermen were afraid to go out because of mines. As the Republic shrank in territory, it increased in population, and was much greater than on the other side. Every town and village was swarming with people, women and children, old people, gypsies, all the poorest of the poor, all helpless and without possessions.' So much of what Kate writes about is bleak yet neither the elegance of her prose nor her sense of humour flag. She captures the shambolic improvisation of the popular militias in quoting a remark by her sister Greville: 'Oh, we encourage fancy dress in our column,' she said, 'it keeps up the morale. Some people wear fur hats like Cossacks, and some big straw ones like Mexicans, and some have feathers like Red Indians.' Her priceless description of the journey from Lisbon back to London in July 1936 includes the comment: 'Several of the stewards were actually sailors recovering from appendix operations and thus given over to light duties such as spilling soup over people.' Regarding one extremely serious issue – the opposition to the military coup by the miners in the northern part of the province of Huelva, as recounted by the Portuguese press – she cannot restrain her sense of humour: 'The Río Tinto miners were described as having joined forces with the workers in a sausage factory and, armed with sausages and sticks of dynamite, were said to be running about in trucks terrorising the countryside.'

Beyond the specifics of the press office and the hospitals, Kate also captures something important about the spirit of the Republican war effort. Despite overwhelming odds against them, millions of ordinary Spaniards went on fighting to defend the Republic that had given them educational opportunities, women's rights and social reforms. Kate, even as a foreigner, present only for one year of the war, seems to have felt this. She writes: 'All through the war, one had a wonderful feeling of freedom from the responsibility and individual worries of ordinary life. Once I got used to it, I never worried any more about possessions, or money, or when I would get anywhere, or where the next meal was coming from. Possessions did not seem to matter; I had very few with me but nothing I clung to except my typewriter.' That sense of exhilaration seems not to have survived the difficulties that she faced in getting Jan back to England. When they reached Paris, she reflected, in what was a terrible epitaph for Jan and the International Brigades as a whole: 'Jan had done something which a few people thought heroic, to which many Spaniards were indifferent, and which had to be hidden, like a crime, in the country to which he returned.'

Chapter 1
Summer in Portugal

It was June 1936 that Jan and I took passage to Lisbon. We had a peculiar send-off as a group of people assembled outside our carriage at the station in London and sang *For Those in Peril on the Sea* and other hymns. There were some evangelical missionaries in the carriage and, on the boat, I shared a cabin with one. She was always on her knees and I always fell over her as I opened the door. She was bound for Angola.

At Southampton, the Poles came aboard, and many more at Cherbourg. They were emigrants bound for South America. They were mostly Catholic peasants, big people, blond and snub-nosed. The women and little girls wore flowered kerchiefs over their heads and a great many petticoats which increased in number when the weather was cold. The men and boys wore high-crowned black felt hats or caps with very long peaks. Their baskets and bundles were labelled 'disinfected'. They slept in 'family' cabins with eight or more bunks, very stuffy, emanating a stable-like smell. They were very seasick and broke indiscriminately into lavatories for either sex and the boat was always in a filthy mess. They carried chunks of bread and garlic about with them which they gnawed from time to time.

As a rule, I have found that third class passengers and stewards on boats are inclined to behave as equals and fraternise, but in this case the stewards evidently considered themselves quite a cut above the passengers socially. One particularly hideous peasant woman, who bared her teeth rather than smiled, was the object of pleasantries from a steward who amused himself by flirting with her in a language she did not understand. 'Have a bit more, my pretty dear,' he would say, winking at us. The food was vile. Whenever the Poles seemed unhappy, plates of pickled cucumbers were put on their tables. These disappeared in an instant and seemed to have a soothing effect.

Besides the Poles, there were a few tall Russians and some orthodox Jews on board. When we had lifeboat drill the interpreter had to give instructions to the different groups. We got into the wrong group and had all the shipwreck arrangements explained to us in Russian. There was an old Jew, with side-whiskers and a little black cap, whose life-belt was tied at the back to a fat old woman by some sportive boys. He made a terrible row in Yiddish at the indignity as they struggled vainly to separate.

After three days with these assorted shipmates we reached Portugal.

* * * * *

Kate and Jan in Portugal, Summer 1936

Portugal in Baedeker signifies many historic monuments and picturesque scenes. We had a Baedeker – Spain and Portugal – and studied it often enough, particularly the maps, trying to discover what the scenery would be like for painting and, later, the terrain for fighting.

To us Portugal signified fish, police and poverty. There was the usual evidence of modern progress it is true, fast automobiles knocking down poor old washerwomen and rickety children, and a blaring radio in the square day and night.

There were several dilapidated, uninhabited palaces, one a faded pink with statues in the park, imitating Versailles, one with onion turrets on the corners and one with immense Moorish chimneys like Kentish oast-houses. Officious officials pursued us in every field and garden driving us off, forbidding sketching or photography or merely walking. Everything appeared to be owned by the absent duke of this or the count of that.

Whenever there were trees, which was not often, Baedeker spoke of 'luxuriant vegetation'. There were desolate, dusty, wayside halts where we changed buses, beset by flies and starving mongrels. Peasants stood and stared in hostile fashion, looking fearsome in their black, stockinged caps.

The police were everywhere, even on the beach when the bleary fishermen, slopping up to the waist in the cold Atlantic in their faded tartan trousers, landed the catch from their unwieldy boats through the breaking surf.

The fish, many and strange, with queer faces like dragons, looked like things from the pictures of hell by Hieronymus Bosch. Some were long and thin and shining like writhing swords. There were sacks full of crabs, some crawling out at the top while others could be seen through the cloth, slowly turning and struggling.

Sometimes at night the fish were ranged in piles on the wet sand and, by the infernal light of flares, the buyers screamed shrilly bidding for them. Fishwives, barefoot, in blue-green patterned kerchiefs and short, black skirts, oval trays on their heads, tramped about with their wares. Superannuated fishermen smelling like the beach and everything else, of a mixture of dirt, tar and fish, were vending grey shrimps. In back streets the fisherfolk fried the unwanted residue on charcoal braziers.

Great monsters of the deep were hacked up with a chopper on the battlements of the fort where we stayed and there was an octopus hanging in the sun to dry from a turret like a malefactor.

Sesimbra, or Cezimbra (the Portuguese themselves are undecided) is a picturesque fishing village among bare hills surmounted by creaking windmills. The boats are vividly painted, with almond-shaped eyes on the bows. The place is frequented by one or two Scandinavian artists. The bed bugs are legion and infest the entire village. However, one can buy Japanese insect powder and the man at the café makes his own potent poison gas which knocks out bugs for some hours but may have the same effect on humans.

There the *pensión* was over a shop. Someone died so the shutters were put up and the sewing machine was busy on shoddy black clothes smelling of dye. In spite of this, the stumpy girl, with red eyes, hung round our table urging us to eat more.

The nights were tropical and moonlit; we were afraid to go to bed and spent them, until the small hours, in an outdoor cinema. Along the whitewashed walls were ledges on which grimy urchins slept in heaps on top of one another. Occasionally, one would wake and nudge the next one, the nudging and pushing would run down the whole row and all would sit up chattering and scratching.

We took the ferry across the Tagus as there was said to be a fine view of Lisbon from the other side. A fat rat ran out and along the railing of the deck. The fish-wives screamed and lifted their skirts in dismay, huddling into the opposite corner. A man with a stick ineffectually chased the animal which quickly disappeared below again.

We took a bus along a corniche road, described with enthusiasm for its vista in Baedeker, and ended up with an unexpectedly macabre view. Past a white, dusty quarry, under an archway up against a cliff, we were confronted by pale and ghastly faces peering through the barred and slit-like windows of a fort which had been turned into a sanatorium for the tubercular poor.

In Cascaes, we saw children in spinal carriages with umbrellas fixed over their heads. The cook there was fat and had epileptic fits and her narrow-faced, narrow-chested little daughter was consumptive. The child was olive-green round her burning, dark eyes and was given to silly giggling fits.

There was a little girl who sang on the street in a harsh, cracked voice, strained from premature usage but extraordinarily penetrating for her size, an endless, monotonous song. She also sold song-sheets.

But I am forgetting the high life which existed in Estoril and, to a lesser extent, in Cascaes. There was an English colony, mostly elderly and eccentric shrivelled hags, people fond of the bottle or with other vices; much the same as one finds in every sunny, southern resort.

Then there was the Spanish colony. Some of the Spaniards had been long in residence but the majority had either been warned and fled just before the Popular Front Government got in or very soon after, smuggling their wealth with them. As 'refugees' they looked very flourishing but wailed and complained about what they had suffered and lost, demanding sympathy as such refugees always do and abusing their enemies with unusual vindictiveness and arrogance. They were fat and well dressed with big motor cars and numerous polite, befrilled children, servants and foreign governesses. They played at the Casino, or sat on the beach with much paraphernalia in the way of sunshades, tents and bags, the aproned nursemaids standing at the water's edge, towels in hand, ready to wrap their charges as they came out.

The beach was patrolled by a sailor of the Portuguese Navy armed with a sword, who arrested men who uncovered their chests. Plump, smiling girls came round with tin ovens on their heads containing trays of fresh and fragrant cakes. This was Cascaes. Estoril was more cosmopolitan and one might even wear shorts there.

Estoril was a brand new, imitation French Riviera resort. It was bare and glaring as the ornamental trees and shrubs had had no time to grow up and everything else had been hacked down to make room for new roads and those desert wastes known as development sites. There were white marbled arcades with very expensive shops and, up a quite unnecessary number of flights of steps, the Casino, shadeless and floridly hideous.

In this atmosphere and environment we saw nothing sinister, no signs of plotting. We saw, of course, that all the high society was very reactionary, very bitter about the Popular Front and very angry at the decrees passed restricting people from taking their wealth out of Spain.

Kate and Jan in Portugal, Summer 1936

It was perhaps our last carefree holiday when, bronzed and healthy, we had no qualms of conscience nor nervousness at the sight of ships, aeroplanes or newspapers. Now, anywhere on the blue sea, in the warm sun, amongst the summer villas, I think of similar places on the same sea that seemed equally peaceful and idyllic, where old people had settled down to idle away the rest of their days – and I think of what happened there. As I watch a harbour being deepened and a mole built I remember autumn 1935 in Pollensa, Majorca; there I watched the harbour being enlarged and never dreamt that by the following autumn it would be a base for submarines. I sat there convivially in the café with Republican *mallorquines*. Where are they now? Probably dead, like most of the finest people in this story.

However, the Spanish colony of Portugal is not dead, but flourishes like the green bay tree in all its parasitical uselessness and vulgarity. It seems that all the well-intentioned, humanitarian, liberal people like ourselves were deaf and blind to the tragedy that was brewing.

Before that fatal date in July we took walks past the antiquated fortress barracks, where the scrubby little soldiers with olive faces and olive uniforms hung over the battlements, watching the officers play tennis in the dry moat; past the marble war memorial of a soldier lunging forward with a bayonet, which economically commemorated the fallen both in the Peninsular War and the war of 1914-1918.

At weekends, on the promenade between fort and sea, was a fair where one spun a wheel and could win live prizes: rabbits, ducks and chickens. Jan won a very small, skinny chicken which we had to carry about all evening and which spent the night tied to the leg of our bed and made more mess than one would have thought possible for its size. At the fair, Jan was quite a champion at rifle-shooting at little earthenware pots dangling on wires. He was so good that a crowd collected and shouted, 'He is wasted here, he ought to be in a war!'

* * * * *

We were bored and decided to go to the south of Spain though our acquaintances darkly predicted trouble and tried to dissuade us. We paid no attention as we knew they were reactionary and afraid of the Popular Front. Though consuls regarded us oddly we went through the necessary formalities and reserved seats on the Lisbon-Seville bus for the Monday. On Saturday alarming rumours were afloat; we were told *tudo chave* ('all shut', meaning the frontier), which Thomas Cook's confirmed. We still did not take it seriously. We thought it would blow over in a few days. The Portuguese authorities were always nervous and that year had already closed the frontier for a bit just after the elections.

The international trains were no longer running and news now came in only late and slow, by boat. Morning and evening we pored over the *Noticias* and *Diario* and tried to understand the Portuguese radio. It was all about the 'glorious liberating movement' and fantastic atrocity stories about the 'reds'. Many days later we tried to get at the truth via the columns of *The*

23

Times which at least printed the assertions of both sides. We then first heard of Generals Franco,[3] Mola[4] and Queipo de Llano.[5] The papers were saying that Franco was about to make a landing from Morocco and Mola would march on Madrid.

The English residents, the Spanish colony, the South Americans and the Portuguese exhibited such a deplorable morale that it certainly was not through any such people that Franco obtained his success. They alternated between panic and a quite despicable terror of the 'reds', chiefly the very obvious terror of losing their worldly goods; and the most crude and vulgar exultation over the victories won for them by the mercenaries, and the executions that were reported. I never believed in a decadent and useless aristocracy until I witnessed the behaviour of the Spanish colony in Estoril, their shameless egoism, their abject cowardice and their ruthless *sauve que peut* in moments of depression.

Most young Spaniards there, fat and spoiled, were not inclined to fight for the movement but only to talk in cafés. 'Let the Moors and the *Tercio* do the dirty work' was their attitude.[6] They would wait until they saw which way the cat was going to jump and then hope to return in triumph and claim their estates.

The first tangible sign of the war was a bullet-scarred car which was left for some days parked in the square. There was always an excited crowd round this trophy. It was said to have brought a family from Badajoz and only the chauffeur had been wounded. On the windscreen was pasted a very amateurish-looking label: *Médico*, I suppose for protection. We examined this vehicle carefully. Inside there were no bloodstains, nor was the upholstery damaged. There were bullet-holes in the roof but the metal was torn as though someone had been firing from within the car. No glass was broken.

Some wealthy South American acquaintances made a hasty trip by car into the province of Cáceres to see about some securities they had in a bank there. However, at first, most of the movement of private people was in the other direction; more Spanish refugees than ever of the upper classes, all with horror stories. We kept our heads but most of the foreign residents fled for home. I have seldom so despised my countrymen.

One day, the South Americans were having tea with us; a stout, moustached lady powdered mauve, with a beautiful, juicy, marriageable daughter in satin, and several male hangers-on. The mother held an imaginary rifle to her shoulder and closed one hard, black eye as she said with astonishing ferocity: 'Ah, if I had one of those reds here I would shoot him, so!' The face and gesture were reminiscent of that of the daughter of the wicked *hacendado* in Eisenstein's film *Thunder over Mexico*; the same huntress of the humble, the same hard-boiled frivolity.[7] Women have least mercy. She did not suspect what kind of neighbours she had; Jan said not a word.

Tea was just served when we were surprised by the sound of a plane passing overhead, which was very unusual in Cascaes. Perhaps ten minutes later the fire bell was rung furiously. We all hung over the balcony as the house looked over the main square and commanded an excellent view of the fire-station. Only a short time before, the firemen had given a demonstration of their skill in saving people from shipwreck which was a complete failure but, fortunately was only a pretence staged for the benefit of the president, who was on a warship lying off the rocks. He had grown impatient, however, and left long before they arrived. On this occasion they rushed out, buttoning their uniforms, and rattled off somewhere in a great hurry.

The plane was a private one which had been taking General Sanjurjo, Marqués de Riff, to insurgent Spain. It was leaving from a small, private woodland when it caught fire. The pilot jumped out and escaped with broken bones but the General, who was strapped in, was, as the papers said, 'totally carbonised'. All the Spanish colony had turned out to see him off and witnessed the scene. He had a big funeral mass in Estoril with a uniformed guard of honour who stood with arms upraised.

It is difficult to remember the sequence of events as, at first, the war moved distressingly fast. Vigo and La Coruña fell to the insurgents but, for a longer time, the country on the southern frontier of Portugal held out.

The Río Tinto miners were described as having joined forces with the workers in a sausage factory and, armed with sausages and sticks of dynamite, were said to be running about in trucks terrorising the countryside. Jan badly wanted to join them but it would have been madness. If he had succeeded in avoiding arrest at the hostile Portuguese frontier he stood a chance of being shot by the Spanish miners as a suspicious foreigner since he had no credentials to prove his intentions and was not fluent in Spanish. Not long afterwards we read that the Río Tinto bands had been 'cleaned up' by Franco. I do not remember whether this was before or after the fall of Badajoz.

That was greeted with open rejoicing; the newspapers gloated over the massacres and boasted that the streets were running with blood. I wish that I had kept copies as evidence; not that people ever heed such evidence. After the fall of Badajoz, which is not far from the frontier, a sightseeing bus was run from Lisbon to look at the ruins.

We felt imprisoned in this narrow strip of country between the sea and a burning Spain. We read the headlines: '*Málaga en chamas*' (Málaga in flames); residents of Gibraltar said the sky was red with burning churches. That town must have been burnt more than any other, at least by report, for this was only the beginning.

We were terribly restless and unhappy. Jan spent all his time trying to find a way to go and fight for Republican Spain and my approval did not decrease my anxiety. The final decision was taken after going to the cinema. It was an open-air performance and a windy night and I caught a fearful cold. We saw the French film about the Spanish Foreign Legion called '*La Bandera*', made under the auspices of General Franco and General Millán Astray.[8] It showed an officer, modelled on Astray, with one arm and a sinister black patch over one eye. I suppose the Portuguese thought it topical as we were reading daily about the 'glorious *Tercio*' entering towns in triumph. The hero of this film, played by Jean Gabin, is a murderer escaped from justice. The heroine, played by Annabella, is an Arab girl in a house of ill repute. Jan was influenced by the film. It was not that it inspired him with animosity against the men of the Legion but it made him want to lead such a life, and perhaps death, of hardship and comradeship in a cause he believed in.

He returned home much excited and we talked it over that

night. I was very sad but quite agreed with him. He said he would never forgive himself if he did not help to fight fascism. The issue was quite clear to him. He planned to go from France to Catalunya. I stipulated that we should have a couple of weeks more together, but throughout that time he was impatient and fearful that Madrid would fall and the war would be lost before he could get there. He said he would not go if it seemed useless suicide to do so.

*   *   *   *   *

This last period was spent in a lonely fort transformed into a inn. It was the most romantic place and the time there had the double sweetness of the last of summer and of our holiday and uncertainty about the future. We pretended to ignore the outside world as we rambled along the vast, sandy, deserted beach picking up stones and seaweed and fashioning surrealist objects out of them.

In jest, Jan posed for a photo outside the sentry box or lookout post on the roof, holding a stick instead of a gun. Looking out of our solid, hewn-stone room at the sea was like being some story-book prisoner; it was like living in the Château d'If.

On moonlit nights we watched the pale green, curved fishing boats, like gondolas rowing round the point on which our castle stood, always a hard pull as the current was especially strong there.

In the wooded mountains behind the fort was an uninhabited monastery, white in the midst of dark evergreens, the spread of buildings looking, in the distance, like a town. It was a steep climb under a shady tunnel of ilex. At the top was a wonderful cold well. The entrance to the monastery was concealed. Over the inner door was the figure of a monk in a brown robe and hood, blindfolded, his ears stopped and his heart and lips padlocked. Lying about were a mass of distorted, bearded, broken statues, one on horseback, which Jan used to paint. They looked like the remains of a crowd after a bombardment.

The weather was breaking; we sometimes had mornings with white sea-fog, and a gale round our castle at night. We, with the thinning ranks of summer visitors, were quite cut off from news.

When we returned to Cascaes we read of the landing in and failure to take Majorca which had been attempted from Barcelona, and of how a Catalan column was marching on Zaragoza but was stuck for so long on the outskirts of Huesca. Jan foresaw then the serious consequences of the loss of Majorca and that all the east coast would be exposed to air attacks.

The day we were leaving we read of the fall of Irún. A few days later there was an unsuccessful attempt, on the part of the Portuguese fleet, to mutiny and leave the Tagus to join the Spanish navy which remained loyal to the Republic.

In Paris we saw a terrible newsreel, before the censor had taken the Spanish war in hand, of the attack on Majorca. I remember the helpless, canvas-shod feet of wounded men approaching the camera as they were carried down the gang-plank of a boat. At Irún there were men throwing tins of dynamite and there were handsome girls with rifles at impro-vised barricades.

Our company on the boat, which came from South America, was very different to that on the voyage out. It included a phenomenal number of bed bugs, particularly in the dark inside cabins, which the steward asserted were introduced by the emigrants. He said he had burnt the springs of the bunks with a blow-torch and all to no effect. 'We don't like them either, they are nasty things,' he said. I wondered how they were prevented from straying into the second and first class, since bugs are no respecters of persons. It was an old ship, long since broken up.

Besides what Baedeker calls 'the enemies of repose' there were Spaniards of various kinds all looking askance at one another, unsure which side they were on, who were hurrying back to Madrid to look after their interests and find out what was happening. There was a multitude of South American newspaper correspondents commissioned to get at the truth, for it was a time of general confusion. There were survivors of a shipwreck and there was the adventurer. Several of the stewards were actually sailors recovering from appendix operations and thus given over to light duties such as spilling soup over people. The number of these appendix cases must prove something or other about the British merchant service.

The ship had been a French one. The crew, including the fat, jolly cook, all wore very dirty and crumpled clothes, being all they had; the stewardess, a noble, angular woman who had been decorated for her heroism; and the ship's tabby cat, were all being repatriated. The cat was a great pet and wore a tricolour ribbon. The stewardess also wore a tricolour ribbon across her bosom when we had a party, and she sang about the flowers in the spring in a very quavery voice. The ship's crew sang indescribably lewd songs.

The adventurer was English, strikingly handsome and sun-burnt, with a moustache. He wore a tropical suit and said he had lost his money on a fruit farm. He was cheery, a good mixer, and knew all about the passengers. It was not the last we saw of him. In Spain, I considered anyone who I could call on for help as a friend, and he was one of them. I cannot betray his real name because I never knew what it was. We called him 'the Man from Buenos Aires'.

The boat stood off Vigo for a few hours while cargo was discharged. In the distance on a hill, outside the town, probably outside the cemetery, I saw the tiny figures of a firing squad at work.

The only other military event which occurred between our return to England and Jan's departure was the siege and relief of the Alcázar at Toledo which we followed with hope at first and could not understand the final outcome. The real story was by no means revealed in the papers.

Chapter 2
London—Barcelona

Seeing one's man off to the front must always be bad enough but, under normal circumstances, when one can be openly proud of the hero and the bands are playing and there is sympathy and glory, there are some compensations. At that time, Autumn 1936, the International Brigades were not yet organised or acknowledged.[9] Jan went off to Spain secretly, like a criminal, because of the decision of the Non-Intervention Committee.[10] He absolutely forbade me to speak of it until I had heard from him and he knew he had crossed the frontier safely. My grief and gnawing anxiety had to be suppressed. I was not even allowed to see him off in case suspicion should be aroused.

By one of the chances of a bohemian existence we happened to be staying in the top storey of an empty house which was being redecorated and only contained a minimum of furniture. The night before Jan left he had to go out so I too accepted, unwillingly, an invitation. I went out in evening dress, the last time for many months, to a hotel dance. Like Cinderella, I fled at midnight pleading indisposition, just as the lights went down and the cabaret was beginning. I had gulped my champagne and hiccupped slightly as I got out of the taxi and approached the tall, dark house through the autumn fog.

Jan was tired from running around on last minute errands; he had been to a show with friends, and he was feverish from a typhoid injection. I tried not to jostle his swollen arm and lay awake most of the night in order to be sure of waking him in time. The electric light was not working and we lay watching the wintry dawn outside the curtainless window. As our room was the only one in any semblance of order I brought up our breakfast on a tray.

I had promised not to cry and kept a frozen face. I made conversation about trifles. In a final fit of generosity Jan kept pulling things out of his half empty bag and giving them to me. At last he had little more than woollen underwear, a pair of overalls (the militia were fighting in overalls) and a pocket edition of *Hamlet*, a strange choice for a man of action. He was so afraid of a scene, it was only the day before that he had broken the news to me that he had really arranged to go.

I stood in my dressing-gown, my hair uncombed, probably looking my worst. I was oblivious, listening to his steps echoing down the uncarpeted flights of stairs. I waited for him to appear at the door and walk down the neglected garden path. At the gate he turned and waved. I watched him in the grey mist walking to the tram-stop where he stood waiting, with his small bag, his old felt hat jauntily on the back of his head, his mackintosh over his arm. He stood among the early people going to their business in the City and none of them knew he was not one of them; that his business was to go off, quietly and unobtrusively, to a war. I hoped he would turn his head again but he did not, he just got on the tram with the others and was lost to view.

After he had gone I remembered other things he should have had and I sped down to Camden Town to buy army socks and a bottle of iodine so small I realise now it would have been useless for more than a scratch. These, with a thick fisherman's jersey, I did up in a clumsy parcel with a note and I went off to try to dispatch it. The post office refused parcels for Spain; so did the American Express in Haymarket. I went, shabby and dishevelled, to the Park Lane Hotel where I got it on an Air France plane, sending it care of friends to Paris.

He sent a note from Paris, thanking me and sending also a book of Pompeiian paintings which we had admired together. Then I heard no more. I wrote several times to different pre-arranged addresses in Barcelona. I even sent a card (of a Gauguin) suggesting that if he had time he should go to the art museum at Montjuich!

* * * * *

From the time Jan left, I intended to go to Spain though I never told anyone the real reason. If getting to Spain had entailed an interview with the Prime Minister or the Pope I should have had no hesitation in trying it. Lack of money and a complete lack

31

of 'Left' political affiliations did not hamper me.

I approached everyone who had any Spanish connections, either directly or by scraping an acquaintance with them where possible or, failing that, I bullied friends to approach them. I offered to work for the cause, of course. Fortunately I found an excuse to go to Spain as it was decided that someone should go and bring my little niece back to England. I obtained an introduction to the Spanish Ambassador to ask for a safe-conduct, and I offered to take out supplies for the Spanish Medical Aid. This offer was refused in the coldest terms – I was told 'we have our own channels' and they would not even divulge the address of the Medical Aid in Barcelona. In those days political suspicion and generally exaggerated mystification were the rule in anything connected with Spain and I survived this rebuff. I may say that most of those I approached were as discouraging as possible, doubted my intentions, and described many dangers and difficulties which never materialised. I had no idea what to take with me as some people seemed to think there was already a food shortage or that one must dress as for the trenches.

I never received a safe-conduct as I was told that I did not need one. I was, of course, unaware that at that time the frontiers were not in the charge of the ordinary police and customs officers but of the anarchists, to whom a paper signed and sealed by the Embassy in London (appointed by the Madrid Government) would mean exactly nothing. I was a bit uneasy about my ability to penetrate the frontier and went to the Spanish Consulate to get a visa which, to pacify me, the Embassy had suggested. At the Consulate a young, rather public school, Englishman came in and asked if he could go to Barcelona to fetch some valuables for some Spanish friends who were afraid to venture out there. He carried himself with rather the air of a Scarlet Pimpernel but became deflated when the little vice-consul very civilly pointed out a printed list, just received from Spain, showing that it was prohibited to take all kinds of valuables out of the country.

'I should not advise any attempt of the kind – you would very likely get into serious trouble,' said the vice-consul, with that equivocal smile, worn by officials outside Spain, that never revealed on which side their hearts really lay.

I reached Paris in a fearful state of nerves. I had very wise friends there, much more experienced in war and revolution than I, whose only advice was not to confide in anyone and not to speak to strangers on the train or allow them to make friends with me, as there would be many spies and bad characters about and innocent association with them could get me into trouble. I am afraid I did not heed this advice. Lonely and worried, I longed to talk and was also devoured with curiosity about the business of other people travelling in the same direction – as they were about mine.

One always arrives at the Spanish frontier at a disadvantage, worn out with travelling all night. This occasion was merely more harassing than usual. Wrought up as I was, I noticed details more vividly. There was, to greet the traveller on the station, the photographic poster of the Catalan rope and canvas peasant shoe breaking a swastika underfoot on the cobblestones, with the legend: '*Aixafem el Feixisme*' (Crush Fascism), which I found very moving. On the desk of the passport officer were postcards for sale, photos of plump, laughing boys and girls in overalls, waving flags and rifles with the lettering CNT-FAI.[11] CNT reminded me of TNT and FAI of 'Fee, Fi, Fo, Fum.' Beside the packets of cards was a tray of money labelled: '*Pro-Milicias*', into which travellers threw small change and one *miliciano*, back from leave in France, who said he was penniless, was carelessly given a handful of it.

There were two customs men. One was small, desiccated, with beady black eyes, lively as a flea; he wore a little forage cap, half red and half black, that made him look as if he came out of a circus. The other one was very pale with a scar, a high-necked jersey and a beret rammed down like a skull-cap; he was much more reminiscent of the French Revolution *à la lanterne* and as though determined nothing should betray him into a smile. Everyone wore revolvers strapped over blue cotton overalls.

A gentle, blond young German in a floppy beret sat beside the passport officer as an interpreter, flushed and embarrassed. I am convinced that many such Germans were neither Nazi spies nor left-wing agitators. Germany had its troubles and Germans were always inclined to seek their fortunes abroad. They were always numerous in Spain and many, as good linguists, were attached to travel agencies or hotels. In the war they tried to go on earning their livings, preferably without risk of being wounded or killed, and of course were soon hopelessly compromised one way or another.

There were few travellers. I particularly noticed one couple from Marseilles. They were short and very stout with big heads and the woman had a bush of untidy, black cropped hair. Both wore red neckerchiefs and their passports were trade union cards, which they waved, talking glibly and pushing to the front. They said they were taking clothing, linen and dressings to a wounded brother. For the first time I saw evidently working class people at a distinct advantage to myself.

Though I was under suspicion, I was allowed to go out in the town and walk on the beach. The anarchist officials even advised me of a good restaurant where they sometimes lunched themselves and nodded in a friendly way when they saw me there. No watch was kept on me during my walk. I sent a postcard home and bought the only newspaper I could find which was not in Catalan. It happened to be *Solidaridad Obrera*, a trade union paper with anarchist leanings. There I saw a long column of advertisements, inserted by anxious relatives, asking for information about militiamen, last heard of in such and such a locality with such and such a unit. It dawned on me that it might not be so easy to find Jan.

Only two people were in serious danger of being held up and they were myself and a lady who, I must say, filled me with misgiving also. She tried very hard to throw in her lot with me but I shook her off quite heartlessly eventually. She was well-dressed – a fur-trimmed outfit, high heels, neat hat, cosmetics, smart luggage. She said she was Austrian, she may have been Jewish, and did not look young enough or unworldly enough to have come to Spain just for a lark. She appeared to be about thirty-five and said she had come all the way from Switzerland just to offer her services to the Republic and did not belong to any political party. She was a linguist, fluent with a bad accent, and had considerable previous acquaintance with Spain. I suppose I should not have suspected her any more than she should me, but somehow I did not believe her story and she looked as if she expected trouble.

We two were finally poked into a dirty first-class carriage (I do not think we even paid the fare) and sent off with our passports in charge of the guard. We whiled away the journey by talking to a middle-aged militiaman with merry black eyes and plenty of crow's feet round them, who had been a professional soldier. He said he was returning from sick leave and had been twice wounded, once at the taking of La Zaida in Aragón. He was from Oviedo and his family was still besieged there, about which he was philosophical.

It was late and dark when we arrived. I was met by Manolo, my brother-in-law to whom I had wired with only the faintest hope that he would be in Barcelona or receive the wire.[12] The other woman and her luggage clung to us and we were all driven straight to the police station under an escort of two and at a furious pace. I realised later that Manolo, a Catalan, was both bourgeois and a firm believer in self-preservation and that he was, therefore, going through a good deal for me. For, though we were kept waiting for a couple of hours and chivvied from one office to another, he bluffed boldly and his Catalan was invaluable in extricating me.

Finally, I was shown in to a great man, who appeared to have the power of life and death in his hands, to be interrogated. He was small and rather like George Raft in a gangster role.[13,14] Snake-like, with a terrifying manner laid on, he had several synthetic blonde, highly painted secretaries in white linen suits, also reminiscent of Hollywood. I emerged safely, probably because of my sex, and at this point we abandoned the Austrian woman.

In the great man's ante-room there was an old bourgeois in sobbing hysterics because he had been told he was being taken to prison and he thought he was being taken for a more sinister ride. This must have scared Manolo. I do not know if the old man was really going to be shot but he was protesting and struggling as they pushed his resisting round shoulders and dragged him out by force, his unshaven face green with terror. I did not feel much sympathy since he looked like a money-lender to me.

I was very tired and we had a hard time finding a place to sleep as everywhere seemed to be full up or requisitioned, but at last I was planted in an expensive hotel.

* * * * *

The next morning was so light and bright that, tired as I had been, I woke early feeling fresh and elated. The hotel was on the Calle Santa Ana; while I was there the name was changed to Calle de los Mártires de Montjuich. I do not know who the martyrs were but the place is associated with prison and execution. It was a very narrow street and on it was a clock shop which advertised itself with a big clock suspended across the street. I opened my shutters and saw to my astonishment that by this clock it was only nine, though the bustle and brilliant light made me think it must be noon.

I went to the café on the corner, the Rambla. At that time, though I did not know it, this was a rendezvous of English Medical Aid people and foreigners generally. People, aspects of towns and life changed so quickly in Spain then that everyone's daily habits were different a month later. This rapid shifting undermined all certainty and even one's individuality seemed to melt and alter.

Afterwards, I was constantly finding myself in dispute with others who had also been in Spain. Usually they protested violently that their impressions were true, mine quite erroneous. This I attribute either to their having been at the same time in a different place or in the same place at a different time.

That October morning it was still possible to order what one liked from the 'Collectivised Gastronomic Industry' and I was having *café au lait* and *croissants* and scanning the crowd that streamed up and down the middle of the Rambla. All working class people were on the promenades at that epoch and every day looked like a *fiesta*, there were so many flags and banners and processions. I watched intensely all the militiamen with girls and felt a pang of jealousy when I saw a fair one whose back view resembled Jan.

36

In the café was a dark, curly-haired militiaman in a neat khaki overall, with a clenched fist badge in his cap. I suppose we both stared. I have no recollection of who spoke first, but he was English and, in a moment, he had joined me at my table and I was pouring out my story. Everyone in Barcelona, and indeed all over Spain, who ran into me must soon have got heartily sick of this story. The stranger was charming, very serious, and I think it was only a concession to appearances – soldier with girl in café – that made him insist on buying me carnations from a whining, flattering old crone, a survivor of the old régime who, to suit her wares in revolutionary times, now sold only red flowers. My new friend wrote down Jan's name and listened carefully to his description, but he had not seen him.

'He's not in my barracks anyway.'

'Could he have got up to the front yet?'

'It's very unlikely he would be so lucky. I'm longing to get a whack at the fascists but I'm kept here training.'

'How can I set about finding him?'

'Would he have joined an anarchist column? If he has that's pretty hopeless as their organisation is so bad.'

'Oh no, I'm sure not.'

'Member of any political party, either of you?'

'No, unfortunately not.'

'That makes it more difficult. But go to the Hotel Colón and, if you can get by the guards and inside the door, go to room 25 and ask if he has passed through there.' The Hotel Colón was then the headquarters of the Unified Socialist Party.[15]

I was profoundly grateful to this boy and felt my troubles were nearly over. I ran into him one more time, in a bar in Madrid. He was a bit drunk, his hair was tousled and his eyes shining. I hastily outlined to him the latest developments in the Jan story although his attention wandered. He had achieved his ambition and got up to the front with the Thaelmann Battalion[16] and said, 'The Germans are the finest comrades in the world.' He only lasted a week or two.[17] He was a promising student at one of our universities. I have always to struggle with a sense of incredulity by repeating to myself that certain characters who I remember vividly are dead – they seemed so buoyantly alive.

Before breakfast I had had another setback. I had called, as soon as the doors were open, at the bank where we had arranged to send letters. There was nothing for me but two or three for Jan; I recognised my own handwriting and they went back into the pigeon-hole. This was only the first of many, many times I called at that bank, ashamed to be seen so often, trying to make it seem casual, but there was never anything either direct or forwarded from home. The previous night Manolo had told me that he had seen nothing of Jan, but there were letters for him waiting at his office, so he must be expected to call. These letters were also in my handwriting; they remain there to this day as far as I know. I expect the bank was closed later. It was not doing much business then as it had departments for travel and foreign exchange which had both collapsed, of course, and ordinary money transactions came under very severe control.

After my meeting with the English stranger my hopes sprang up again. I spent a nervous half hour, however, before making up my mind to put his advice into practice. Slowly, slowly I walked up the Rambla past the newspaper kiosks, under the banners: 'The Germans at the front are cold.' (*Germá* is Catalan for 'brothers' but I thought it meant Germans).

I loitered in the Plaza Catalunya where people were being photographed and pigeons were fluttering. *Els Boy Scouts* were encamped in the middle and collecting for something or other. The last time I had visited the Hotel Colón it had been with Manolo, to the Bodega, the night club underneath and he, who knew Barcelona society, had pointed out all his acquaintances and their mistresses and ex-mistresses. Now both gigolos and mistresses were conspicuous by their absence. Here and there the shattered windows bore witness to the July fascist defence of the building. A huge banner, with rather forbidding portraits of Lenin and Stalin, was stretched across the façade now. In front was a bookstall of Marxist literature where I bought the Communist Manifesto in Catalan by mistake and had to change it for a copy in Spanish. There were guards with rifles outside the hotel.

At last I left off fingering pamphlets, plucked up courage and marched boldly in without opposition, probably because I seemed so sure of myself and knew just where to go. The first person I met in the hall, before I had decided whether to look for room 25 up or downstairs, was an English friend who was there for a wedding.

'How did you get here – and inside this building?' he cried.

I gave a sketchy explanation and he took me up to the Department of Foreigners, where a nice young German with a moustache and soft brown eyes tried to be very helpful and shuffled vaguely through records – but there was no Jan.

I left with the Englishman, Bill, to have a vermouth.[18] I was in a strange mood, dreadfully disappointed and, at the same time, very wrought up by the exciting atmosphere of those days and full of nervous energy. Needless to say, Bill too had to take down the name and description and promise to look out in the Sarria and the Carlos Marx barracks, to which he had access but where I, as a woman, did not dare to go poking around. It seemed as if I was destined to meet instantly, without the slightest difficulty, all my friends except the one man I was seeking. Bill invited me to lunch at a hotel and there we were joined by another journalist and old friend, Humphrey Slater,[19] and by the French surrealist painter, André Masson, up for the day from Tossa where he was living at the outbreak of the war.[20]

Masson, short, fat, red and excitable, was very full of events. He was pro-Republican but said the defences of Tossa, a tiny fishing village, were quite neglected.

'But today,' he said, taking a draught of wine, crumbling his bread and leaning forward over the table, 'I saw the Thaelmann Battalion marching through town. They give one confidence indeed. What a fine set of men, what a martial air! I have seen plenty of volunteer militia but these were the first real soldiers.' He squared his shoulders in imitation of smart marching. 'People were staring at them in admiration.'

It was the first I had heard of these Germans, mostly already living in Spain, who had been fighting in Aragón.

All these friends seemed determined to give me a gay time while I was bent on breaking my heart over Jan. All sorts of possibilities crossed my mind which, I confess, easily the most depressing was that Jan no longer loved me and, therefore, had neither written nor called for my letters. Other alternatives were that he was kept in barracks and had no chance to get into town to collect mail, or that he was sworn to secrecy and forbidden to write. Also he might not have got across the frontier, but then I thought he would have written. The idea of his being detained in a French prison, as some of the volunteers were, did not occur to me.

No one seemed to think it likely that he had already got himself killed, as casualties in those parts, on the Aragón front, were not high and were mostly known about. No one was taken prisoner then; they preferred to commit suicide, like Lina Ódena.[21] The general view seemed to be that Jan might easily have changed his name and not dared to make any communication with me.

* * * * *

It was a busy week, partly employed in visits to the British consul and the gangster who then controlled the Catalan passport end of things, in connection with my public mission – the child I was taking home. Then there were telegrams to England to ask if letters had come for me there, and the rest of my efforts were devoted to making sure, since I had to leave my quest unfulfilled, that I could get back again.

I took most of my troubles at first to Bill, who was not young or attractive and was sentimental about two young people. My eyes would fill with tears and so would his and we would clasp hands across the café table. I actually think I trusted the wrong person in that instance, though he did seem to try to help me. He told me he had been to the biggest barracks and a man had been found with a similar name but when he was called out of the ranks he turned out to be quite bald and never to have heard of me. I said that if Jan had lost both his hair and his memory in so short a time I did not want to see him. After that I gave up the quest until I could get back again with further details to help enquiry.

I fear that many of the men I knew pretended to sympathise about Jan because they thought I would tire of the quest and console myself – perhaps with him who had seemed most sympathetic. As for women, except for those who knew and had a more than passing interest in Jan, they were even more useless, for they were always completely absorbed in their own romances and had no time for mine.

When I consider my state of passion and despair I am astounded now that I managed to lay and carry out plans with such coolness. I found that women were very much at a premium in Spain, particularly those who could talk to foreigners in their own language. It must have been ideal for female spies. For no good reason everyone seemed very trustful, and just because I had been seen with one person who was *de confianza* (trusted) I was accepted as all right by everyone without further enquiry – though of course, there was plenty that was concealed from me. It was assumed that I was politically sound and well-intentioned, 'valid' but naïve and untrained. This was true, but I was even more ingenuous than people thought.

Within a couple of days I had two or three men throwing themselves at me and, though a bit surprised, I did not hesitate to take advantage of this. I led on, as far as I dared, people who I thought might be useful in my scheme to return and remain until I found Jan. I made friends with a man from Central Europe (whom we called 'the cloak and suit man' because he looked like a tailor) with whom I could only communicate in bad French. For this reason, perhaps, he did not seem to doubt that I had the political and professional background to undertake propaganda newspaper work.[22] I had never enough to undertake anything and was canny enough not to give away my ignorance to him, while busy poring over Marxist literature in private. There were so many sets of letters in use than that I felt it quite dangerous if one casually mentioned any combination of the ABC without learning the significance of this new alphabet. The PSUC, the POUM, the UGT, the CNT-FAI, the JSU, were only some of them.[23] It seemed as if all the banners in town were bristling with mysterious initials.

I wore a hammer and sickle badge – such badges were sold on the street and one could join anything one fancied for a few cents. I wore a red handkerchief round my neck and a red ribbon round my hair. With most people I was tactful and patient and forbore to pester them about Jan when I saw it was of no immediate use. As far as newspaper work went, I was confident I could do it though I had no qualifications apart from French, some Spanish, and a short Pitman's secretarial course!

It was a strange week. I found out that lots of people stayed in the best hotels without paying except in paper *vales*, and that it was quite easy to get hold of a flat rent free. Barcelona and its suburbs were then full of fine empty houses and flats, many of which were later requisitioned as homes for refugee children.

The English Medical Aid, so elusive in London, was quite welcoming at its requisitioned flat in Muntaner, a place sumptuously decorated with vases of tin lilies, a library (from which I borrowed books still on my conscience) and a nursery of imported toys.

One afternoon I went with friends to see a girl in the hospital at Montjuich. There was a splendid view from up there in the hills. I had always associated Montjuich with those steps, fountains and gardens left over from the Exhibition and with the fine museum of Catalan art which I had recommended to Jan. It was closed during the war and most of its treasures were stored in the monastery of Monserrat. Since the war I have associated it with the hospital, all clean and white and hygienic (lucky patients) and with the prison, for which Montjuich was, I found, chiefly famous. All Catalan patriots had spent a term there, and later it was well filled with fascists. Many bourgeois purchased immunity for themselves and showed their good faith to the Republic by denouncing a relative. They probably selected some tiresome, unwanted aunt or a domineering father-in-law and the prisoners were not badly treated.

* * * * *

Humphrey had come from Madrid with a white Rolls Royce, a dreamy Andalusian chauffeur and a handsome interpreter who had been a sailor and was politically valid – at least while he was not in physical danger. The Rolls was really a white elephant; it was dreadfully noticeable on the battle-field and swallowed an infinite quantity of petrol. He took me to my first political

42

meeting. Meetings and processions were usually on Sunday mornings, instead of church I suppose, and this was a '*Monster Mitín*' to celebrate the UGT-CNT pact, the first sign of unity between the two trade unions.

It was in the bull-ring and we had the greatest difficulty in getting near the place as the crowd was so dense. We tried entrance after entrance, walking the whole way round the circumference and at last, after making a lot of fuss about being 'Press', got in through a back way and began climbing the stairs. There was to be a bullfight in the afternoon and we found ourselves on a platform projecting like a jetty over the pen where the animals were kept. A few *aficionados* were hanging over the rail judging the beasts regardless of the excited roars from inside the arena.

At last, we reached the top behind the platform; every nook and cranny was crammed with people and we had the utmost difficulty in insinuating our heads and one foot apiece into an opening from which we could get a glimpse of the ring, though our view was greatly obscured by the folds of a vast red flag which hung behind the speakers.

We were opposite a phalanx of JSU (Unified Socialist Youth) who made a colourful block in their bright blue shirts and red ties. It was impossible to hear a word as all was blurred by amplifiers and drowned by applause. Everyone seemed intensely enthusiastic and I have found political meetings in other countries terribly dull, dreary routine affairs after those in Spain. In England, they may be more professional and efficient, resolutions may be passed and agreed upon, speakers with nothing new to say repeat phrases without conviction. Perhaps I am unjust, they may have things of importance to say, they may have earnest convictions, but somehow one feels a profound discouragement in both speakers and audience.

In Spain, I suddenly felt that I was in the presence of real freedom and truly self-governing people. They cared about what was said because they knew it would be acted upon. Their discussions might be amateurish and their efforts bungling but they were at least out of the field of abstract demagogy and in the field of practice, everybody taking their part in trying to improve society and win the war at the same time. There was a terribly bewildering welter of opinions and talk but it was all so alive and there I grew keen on politics for the first time and was convinced that if ever these people should be conquered and suppressed it would be a scandalous waste and shame, for they had just begun to live.

Humphrey was in Barcelona on a rest from Madrid. He said being in Barcelona was like coming home to Blighty because there was so little sign of war and one could still have milk-coffee for breakfast and there was still no blackout. I spent several jolly evenings with him and Manolo, mostly in eating and drinking.

Manolo I had known as long as I had known Barcelona and to me he epitomised that city. He was a salesman and a very plausible one. He lived in a good neighbourhood (though he moved frequently) and he ate and drank where he had credit. He was well built, good looking and very much the man about town. He knew his way about everywhere and was on good terms with most people, though there were always a few creditors who had to be avoided. He used to take us to the *barrio chino* (Chinatown), behind the *Atarazanas*[24] and scheduled for slum clearance, where there were low cabarets, the gypsies, the Buena Sombra and its parody the Crioll across the street where the performers were all boys. Since the start of the war they had vanished like ghosts at cock-crow.

However, Manolo was very much in evidence. He was wearing a leather jacket and a UGT badge. He was very busy over the cause and carried a copy of *Das Kapital* under his arm. As usual he had a smart car, a sports model, to run about in.

With Humphrey and Manolo I went to little restaurants on the port, where it seemed strange not to see the smart, white Palma boat in dock, which used to leave at nine each night, and to think that once familiar island was now hostile and inaccessible. We did not then think of air raids from the island of *ensaymadas*, those round cakes, packed in a kind of band-box, which were its most noticeable export. The Palma steamer service belonged to Juan March, the last pirate of the Mediterranean, who had the tobacco monopoly and supported Franco.[25]

At the port we still had to drive round the remains of

44

barricades that had been used in the street fighting of July. On the way to the port, next to a theatre, was the POUM headquarters, with its own transport parked outside; its adherents, in navy blue overalls with lettering on the collar, intellectual-looking men and girls, frequented the cafés about there. Manolo, with his wonderful instinct for not doing the wrong thing, avoided the district as he did not want to be seen speaking to former acquaintances who had joined that group.

Down a dark back street, to the left, was the Caracoles restaurant, a rambling old-fashioned place with awkward spiral stairs, a sanded floor and wonderful, sizzling, garlic-flavoured cooking, where one waited interminably to be served among the new, sweating, shirt-sleeved proletarian clientele.[26]

'Let's go for a drive up to Tibidabo,' said Humphrey, after we had achieved dinner at Caracoles and Manolo had gracefully allowed him to pay the bill.

'I hear it's a bumping-off place,' said Miguel, the interpreter, nervously.

'No, no,' said Manolo deprecatingly. He was a native of Barcelona and felt he must stand up for his home town. 'I wouldn't say that. A few people may get bumped off but at least we are not so bad as the other side – they shoot women and children. But it might not do to go out to the suburbs after dark. Come round to my flat.'

'Did you ever see any of these bodies one hears about?' I asked Humphrey.

'Yes, I saw a few, in University City, outside Madrid. But one has to be up early to see them, they are all cleared away by nine. I don't know how the game goes here. A lot of old scores being settled, I expect.'

We went to Manolo's flat. It was in a big office building and we had to grope our way as the electric light was not on in the main building. He had it rent-free. It had been a businessman's love nest. The decorations were incredible. All the rooms had naughty pictures on the wall and the sitting room, overloaded with divans and cushions, had a lamp in the form of a skull. There was a bar, still with some drinks in stock, mostly Chartreuse, and barrels to sit on, and quite a lot of revivers and pick-me-ups. There were murals of brothel scenes and written signs with double meanings. The drawers of the desk contained nude photographs.

We sat round listening to the gramophone and Gabriel, the Andaluz chauffeur, looked dreamy during the flamencos. We got quite a kick out of thinking that the owner of this abomination had probably been shot. How Manolo could bear to wake up in the morning surrounded by dirty pictures and Bromo Seltzer I do not know.

* * * * *

When I left Barcelona I thought I was all set; I had a job promised and I had papers to return. I had already discovered that in Spain 'papers' are everything. One must have plenty of documents from every conceivable source and carry them all about constantly.

I rushed back to Paris, handed over my little charge and then rushed back to Barcelona. I was rather frightened at Port Vendres by false rumours, confidently asserted by the French railway officials, that Port Bou had been shelled and the line had broken down. When we reached Cerbère, the French authorities made us sign a paper giving a home address and taking all responsibility for risking our lives. The French were not risking a valuable train anyway, and we were transferred into an ancient and battered one, that must have been retired from service many years before, in order to be conveyed through the tunnel and across the frontier. The porter pointed out a few dents in this relic and said it had been hit on a previous trip, but really it was just old age.

The rumour had been started by the random shelling of Rosas from the sea. This was the first enemy action against Catalunya and it was not followed up for many months. No one was hurt in the village but the peasants were in a panic and evacuated the place wholesale. There were no defences and they thought the fascists would land there from Majorca. Old and young piled on to the Barcelona train with their belongings, though the more educated passengers assured them it was foolishness.

Chapter 3
Autumn in Barcelona

La Reina vol corona? Corona li darem,
que vingui a Barcelona i el coll li tallarem![27]

This is the song I found popular in Barcelona in Autumn 1936. It was sung to the tune of the Republican anthem.

I returned armed with a smiling photograph of Jan with open collar, taken in the summer holiday. I was really on the print too but I cut that part off, and the name of the man with whom he had left England. It was only afterwards that I realised that Bill was consciously, or from a subconscious wish, double-crossing me. He was the first person to whom I presented these additional clues to the mystery. Again we were sitting in the sun, in a café.

'Why I saw this man only a few days ago, it must have been while you were away, sitting in the Rambla café with the other chap you mention.'

'It's not possible,' I faltered, 'are you absolutely sure?'

'Well I couldn't be sure about your friend as I don't know him, but the man he was with I know and there was no question about him. They were talking and your friend stared straight at me.'

It never occurred to me to doubt such a circumstantial story, but this was the blackest news I had heard yet. Jan had been in Barcelona, he had not called for my letters or left a note for me, though only a stone's throw from the bank while at the Rambla café. Perhaps it was at night and the bank was shut, but still . . . and he had been at the very café I frequented only a day or two before, at the very time when I was unlucky enough to be away in Paris.

I was quite stupefied. As a result I took to sitting for hours at the Rambla and, whenever I had been obligated to leave the spot for a meal, I hurried back imagining I had just missed him. I am sure that if Bill was aware that he was recounting to me a pure fiction he must have been struck with remorse at my reception of it. He asked to borrow the photograph for a few days to show people and, very reluctantly, I let it out of my hands. I heard this tale within a day or two of my return.

I found everything different in Barcelona after only a week's absence. Most of my friends had gone away somewhere else. The first morning, the sun was still hot and I walked miles up the Paseo de Gracia, past the statue of Christopher Columbus to the office of the Central European. I was waiting with nerves at the prospect of having to impress, yet certain I had a job awaiting me. I found everything had gone wrong. He had discovered he had no right to engage me, it all depended on someone else.

Off I went to see the someone else, a Catalan, having engaged the services of Manolo, whose ability in getting himself jobs was so remarkable, but all to no purpose. It would have been all right except that I was a foreigner and, therefore, always landed back again at the Department of Foreigners, Hotel Colón.

I suspect that really there were a lot of intrigues going on. I was very glad afterwards that I never got stuck in Barcelona in this job, which would have paid only a militiaman's wages, ten pesetas a day without keep and, with rising prices, this was very soon not a living wage. I found that in my absence the job had been given to someone else, said to be more experienced, as well they might be, though later sacked as incompetent and the job was abolished and metamorphosed into something else. The Central European left, rather in disgust, as he was a big shot.

I kept complaining to Bill, and trying to get him to find me another job, and he kept saying he would, though I believe here he was sabotaging me again, as other people who wanted to employ me said he objected.

I spent most of my time in cafés studying, trying to improve my Spanish, and talking and making friends with any International Brigaders who happened to be loitering around. They were mostly French, very unpleasant and quite hard to shake off – but I always hoped I might hear something of Jan.

I was rather worried about money. I had brought back what I could but it was not often possible to get a favourable rate of exchange (clandestine, as it was officially controlled) and after shopping round here and there privately I would have to part with yet another precious pound, for fifty pesetas, with no prospect of ever getting another. At no time did I make good contacts with the black market.

As economy was of the first importance, Manolo fixed me up in a tiny room in a modest *pensión* at 8.50 pesetas a day. When I got there I found a candle burning before a holy image in my room.

'What is this doing here?' I asked the proprietress, a fat, florid ex-actress from Madrid. She hastened to remove it.

'I was praying for more guests as business is bad,' she admitted, with a guilty smile.

'But surely you, a woman of the world, don't believe in such nonsense?'

'Well,' she said, a bit shame-faced, 'it worked, didn't it? You have come, haven't you?'

The *pensión* was in the centre of town, high up, in two adjoining flats. The hall and dining-room were economically furnished. Hard wooden benches had been fitted into a series of alcoves and given a spurious air of comfort by thin, flat cushions covered in a blue and white cotton material patterned in irregular stripes, which had rather the effect of ink spilled on blotting paper and was a great favourite in Catalunya. The various doorways were curtained and on the table in the hall lay an obsolete telephone directory and a number of very out-of-date, torn and greasy magazines of women's fashions and beauty hints.

Manolo had lived in this *pensión* when down on his luck and he still owed the proprietress money, but he had a way with women and they were all much attached to him and gave him a big welcome. There were two girls who helped the *señora*, a horse-faced bleach blonde, and a pretty little one called Montserrat. Manolo chucked them familiarly under the chin, called for a bottle of rosé and went to the kitchen himself to see the preparations for supper, from whence I heard laughter and merriment while I was taking a tepid bath. He then came back to my little room, which he had once occupied himself, helped me to unpack, showed me the few conveniences (hooks and shelves), switched on the bedside lamp with an artless pride, and asked me the news of the outside world.

Always the same questions. 'What do they think of the war out in France? Do they think we shall win? We must win. Will they send arms?'

I shook my head at the last question. 'They think you're putting up a pretty good fight,' I said. 'I'm sure it surprises me. I bet if the regular army turned on the people and attacked them, there would be no street barricades in Liverpool. I don't believe the Labour Party, or the trade unions, or the farm labourers would form a militia, or take over industry and turn the Morris works into a munitions factory. I bet they would just give in.'

'The damned central government didn't want to distribute arms to the people,' said Manolo, who was a thorough *catalanista*.

'Maybe not,' I said, 'but they had to do it. They might not have made a stand against the rebels at all. Liberals always waver between fear of fascism and fear of the mob and often fall between two stools. But with the drive of the mass of the people they just had to put up a fight. We think it's impressive.'

'Dinner is served,' said Montserrat, smiling at the door.

After this I always stayed at the *pensión* when in Barcelona. The girls and the *señora* were kind and pleasant, but as the guests who lived there were middle class and thought the end of the world, their world, had come, the atmosphere was depressing.

* * * * *

What was particularly strange was the rapid change of fashion in Barcelona. I suppose it was partly fear that made all the bourgeois at once dress and talk like the working class. Only the older people were unaffected. The shops all produced revolutionary wares, badges, ribbons and Left books. Everyone used the familiar 'thou'. No one said '*adiós*' any more, only '*salud*'. Few people addressed one as 'sir' or 'madam'. I suppose it has all slipped back again just as quickly, and the fascist salute has replaced the universal clenched fist.

Manolo took me to a music hall where a comedian made a favourite joke. He came on with a stooge dressed as a peasant. The peasant kept saying '*adiós*' but at last remembered to say '*salud*' whereupon the other exclaimed, 'at last, *gracias a Dios!*'

The comedian imitated natives of different regions of Spain. When he came on in a shiny black hat and began to talk with an Andaluz lisp, representing a *sevillano*, he was hissed off the stage. The audience did not think of José Diaz, a former baker, secretary of the Communist Party and a *sevillano*,[28] but only of the headquarters of Queipo de Llano. In Catalunya the word *sevillano* was used to designate a false coin.

I went once to visit Manolo's family and there life looked quite different. His aunt, a courteous old lady in black, and his unmarried sister found the war and revolution most trying, though they still had a servant who was as deferential as ever. But friends of theirs were in prison as enemies of the régime and they complained of money difficulties and scarcity of food supplies. There was no scarcity then but middle-class Spaniards are used to such groaning boards that meals much larger than in England seemed scant to them and they apologised profusely for serving a miserable four-course meal.

Manolo had another relative in the background who was too shy to emerge while I was there, a nun they were sheltering. This old lady, I was informed, was perfectly happy because she believed herself to have been especially singled out for religious persecution. She had been obliged to flee from two convents, one in Mexico and one in Spain and now was sure of heaven. She had taken the veil at least thirty years before and had been flung abruptly out on the world in the same quaintly old-fashioned lay dress in which she had entered the convent and was naturally now unable to adapt herself to visitors.

Manolo described to me the departure of some hundreds of nuns who were allowed to leave for Italy in the early days of the war. They were all grouped on the dock in some sort of lay garments and whispering to each other timidly: 'Be careful what you say, sister. Hush, hush, or people will recognise us as nuns.' It was obvious enough that these ladies were from convents, but their demeanour only produced pitying smiles and no molestation from the toughs of the port.

* * * * *

The one point of accord between bourgeois, communists and socialists, a point that drove many like Manolo into the UGT because they thought that in those times it was safer to join something, was fear of the anarchists. The CNT-FAI were bogeymen to them who went in for irresponsible shooting and looting and I have seen them tremble on even mentioning them and only doing so in whispers. It is strange that for every Left-winger there is still something too far Left! Those in England who think communists are Reds would be surprised to witness the aura of respectability that surrounded them in Spain.

Another area in which communists encouraged the bourgeois was Catalanism. The chief exponents of Catalanism were the rich farmers and peasants and the shopkeepers of Barcelona. They were members of the *Esquerra, Unión de Rabassaires and Estat Català* (Catalan Left Republicans, Farmers' Union, Movement for Complete Autonomy).[29]

The communists had a theory about encouraging national minorities when these were progressive and at first the Catalans fitted this description. Later, great efforts were made to bring them under the control of the central government for war purposes while leaving the Generalitat in nominal control.

The PSUC flattered them by using the Catalan language for their newspaper and so on, the POUM tried to do the same though it was rather an affectation to pretend that what was so largely a foreign movement had enough local support to warrant the use of Catalan.

The *catalanistas* seemed to me far from genuinely progressive. Their sentiments were largely founded on jealousy of the Spanish aristocracy, whose pride and snobbery infuriated the good *barceloneses*, and the idea that Catalunya would do better commercially if free of the poorer parts of Spain. They were narrow-minded in so far as the ultimate good of the region was concerned.

The anarchists, on the other hand, were genuinely proletarian. Many of those in their ranks were from Murcia and other parts of Spain who had come to work in the factories. They were therefore obliged to use the Spanish language and to eschew regionalism except in so far as they favoured a federal system for the whole Iberian peninsula.

I only made one excursion among the anarchists. My relations with them were distinctly hampered by the hostility of most of my acquaintances, who were socialists, and I was afraid that if I saw too much of them I would get a bad name and never capture that job – hopes of which were still being held out, if only I could afford to wait.

One night I chanced to meet two old friends, Werner and Greville.[30] Werner, formerly a mild, scholarly young man, now had blossomed surprisingly into a bloodthirsty buccaneer with a red neckerchief and a beard and a fine assortment of Spanish swear words in most of which the Virgin featured. Most of the militia wore beards then, luxuriant and black, which gave them a violently masculine and strangely Elizabethan appearance. One could easily tell which were young boys by their lack of beards.

'We've just been paid,' said Werner, 'let's go out and have a bust.'

We went to a restaurant and they ordered a bottle of champagne. They looked like a couple of healthy tramps.

'What are you in?' I asked.

'Well, we joined the anarchist militia. At first we belonged to the POUM, because in the early days it opened a recruiting office for anti-fascist militia and accepted everyone, including foreigners, and no questions asked, but it didn't pay wages when the time came, and it doesn't count at the front, and is such a sinking ship.'

I told them about Jan, but they had not seen him, and also about how I hoped to get an office job.

'You're an *enchufista* then,' said Werner.

'Whatever is that?'

'Somebody who wangles a cushy job,' said Greville, 'it's a grand word.'

'I think *bufanda* is a great word,' said Werner, 'it means a kind of shawl that you wrap around your mouth.'

Spaniards are very superstitious about cold air getting into their mouths. Children with bare legs and no warm coats will still be seen going out with scarves around their faces.

'You don't wear uniform,' I said, surveying their motley

garments. Greville was in trousers.

'Oh, we encourage fancy dress in our column,' she said, 'it keeps up the morale. Some people wear fur hats like Cossacks, and some big straw ones like Mexicans, and some have feathers like Red Indians.'

'Doesn't that make them rather a good target for the enemy?'

'Well, it would, only we don't see much of the enemy, to tell you the truth.'

They had been in Aragón for some time and described an idyllic life of swimming in the Ebro, keeping guard on moonlit nights and making raids into no-man's land where stood deserted factories and big houses from which sewing machines and other objects of value could be salvaged. Life there seemed to be very pure and ascetic. They taught the villagers to read and made them pool all their wheat together. On their front there were no tanks, no aeroplanes, no officers, only 'military advisers'. They had meetings to decide what tactics should be adopted. Everyone was represented by a delegate, including the mules. The mules, however, were unjustly not represented by a fellow mule but by a human.

Werner and Greville had a great ambition which was to acquire a pair of field glasses to see the fascists with. I remember sitting with them in a café one night and discussing with another friend, Tom Wintringham,[31] something of an expert on military matters, what ought to be done on the Aragón front. It was then so thinly held, on both sides, that they sometimes used to wonder if there were any fascists on the other side! Café strategists drawing maps, and then hastily destroying them, lest it should look like spying, decided in October 1936 that the best thing would be an offensive to take Belchite – something which was not actually carried out until about a year later.

Then I discovered not only that politics were interesting but also that methods of waging warfare were also interesting when one had one's heart in the cause. We went to the war newsreels as they appeared and Werner and Greville, my two formerly pacifist friends, were excited by them, particularly one about the taking of Siétamo (an Aragón village) because they knew the country and sometimes the individual soldiers shown. Parts of these films were faked, of course. The one on the Majorca landing, reconstructed long after the event, was particularly bad but on the whole they were thrilling. It was partly because they were war pictures, partly because they were experiments in cinematography by people who had just taken over the industry and were not then hampered by lack of money and materials. They contained beautiful photography and I was surprised that so few found their way abroad. I suppose they were barred for political reasons. For a long time the anarchists had a complete monopoly of the entertainment business and made a very good job of it – except financially.

Werner and Greville took me to an anarchist lunch but perhaps some points about it were typically Spanish rather than anarchist. It was all very late and everyone made conversation and no one seemed to mind the lateness except myself. We were shepherded onto innumerable trams so that, to this day, I have no idea of the district in which it was held. I thought all the guests would never be collected together. At one point we were all photographed in a group on a vacant lot which made a very unpicturesque background of rubbish.

Then we all walked a long way and I talked, some of the time, to a Neapolitan cook who spoke bad French and the rest listened to the varied prison experiences of an elderly man who was the head of a fine old anarchist family. As we walked through the streets among the flags and diagonally painted black and white trams and taxis and noticed that even the small urchins had parti-coloured caps, neckerchiefs and badges, the old man remarked: 'One would say the city was celebrating a carnival, but it is a ghastly kind of carnival.'

This was a family that might have come from *Seven Red Sundays*.[32] The mother, fat, kind and motherly, talked of the worry it had been when she often carried bombs concealed in her shopping basket, and there was a blind brother who used to make hand-grenades, the kind in old tins, in the cellar, as he was not good for much else. There was a pretty younger son who clung to his father's hand but was already a good shot, so his old dad boasted, and there was a thin, straight and beautiful and forbiddingly serious daughter who was a militiawoman, and a fanatical, spectacled son, also in the militia, who was a school-teacher. The young people were just back from the front and they were much more dogmatic and ascetic than the old. They were *naturalistas*, that is, vegetarian, and did not drink or smoke. The old man said he liked a smoke and the mother said she had no patience with the children's fads.

We drank orange juice and ate pomegranate and brown bread and cheese. At about half past three I made a polite speech of thanks and hurried away to get a ham sandwich.

The luncheon was held in a fruiterer's shop. Our host, the fruiterer, had rather frightening gold teeth. He was a talented man and had decorated the restaurant at the back of the shop himself. To make it naturalistic like a garden he had put up trellises with paper roses, and he had painted a mural symbolising all the needs of man. These included a guitar (music), a book (literature) and a banana (for the body). Out of these ingredients a pure flame arose to heaven. There were many apologies because the banana element was lacking in the meal; but bananas came from the Canary Islands, unluckily in rebel hands.

* * * * *

There seemed to be some sort of break-up in the 'column' to which Greville and Werner were attached, which was called *Los Aguiluchos de Las Corts*.[33] Like all units of the early militia it was called a 'column' but composed of no specific number; smaller units were called '*centuria*'. It was paid up and let loose in Barcelona for weeks. This distressed my friends as it was demoralising and they were afraid all the country boys would catch venereal diseases. The anarchists were very strong on propaganda against prostitutes and social diseases. I was rather staggered by a huge poster that was flashed on the screen, in the interval at the cinema, representing a soldier looking longingly up at the Venus de Milo with the caption, 'This is worse than the enemy's bullets'.

At that time in Barcelona, the general public was no more aware of what was going on in Madrid than on the moon. This was perhaps hardly surprising considering that the public in

Madrid itself did not know how seriously they were threatened either. However, there were rumours that things were bad and that all troops, trained or not, were to be sent up there. Greville and Werner, however lion-hearted about the stagnant Aragón front, rather funked Madrid when they heard the stories of Humphrey and other journalists of the disastrous retreats, or rather routs, that were taking place.

According to Humphrey, there was nothing to eat but beans and bread and vast masses of troops could not possibly be fed. The medical services were chaotic and he described men lying on stone floors in pools of blood with no bandages, and legs and arms being amputated wholesale because there was no time to try to save them.

'No one comes out of the front line there until they are either dead or very badly wounded,' he said. Also he said that there it was real war, and tough, and no girls would be allowed up to the front. Already girls were beginning to be eliminated from the militia; they were requested to retire though not yet forced to do so. Those who insisted on sticking with the troops would be relegated to cooking and clerking jobs.

I spent sleepless nights after hearing these stories . . . Jan was not here, he was not in Aragón, he must surely be there.

Greville and Werner did not like the sound of it. They had always been together and she did not want to let him go to Madrid alone. The whole situation seemed worse to all of us because, though we all happened to be on familiar ground in Catalunya, we had never been to Madrid. It was strange and very far off to us. Werner, moreover, was tempted by the educational experiments that were going on in Barcelona; his *métier* was that of a teacher. There was still no compulsion and he and Greville did not like the sound of military discipline either, which was just being introduced.

Finally the column received new outfits, of which there were then plenty in Barcelona, and went off to a small town to be re-formed. I saw them off in their new corduroy breeches, imitation leather jackets hung with tin pans, and big boots, Greville doing a tap-dance to the tune of *Popeye the Sailor* in her boots. We bade farewell as if they were going heroically to their deaths but they never went into action again. Later they found work behind the lines in Refugee Children's Colonies.

* * * * *

Meanwhile, I picked up temporary jobs as an interpreter. It was much more exciting than I had expected and I had to acquire a new vocabulary. I had to drop the polite third person, which I had hitherto used exclusively, and learn a lot of different parts of verbs now that we had all become *poco formal* (very informal) and everyone was a *camarada* or a *compañero*.

I became interpreter for a man who behaved and looked so much like a professional revolutionary that I still cannot believe that he was one. He immediately informed me that the name he went by was not his real one; that he had several passports and credentials sewn inside his clothes and that, if he wished, he could disguise himself as a gentleman (which I very much doubt). He had an accomplice who wrote his name on a piece of paper which he promptly tore into small pieces and scattered to the winds. Both of them were liable to produce confidential messages that could only be carried out of Spain by hand.

I will call my employer Zachary.[34] He hinted that he secretly occupied a position of great importance, and went about looking like a conspirator. Unfortunately he was very tactless and bad at humouring Spaniards and I sometimes trembled for his life. I do not think he was a coward though he thought his life very valuable and never risked it knowingly. He boasted that he travelled a great deal and had unlimited funds to draw upon and suggested that the advantages of friendship with him were very great.

He was rather an old-fashioned revolutionary. It is a profession that dates quickly, and he used the technique that the best way an earnest girl could serve the cause was to become his mistress and secretary. I found this rather disillusioning as I had thought that revolutionaries were above such things and particularly that they would not play on one's political ambition as he tried to do. He promised an education (I was still classed as a political illiterate) and better jobs. I did a good deal of work for

58

this man while staving him off personally and I expect I learned something, if only that not all reds are idealists, but I never got more than free meals and promises of payment.

One day when I was lunching at the Oriente, where Zachary had acquired a free billet, he pointed out Durruti, the great anarchist leader who was lunching with his staff. He spoke under his breath, as always being conspiratorial, and I had to ask him loudly to repeat the name twice, and then I was none the wiser. I had never heard of this redoubtable figure![35]

It was a very sad and lonely time for me. I remember one of the most solitary days was that November Sunday on which I stood and watched the procession to celebrate the anniversary of the Soviet Union. It took four hours to pass, and everyone was in it, that is more people were in it than watching. There was a first detachment of child refugees, the *pioneros de Madrid*, with cropped heads and those striped pinafores that make Spanish boys and girls alike, who were loudly cheered. There were Red Cross nurses holding out sheets for pennies, ambulances painted with scenes of blood transfusions. There were all the political parties and organisations including the POUM, very highbrow with banners written in Russian. There were endless trade unions carrying the tools of their trades and some of those embroidered silk banners that look like those in churches. Manolo complained afterwards that the anarchists had sabotaged the procession.

'How do you mean they sabotaged the procession?' I asked. 'They took part in it.'

'Yes, but they sabotaged it by walking along looking bored, with cigarettes in their mouths.'

The evenings were getting dark early and at about seven I would creep out to buy *La Noche*. The news was bad, what there was of it.

One night a great batch of soldiers was going off to Madrid. I stood and watched with two friends, holding my frozen fist clenched in the air for the first time. I did not know which fist or if the thumb should be inside or outside. Everyone stood watching in this manner. The men were fairly well and warmly equipped, with cloth caps with ear-flaps and some had puttees.

59

They were of all sorts, shapes and sizes, for they were volunteers and had to pass no medical boards. There were very old and very young, one hunchback with his pack on top of that, and two or three girls looking very small, enveloped in long cloaks with hoods. There was at least one dog mascot and several guitars. One man was waving a doll and shouting, 'No pasarán.'[36] Most of them were Spaniards but there were a few foreigners transferred from other fronts or newly trained. Some had their girls running beside them to keep up with the marching and still holding their hands. It took a long time for them all to go by.

Tom Wintringham made some remark about, 'a pity they could not have given those water-bottles a lick of paint, they catch the light so.' We did not know what to say. I had such a lump in my throat I dared not speak. I tried to look at each individual face but in the dim light and multitude it was impossible. I stayed there until all had gone by and then felt a terrible sense of loss, foreboding and abandonment, as I had felt when Jan left England.

The next day, after lunch, I was sitting at the café and my attention was attracted by a German girl. Everyone seemed to be trying to be very kind to her. Two young men were pressing to take her out that evening. Ilse was a plump, deep-bosomed girl, shabbily dressed, hatless of course, with thick brown hair that fell in a lock over one side of her face. She had steadfast blue eyes and looked womanly for her age. Ilse spoke low and with forced restraint: 'But he did not tell me. I went back to the apartment and just found he had gone.'

I soon heard the story from other friends. Everyone was sorry for Ilse. Ilse was desperately in love, first love, with a fine young man called Karl. Ilse and Karl had fought in the militia side by side from the beginning. Together they had taken part in the Majorca landing. Then Karl got some minor ailment, I think trench feet, and was put on light office duty for a few weeks. They were married and all was bliss. Ilse, a well-disciplined revolutionary, resigned from the militia when she understood that the presence of women was no longer wanted. But Karl was fully recovered and Madrid was in danger. He had left with that batch of troops the night before, unable to bear to say goodbye.[37]

I thought she would be sympathetic and showed Ilse my photo of Jan. 'Oh,' she cried, 'why did you not show it to me before? What a pity! I know that boy by sight; he was with the Germans. But now they are all gone, together with Karl.'

I thought I should go mad that night in my room at the *pensión*, too narrow to pace up and down in. Jan's laughing face in the photo seemed to twist into reproach as if I had not done all I could to find him. The night before I had dreamed of standing outside bars and speaking to him among a crowd of men. If only I had seen him just once, just once again before one of us was dead, even if only in the distance, only a glimpse.

My *pensión* was above a cinema and for some reason the sound apparatus seemed directly connected with my room. Two shows a day, the last ending at midnight, I could hear the same words and music for a week. It was an American college picture which culminated in a football game. This alone played on my nerves through the long hours alone in my room and, that night, contributed to my agony of mind as I tumbled hopelessly about the bed. It would not have been so bad if Jan had not been in that very group I had watched pass. If only chance had been kind . . . if only. Nothing could have been worse or more cruel.

Actually, it was another of the extraordinary chain of mistakes of which I was a victim in Spain. Ilse was not ill-disposed towards me though possibly suffering less than I because she was still supported by such a recent spell of happiness with Karl. She still kept her hopes, she had assurances of his love, and she could not imagine him dead yet. I had gone through long discouragement to reach this stage. She genuinely thought she had seen Jan because the photo I carried either did not greatly resemble him or he resembled many other young men. He was not in the batch I watched go, nor in any batch that left Barcelona and I might have been spared thinking I had only just missed him.

After Karl left, Ilse was a woman possessed, a woman of one idea. She found out that he would be training temporarily in Albacete. She found out every time anyone was going there and would make them carry letters and parcels for her. She also moped and pined to such a degree that her friends finally contrived to send her off to a job in Albacete. She would then be

61

able to see Karl up to the very last moment. She was not sure then if he was already in Madrid but she hoped to get somewhere near him. I saw her, radiant, going off with all her belongings wrapped in a piece of brown paper, to catch the interminable train. My last words to her were: 'Don't forget to look out for Jan and send me news if you can.' She promised and we wrung each other by the hand.

I was quite wrong to put my faith in those steadfast blue eyes. She forgot all about it, and later forgot all about Karl and fell just as desperately in love with someone else. Perhaps this deceptive appearance of reliability and seriousness was something to do with her being German. All her English acquaintances were taken in by it and treated her passion for Karl as if it were Dante and Beatrice.

I saw Karl once more though he is dead now. Ilse is well. She grew to be quite a local queen in those days of woman shortage and blossomed out into something very smart and pretty. She had various jobs, and not a few romances I expect.

I began to hear the name Albacete bandied about. This was just because everyone was trying to keep the place a dead secret, it being the headquarters of the International Brigade. I was too obtuse to think the place taboo; it gave me an idea though. Jan might be in training there. I went off to Bill, who had a good deal of inside knowledge, and plagued him until I had squeezed out of him an address in Albacete that *might* conceivably find a soldier, though the arrival of all letters was problematic in those days.

I wrote a letter to Jan, care of the man with whom he had left England, as I was pretty sure he had changed his name, and I just wrote Jan on the envelope. I composed it many times, trying to keep out any note of the bitterness and blame I felt because he had not made any communication. I wanted it to be the sort of letter that would not hurt him if it were the last thing he heard from me on this earth. By this time I no longer expected he would ever receive it. It was, therefore, only a brief note giving my address in Barcelona. I posted it rather in the spirit of people who put messages in bottles and commit them to the waves.

I began to have a new goal – to leave Barcelona and get some employment elsewhere, Albacete or anywhere. I hated the place where I had suffered such misery and disappointment. Now my only aim was to get nearer to the war and danger – even to get myself honourably killed, perhaps.

I telegraphed Humphrey in Madrid, asking if he could find me something there, and I began a fresh campaign with the Department of Foreigners. That department was stranger than ever. It was in the charge of an odd little German with tousled hair, who reminded me of the Mad Hatter. He was always gnawing on a sandwich, holding a telephone in the other hand and being interrupted. I had to communicate with him in Spanish, the only language we had in common. My opening sentence was all-embracing and vague: 'I want to work for the cause.'[38]

On the wall in various languages was written, 'Few words, much action.' In every version there were spelling mistakes and never was a precept so little followed. There were several husky girls, garbed in overalls though the necessity for trousers in office work escaped me. There was a printed form which everyone had to fill in as soon as they came in and which I filled in several times as they always forgot who one was or had lost the files. It was a form intended to establish one as an anti-fascist but, as it had evidently been drawn up by, and was intended for, political refugees, I found it very hard to do anything beyond signing my name to it. To establish one's good character it began rather astonishingly: 'How many times have you been in prison? When, where and for how long?' It passed from prisons to concentration camps, membership of anti-fascist organisations and ended: 'What refugee organisations have helped you?' In fact it was something very different from the usual bank reference and letters from a professional man or householder required to establish one's character normally.

Everyone in this office was always fearfully busy and everything was chaotic. At first I thought I had done pretty well when I had been introduced and managed to speak for a moment to the Mad Hatter, but of course his attention was quickly drawn away by half a dozen other people and it was impossible to recapture it. Another day I had to be presented to him all over again. I thought I had made great strides when I filled in the form and applied for a job as secretary or interpreter. I soon found that Bill's advice, 'Of course, I'll do what I can to remind them about you but you have to keep on bothering them,' was very necessary.

I prepared my Spanish speech and went in almost every day at the hours I gradually discovered were the most promising. Sometimes I sat and waited for an hour without seeing anyone at all or getting the slightest attention. Sometimes I was fobbed off with one of the husky girls who only waved her arms and said everything was dreadful and 'all our comrades are dying at the front,' as if that fact made my action in hanging about in the office more selfish and annoying than it would have been otherwise. When I did get in front of the Mad Hatter's desk, half the time he would barely look up and say, 'What do you want?' and not wait for an answer before plunging into other business. However, I was determined that at least they should get to know me by sight and perhaps give me something because they were tired of seeing me there.

One evening when I was sitting in the ante-room an English boy got into conversation with me. He was red-faced and Jewish. We were amusing ourselves trying on some new knitted Balaclava helmets which were lying about. When I said I was waiting to see if the Mad Hatter was free to speak to me at all, he said, 'He'll never be free. It's no use being bashful around here, you have to push yourself or you'll never get anywhere.' And he dragged me up to see the Mad Hatter and burst into the conversation. The Mad Hatter looked surprised but that evening I filled in the form again. This Jewish boy had bicycled from France, where he was on holiday, to join the volunteers. He was killed.

Then Zachary was called away, first to Albacete and then, we supposed, to Madrid. He was my last possible source of income. I helped him pack and saw him off. After he had gone his confederate, Dutois, told me that he was so influential that he could surely get me a job in Albacete; also that many interpreters were needed in Albacete. I wrote to Zachary at a guessed address, an hotel where I was told everyone stayed. I also went to the Mad Hatter and clamoured to be sent to Albacete or, I added, 'I'm willing to go anywhere, even to Madrid itself,' hoping that there would not be so many applicants for work in the threatened city. 'I don't want a salary. I don't want anything more than my keep and expenses.'

Then a young male clerk showed me my name on a list of possible interpreters. 'We have sent this list to Albacete,' he said, 'my name is on it too. We are awaiting a reply as to how many they want, but I'm afraid men will get the preference. I'm waiting to hear too.'

I peered over his shoulder at the list, downcast by its length and by the qualifications of the applicants, most of whom seemed to know more languages than I did. I consoled myself that English-Spanish seemed a rare combination, but was terribly jealous of the applicant who knew Russian. Then I was told off for snooping over papers lying on the desk which were private.

Albacete, which had asked for interpreters in the first place, never replied to the Barcelona authorities, but great confusion reigned there, even worse than in the Department of Foreigners, as the administration was only just being set up and they were all spy crazy too.

Much later I met the boy who was on the list and knew Russian. He laughed and said, 'Do you remember that list we were both on to go to Albacete? Aren't you thankful we never got there? If we had ever been let in we never should have got away, you know.' It was rather like that. If one was trustworthy enough to be given a post in Albacete one then knew too many secrets and was kept as a kind of hostage and could not escape.

I had got as far as giving the male clerk my address and telephone number and waited expectantly to be called. One morning I went in very early quite prepared to risk mortally offending the Mad Hatter.

'I *must* get some work,' I said, 'I can't afford to stay here any longer and I no longer have the fare home, nor can I pay my bill at the *pensión*. What am I to do?'

There was no reason why this appeal should have any effect but it did. The Mad Hatter was human. The next day I was sent for and put to work at the former jockey-club, still called the *Equestria* by most of the locals, but now designated the *Casal*

Carlos Marx and devoted to making posters and propaganda.

My luck had turned and I threw myself into the job, which was simply that of a typist, as if my life depended on it, determined to make good, and that the Mad Hatter should not regret his choice. It was a very wet spell and I got to work with my feet soaking and the building was fearfully cold. The others must have been astonished by my zeal. I found everyone very casual and no one scolded me or ordered me about as they had done when I had been employed in more normal countries.

In the mornings, the others drank tea and lemon and ate their breakfast perched on tables in the office. We had our typewriters on a billiard table, which was far from ideal, what with the height and the ledge round the sides and the pockets. One man walked about and dictated with the air of a genius. There was one other girl and she taught me how to make stencils and cleaned the letters with the pin of a badge she wore, a red five-pointed star with the letters PSU on it. Pitman's had never taught me stencils, I was not advanced enough, and the first one caught and creased around the roller somehow, but the rest were all right. I was phenomenally slow being so anxious not to make mistakes and using a Spanish typewriter with the letters differently placed and upside-down question marks and an ñ which confused me. I would gladly have finished by working late but this was not allowed. Hours were strictly limited in Barcelona and if one lingered after seven the cleaners and other employees in the building came and drove one out. The girl who taught me stencilling, an Austrian, later spent a term in prison on a charge of espionage.

It was rather dark in the *Equestria* on account of Carlos Marx's beard. The Union of Graphic Arts had let themselves go on a gigantic representation of the head of Marx with yards of curly beard which stretched from the top floor of the building to the bottom and, of course, obscured all the windows. It was so impractical that it had to be removed later.

Chapter 4
Barcelona—Valencia

Before I had time to settle down behind Carlos Marx's beard, Humphrey turned up again. He found me in the office one afternoon. It was November and we were already working by artificial light, and I was thumping away at a stencil.

Humphrey had exchanged the Rolls for a Ford which had broken down and needed repairs as Gabriel had driven it all the way from Madrid without remembering to put in oil and water. The party was not very flush financially and the hotels were beginning to rebel against the *vale* system. They had had a tussle to avoid a heavy bill on the last visit. After finding lodgings with friends they came to dinner at the *pensión*.

The *señora* came out and plied them with questions about Madrid. Humphrey was astonished to find that I, and people in general, did not know that the Madrid-Valencia railway had been cut for some time past and he laughed at my expectation of being sent to Madrid. However, he suggested taking me down to Valencia. I knew nothing of Spain outside Catalunya but I felt any change would increase my chances of finding Jan. I had, by this time, grown weary of saying this.

Humphrey's descriptions of Madrid were more horrifying than ever. It was the blackest moment the city had known. Miguel, who was not remarkable for physical courage, obviously did not want to go back there at all. This was understandable, since his wife had just come to Barcelona in charge of some evacuees, the children of the employees of a brewery.

'What's the point of going there?' he said, half jokingly, but looking sideways at Humphrey to see how he would take it. 'If we wait here long enough the war will come to us, we don't need to go and look for the war.' Humphrey ignored this prophetic statement.

Gabriel was engaged in a flirtation of a heavy, rustic kind, with the maid of all work, an undersized little person from the country with hard, red cheeks and as sturdy as a bull. Miguel turned his attention to the pretty waitress, Montserrat, and asked her to go to the cinema. She shook her head, 'I am going out this evening with my fiancé.'

We all went out to a café. We heard cheering in the Rambla and stepped out into the street to see what it was. Several hundred international volunteers, who had been assembled together in Figueras after slipping separately across the frontier, were marching up from the station. They had no band, no banners, no uniforms; they were dressed in ordinary workmen's clothes with caps. A crowd was watching, giving them the clenched fist salute.

'That's a heartening sight,' said Humphrey. At first all the men were French, forming, in fact, the majority of the contingent. At intervals they shouted in unison, '*Ils ne passeront pas.*' Then came a small group of Italians who were singing *Bandiera Rossa, trionfera,* which is a fine, stirring song. Last came a compact body of Germans and Austrians, hard and not young, some with their women-folk. The women wore men's caps and were bundled in thick overcoats and mufflers. They were marching in soldierly fashion and singing their own songs.

'We need more of that kind,' said Humphrey, pointing to the last group. 'They are the backbone of the Brigade. It gives one confidence to see these people still arriving. If only Russia would send planes.'

'Sh,' said Manolo, who was with us, with his finger on his lips. 'I have heard that certain aeroplane parts, for seventy planes, arrived yesterday. They are now in Tarragona harbour being unloaded. They only need mounting.'

'I hope you may be right,' said Humphrey, 'and that it is not another rumour to cheer people up.' As he spoke all the lights went out. The Internationals had just arrived at the Plaza Catalunya and were about to be registered at the Hotel Colón. All was confusion.

'I didn't come all this way from Madrid just to run into an air raid,' said Humphrey.

'It's a trial black-out,' said a waiter from the café, where we had registered. 'We had warning there would be one tonight from ten until eleven. We are closing up; you will have to go.'

'Where are we supposed to go?'

'People are supposed to stay indoors – in the cellar if they have got one, I guess,' said the waiter.

We persuaded him to close the shutters but to allow us to remain inside. Humphrey caught sight of a friend, who joined us.

For a time Humphrey held forth on the Madrid situation. Like many people who have lived any length of time in the capital he had become an enthusiastic *madrileño*.

'You ought to go there,' he said, 'you're wasting your time here.'

'I don't see that,' replied his friend, Wintringham. 'It never seems to me that Madrid has the significance that people think. Surely it's only a great, pleasure-loving city, a head with no body, no hinterland, like Vienna. Its position is arbitrary. It is far from the coast. The industries and working-class populations are all round the periphery. Barcelona, Bilbao, Málaga, must all be more important and really more interesting than Madrid. I cannot see that it really matters if it falls. Napoleon took it but still lost the Peninsular War.'

'No, no,' said Humphrey. You're entirely mistaken. There are industries round Madrid and the working classes there are the finest in Spain. You will see.'

'It's easier to defend than this town,' said Miguel. 'It's inaccessible from the sea and much of it is on a height, and then there are plenty of old, narrow streets. Those are the things for street fighting; much better than these boulevards.' We little thought then that Madrid would still hold out when all the ports mentioned by Wintringham had been lost.

* * * * *

We set out for Valencia on a rainy day, accompanied by Manolo who had business there. He made some complicated deal with Humphrey involving Catalan *vales*, which were then unlimited, for petrol. We were in two cars. On the road were the bones of many motor vehicles and Manolo stopped several times to see if he could salvage small and easily removeable spare parts from these wrecks. The number of automobiles smashed up in the early days of the war was formidable, for boys 'requisitioned' cars and proceeded to learn to drive in them on public roads and at great speed. One of these wrecks was near the Roman arch which spans the Tarragona road so, while Manolo was investigating its tool box, we examined the arch. There was a good-sized hole in the base which workmen were repairing with plaster.

'What happened to the arch?' I asked Manolo.

'Some anarchists mistook it for a Christian monument and threw a hand-grenade at it. They've learned their mistake and are fixing it up again.'

We passed a village called Cantallups (which I thought meant 'melons' but Manolo said it was 'singing wolves') and we had lunch at Tarragona. We soon left Catalunya, filling the car up to the brim with petrol at the last village at the border. Darkness fell and rain streamed down. Humphrey's car broke down and had to be towed, so we spent the night at Castellón.

The town was packed with troops and we had the utmost difficulty in getting rooms. Some members of the party had to sleep on the floor. The hotel was overrun and consequently dirty and disorganised, the tables covered with broken bread, grease-spots and spilled wine. Order seemed to have been left behind at Tarragona. As we sat over a late dinner Manolo suddenly pointed to an item in a newspaper. We had not seen a paper that day. He looked fascinated yet horrified, his rather prominent eyes protruding still further.

'It can't be true,' he said, passing his hand over his high, shining forehead in a puzzled gesture. 'But if it isn't, would they dare to print it?'

The paper gave a far from clear account of Durruti's death. It said he had been wounded and died in hospital.

'I wonder if he was murdered and if so by whom?' Manolo said.

Strangely enough, I was plagued by mosquitoes that night and was still very tired when we got under way next morning. The streets, as is usual in Spain, were not arranged for water to drain off and, after the torrents that had fallen the day before, the town was all puddles and mud. It was still grey and lowering as we drove on along the flat roads, through orange groves.

*   *   *   *   *

The first place I was left in was the Wolga café while the others chased round to find beds. The Government had just moved to Valencia and the period had begun in which it was chronically impossible to find lodgings there and the overcrowding was at its most chaotic. The Wolga café was comfortable, luxurious, rather Parisian, with a modernistic interior, white stamped leather walls like a padded cell, red armchairs and a raised balcony. It was a funny place to find in provincial, old-fashioned Valencia. One could still get milk-coffee and buttered toast, or toast hot with some kind of grease on it. It was bombed later.

We had a horrible free lunch at the Europa, a restaurant for soldiers. Dubious-looking dishes were thrown at us. Manolo said, with a grimace, 'This wine has been baptised.'

We found bleak rooms with soiled sheets and no hot water, in what had been a grand hotel – now collectivised.

'Don't pay in *vales*,' the manager implored. 'We are being ruined by *vale* customers. Our debts are mounting. We have no cash to do the marketing. We're only granted a few pesetas a day on *vale* people and it costs much more than that to keep them.'

We listened sympathetically to this revelation of the economic weakness of the *vale* system and agreed, but it was very expensive. We went and stood on the balcony which overlooked the Plaza Castelar. The space in the middle was wet and muddy, the town hall (later burned by an incendiary bomb) was on one side, and the post office on the other. Both were floridly hideous. I took a dislike to the place.

The square was swarming with people milling about uneasily. They were waiting to see Durruti's coffin pass as he was being brought back to Barcelona. For he really was dead, the great anarchist who had rushed with his men to the defence of Madrid. He had been shot at from a window of a hotel in Moncloa, so the papers said. Some said he had been hit in the back by assassins hired by political opponents, some that he had got out of his car on the way to the front to speak to some of his men, some said to remonstrate with them and urge them back when they were fleeing. He had only been in Madrid a few days. He was rash and careless of his safety. His great saying was, 'I will relinquish everything but victory."

In the obituary notices he had had a thousand hair-breadth escapes: he had tried to blow up the Kursaal in San Sebastián, he was wanted by the police in South America, as a railway worker he 'had gone in for sabotage in a big way'. His death, so soon after leaving his old hunting-ground, Catalunya, had filled the people with doubt and rumours. We saw the crowds pressing and surging forward round the flower-covered *cortège* on that grey day and it seemed to portend ill. 'I wonder if the anarchists will cut up rough now,' said Humphrey. 'He was one of the few men who could manage them.'

Afterwards, in the twilight, we paced about among the puddles and sat on chilly, damp, stone seats in the plaza and Humphrey talked about Madrid. He had left at the worst moment and I do not blame him if, like so many other people, he had been rather panicked and exaggerated the likelihood of being killed in bed by a bomb, or by a Moor when the city fell. On hearing this account I began to have doubts about going. I should not have but Humphrey was so solemn, behaving as if I should make my last Will and Testament. He kept pointing out the dangers, and his responsibility, and what would my family say, and did I really feel suicidal, and I must think about it carefully first. I did think about it and was rather ambivalent, chiefly because I had got it into my head that Jan was probably in Albacete and I was casting about for some way of getting there.

In the end I swore I wanted to go to Madrid. Even so it was some time before I got there. The car had to be mended again, which was a slow process, and Humphrey was still reluctant to take me, still suggesting alternative proposals such as leaving me to attend to part of his work in Valencia. I was still thinking he might take me to Albacete. Zachary would have done that but I would not go on his terms, and I did not want to be left in Valencia at any price. It was full of civilians, evacuees from the capital, and did not seem to be anywhere near the war but full of political intrigues.

* * * * *

I was dreadfully bored in Valencia for it rained incessantly and I was hanging about there for a week or so with very little to do. My anxiety about Jan had lifted a bit. I had grown to rely on instinct and superstition and, if these sometimes caused me needless suffering, this time they served me well. I felt convinced that Jan was not and never had been anywhere near Valencia so that I ceased to strain after every face passing in the street.

One day I talked to some wounded Internationals in the café. They were Poles and their attitude surprised me. They said, 'What are you doing here? This is no place for girls like you. Go back home. This is what your boyfriend would want you to do.'

'But I want to go to Madrid.'

'What for?' they laughed.

'Oh, just to see what it's like.'

They shook their heads. 'It's not a joke and an amusement to go to Madrid. People don't go there for sightseeing.'

I felt rebuked and in the wrong. I asked about the militiamen.

'Ah, it's serious now,' they said. 'We don't want girls in it; it's too hard for them. Those we had in the beginning we have sent behind the lines to work in the administration. Why even the cooking is not fit for women. They cannot lift the great cauldrons of soup and our cook's a butcher by profession.'

One of the men said, 'It's not much satisfaction being in the infantry. I'd like to train for the aviation; that's the only satisfying way to fight. To drop bombs on the fascists, that I should like, to get back at them.' This remark was the only sign of bloodthirsty, warlike spirit that either of them showed. I was impressed by their extreme seriousness and stoicism. This seemed to be characteristic of anti-fascists. Accustomed as they were to exile and persecution they had wonderful qualities of self-sacrifice and endurance but they were pessimistic about the outcome. I found a noble but almost suicidal spirit in those chosen anti-fascist fighters who started as political refugees, such as the Germans and Poles. They insisted upon going into the thick of the battle, were consistently brave, but threw away their lives.

I spent most of my time in the comparative warmth and comfort of the Wolga café, reading, taking notes for Humphrey

73

from the papers. While we were waiting for the car to be repaired we had great trouble with the chauffeur, Gabriel. He looked adenoidal and always had a cold. He was from Jaén and miserable in the cold and wet. He was abysmally depressed. He had left his girlfriend in Madrid. He never said this; all he ever said was, 'I'm sad. I've left my underwear in Madrid.' Humphrey gave him some money to go to a brothel but he would not go.

As an economy, our party had moved into a vile, smelly *pensión* where they fed us on obdurate beefsteaks and radishes. In the hall, every night, the radio was turned on very loud, and the programme regularly wound up with the tunes then considered patriotic and complimentary to all sections of the Popular Front, which I soon learnt to distinguish from one another. There was *The Internationale*: 'Let us all join together for the final struggle', which was dignified but sad. Then there was *Hijo del Pueblo*, rather operatic: 'Oh son of the people, throw off your chains', and there was the Republican Anthem, which was an easy favourite with me as it was gay as a polka, one could not have marched to it, only hopped.

In Barcelona I had most heard, played by bands in processions, the anarchist *Hijo del Pueblo* and the Catalan anthem *Els Segadors*, both very sombre and formed in very irregular timing for marching. It was in Valencia that I first became familiar with the funereal *A las Barricadas*, always played on barrel organ and a great anarchist favourite, though they also had their own version of *The Internationale*. *A las Barricadas* was set to some old Russian tune and was sung with other words in other countries.

For some time I was always losing my way in Valencia. It was not entirely dark at night then but the lamps were painted blue. In the centre of the town the streets are so extremely narrow and twisting that it is hard to keep a sense of direction. There was a short cut from the *pensión* to the Wolga and I memorised the landmarks. First one crossed a main road on which a large block of modern flats was in process of construction and where there was a big café with strips of paper pasted in square patterns all over the windows. Then one dived down a dark alley, on the left of which was a restaurant called *Tot Va Ben* (All Goes Well). This sign appealed to my superstitious mind. It always cheered me and I always looked up at it in passing and repeated, like a magic rite, *Tot Va Ben.*

The café with the strips of paper we called 'checkerboard' and was the first of its kind I had seen. Of course it was decorated like that to prevent the glass shattering in case of air raids. The block being built was faced with dark red, imitation marble. We used to joke about it, saying that eventually it would house one of the ministries, that it would relieve housing congestion, until they abandoned work on it and it remained a shell with scaffolding round it.

One morning we were sitting in the 'checkerboard' café when we saw that a number of tables along the wall were reserved and were being laid with spoons, glasses and sugar rations, these last being given out in small paper bags the remains of which people used to save and take home with them. The waiter said these preparations were for the inmates of a female orphanage from Madrid. Refugees were only just beginning to arrive then and there was great competition to welcome and receive them. Soon the girls, in a uniform with a red cloak, trooped in, after driving most of the night in buses on by-roads. They had hot milk-coffee and some fell asleep. One had a nose bleed and some were very excited because they were in a café for the first time in their lives.

At that time people were saying that the only hope was to evacuate Madrid of its civilian population as they could not be fed. Propaganda to that end was plentiful. Yet a million civilians lived in Madrid to the very end, many of them essential for work such as making munitions.

In Barcelona, I had seen chiefly recruiting posters put out by the different organisations, the last one produced by the PSU showing a bleeding man half rising from the ground pointing an accusing finger and saying, *'¿Y tú, qué has hecho por la victoria?'*

In Valencia, I first saw the slogan, 'It is better to die on your feet than to live on your knees' – with its Church implications. I saw the hob-nailed workman's boot, Syndicalist Party, crushing the hydra-headed, top-hatted monster of Fascism. I saw Madrid as a serrated crimson tower which a great green serpent with swastika markings was trying to devour; this reminded me of

William Blake.

There was a saying current at the time which, like 'whistling in the wind' or 'who's afraid of the big bad wolf?' was symptomatic of a rather scared people, 'In Madrid nothing is happening, but if it should it doesn't matter'.

In the Wolga café, great men of the Madrid Government, apparently shrunken in stature and repute since the removal, came in wearing berets and ulsters and looking rather pallid and blue. This complexion was caused by the dark man's chin, plus cold, plus nerves. There was no doubt they had all had a bad fright in the capital and had rushed off leaving all their belongings which they did not expect to see ever again. Many of the more pusillanimous were quite sure the Republican ship was sinking, and they were not too easy about the anarchists here. I saw one or two in a box at a music hall with bodyguards.

In the café, the civil servants and politicians mingled with the Valencian farmers who were holding an orange-growers convention. The orange-growers, plump, rosy and steaming, loud-voiced, with big dripping umbrellas, who clustered thickest after lunch, had apparently no consciousness of the war at all. They were only concerned with the difficulties of marketing their produce that year. One big man was wearing a thick, red signet ring with a carved hammer and sickle, very noticeable when he raised his stubby finger to the side of his nose to emphasise an argument in a characteristic, canny peasant gesture.

Chapter 5
Madrid–The Tomb of Fascism

Meanwhile, the weather had changed. It was clear and bitterly cold. I remember the feeling of anachronism one night as the traditional *vigilante*, an aged man in a frogged coat who let us into the house, said, 'A lovely night for an air raid.'

We then fell into an argument about *serenos* and *vigilantes*, whether they are the same thing with different names in different parts of the country or whether their functions are different. Both are superannuated night-watchmen. Both rely on tips. The *vigilante* is supposed to guard people from robbers, though no able-bodied robber would have anything to fear. He keeps the keys of city buildings and lets people in after the street door is locked late at night. They clap their hands for as long as it takes to waken him from a doze in some corner. The *sereno* wakes everyone up, at intervals during the night, by calling out the hour and weather – all serene, usually – in a nasal, church voice. In a fishing village I knew, he used to wake the fishermen in the small hours by knocking thunderously on the doors and waking everyone else as well.

If we had a nervous fixation about the necessity of arriving in Valencia in daylight to have time to look for lodgings, it was much more extreme as regards Madrid. In Madrid it was totally dark at night and people were not allowed to circulate without special permits. It was essential to know the password or they might be fired at by patrols. Finding lodging was not a problem but feeding arrangements needed special organisation.

We left Valencia in the middle of a freezing, moonlit night. Perhaps our wits were dulled with sleepiness, anyway the car would not start and we thought it was cold. Then, to our despair since the garage bill had just been paid, Gabriel began pulling it to pieces. In fact there was no petrol in it. For weeks we had been hoarding a large tin of petrol in Catalunya which I kept under my bed for safety and shook from time to time to make sure its contents had not been tampered with. The night before, Gabriel had emptied it into the tank and then left the car parked in the street opposite the *pensión*. A thief had syphoned it out.

As Gabriel's pride would never have allowed him to admit that he had overlooked the car's lack of juice, and he would have gone on tinkering with the engine for ever rather than climb down, the rest of us had to walk off with the empty tin and try to get it filled. At last we found a gas station that was open and crowded with trucks from Madrid, and we managed to get our petrol before they announced that supplies had run out.

We were terribly crowded, what with the tin and luggage, and Miguel had added to our difficulties by tying a sack of potatoes on the back, for his family, which was too heavy for the small car. They were not even any use for, when he reached Madrid, he found his family had no fuel in the house to cook with and were just about to be evacuated anyway – but I expect he sold them.

Dawn was breaking when we finally left Valencia and we began to meet peasant cars coming into market with vegetables. Suddenly, without any warning, an old car came out of a side road and ran straight into us nearly overturning us and bending one door and mudguard badly. We all got out and both drivers began to abuse and attack each other. Luckily neither vehicle was travelling very fast. The farmer declared that every day for the past seven years he had driven out of that turning without once having an accident. We talked a lot about the war and important business. Finally all the men managed to bend the car back into sufficient shape to be driven again.

After the outskirts of Valencia, the lack of traffic on the roads seemed to be ominous. This was the only road open to Madrid; the railway had been cut. I expected a constant stream of refugees in one direction and food in the other but the road, as the sun came up and we began to climb the bare hills, was almost empty, quite unlike the Barcelona road. I suppose the explanation was that most people travelled in the dark for safety reasons.

As I feared I should never get another square meal we stopped at several villages to refresh ourselves with coffee and once with fried eggs. We began to pass guards, I think before the magnificent gorge in which the narrow, green river Cabriel runs under a lofty bridge. It was a splendid day without a cloud.

The people in the villages of Castilla seemed very dour; old people in black. There was nothing growing but this was corn country and the harvest was over. We did not see many patriotic posters.

When we were getting near Madrid we heard an aeroplane and the others made me get out and look for cover in the fields beside the road. The country was all open, there were no walls or ditches. Then we saw it was a very old government plane. It was funny how jittery we all were – in my case because I had never been to what was spoken of as 'the doomed capital' before. We asked a man in one of the few cars we met if the Vallecas road was under fire, as it had been at one time, necessitating a detour. He shook his head. Everything was silent as the grave in the direction of the enemy as elsewhere, we saw no people and no animals and it hardly seemed possible that we were approaching a great city.

Miguel, whose emotions were always transparent, began talking about the Barrio Salamanca where his family had moved to, in order to keep his spirits up. The Salamanca district was supposed to be recognised as a neutral zone as most of the foreign embassies were there. So far it had not been bombarded though it was later and the buildings of the British Embassy were hit. That it long enjoyed immunity, at a time when Madrid was subject to air raids shows that, contrary to assertions, it is quite easy to avoid bombing a non-military objective if one wants to, though it may not be so easy to hit a specific target. The Salamanca district at that time was largely inhabited by the *Quinta Columna* of Franco supporters or sympathisers who were waiting eagerly for his entry into the city. They later gave up hope and were starved out, after which the district lost its immunity. Miguel, who was a chronic rumour-monger, was uneasy because he had heard that the Salamanca district was being used in parts as barracks and munition stores which would draw enemy fire.

We entered Madrid rather suddenly and Humphrey began to point out ruined houses which did not look particularly recent and could have passed for slum clearance. On the outskirts, the streets were empty but in the centre they were crowded.

At three in the afternoon, when I had just got into a room in a hotel on the Gran Vía, I heard firing for the first time. It was the castanet-like rattle of anti-aircraft guns on neighbouring roofs which was the first sign of a raid; they no longer sounded sirens as there was no time. I stood on the balcony and there were more aeroplanes in the blue sky than I had ever seen together before except in the movies, flying in formation. A cloud of pigeons also wheeled round, startled by the noise. On the top of a hotel opposite was a statue of the Roman wolf with Romulus and Remus. Bombs fell dully quite far off. I felt hungry and faint but curious and with no sense of danger. Some of the planes were our chasers going up after the enemy; we had only just got some planes fast enough to be any use.

I think I was only a short time in Madrid – two or three weeks – but it seemed infinitely long, so much happened and life was so strange. My imagination is completely baffled when I try to picture how life seems to people who have been living there and have not been out of the city since the war started. They have gradually seen it change, seen the character of whole districts transformed, the once luxurious and fashionable places invaded by ragged refugees, shops, hotels and restaurants closed down for lack of supplies, and dangerous areas deserted.

Before I had really begun to look around me or notice the cold and discomfort, those elements which finally got me down as no danger could have done, my superstitions woke up again. The very first morning I awoke to the conviction that Jan was not far off and no time must be lost in reaching him. I was quickly agitating for Humphrey to take me to the front which I knew was only in the suburbs. There was a row; he did not want to take me or go himself. Even now I do not know why; lots of people since showed not the slightest scruple about taking me to the front and lots of women went. I did not know this at the time and Humphrey's arguments seemed unanswerable and myself unreasonable. I was cast into the most horrible gloom and depression. I worried away at him until he promised to go the next day with Jan's photographs.

All the time I was there I, and nearly everyone else I met, seemed to be in a dreadful state of irritability. I suppose it was part nervous tension and part dyspepsia from the food. I felt imprisoned there. I did not know my way about, the days were so short and the nights so dark that one might easily fall into a shell-hole. Most of the time I was alone typing and translating, my fingers freezing to the machine, while Humphrey was out on interviews and interminable business. Sometimes I sat in the car with Gabriel and waited outside buildings. Then there would be air raids and we would get out and stand just inside a doorway watching. People always watched and got very excited by the air battles and shouted, '*¡Ahora, ahora, baja uno de los pájaros negros!* (Now, now, one of the black birds is coming down!)' Once I looked up and noticed that we were standing under the heavy glass porch of the Hotel Palace, which would have made an awful mess if it had fallen and I pulled Gabriel inside the lobby because I preferred to die outright.

When he was not bound on any dangerous trips, such as to the front, Gabriel was liable to take his girl with him in the front seat of the car and then I felt rather *de trop* when we were parked. She was soft and plump with long hair in a bun, quite without artifice.

The first time Humphrey went to the front we had a bad raid in the afternoon and I must have been frightened, I think, by the noise and vibration of the guns which shook me up where I was working almost on the top floor. Before I knew it, I had gone downstairs where I began to talk to two or three sallow, wizened women who had collected there, to keep my spirits up.

It was very late and long since dark when Humphrey came back and I had sunk into a gloomy mood fearing he would never return, all hope of contact with Jan would be lost and I should be stranded. He came back in a bad mood too. He had not found Jan though he had been among the Germans of the Thaelmann Battalion and lots of them said they knew him from the photograph. Since we had no other information, the quest evidently made Humphrey feel foolish. He was very cross and it was some days before I was able to persuade him to go again, to another sector where there were said to be some English.

The cold got into my bones. Nowhere was there any heating and, though I gave up washing and went to bed in most of my clothes, I was never warm and ached and shivered at night so that I could not sleep. Always at night and again at dawn I heard the artillery bombing and did not know whose it was but supposed it was ours.

The houses had not been warmed since the previous winter and they were solidly built with tile and stone floors. We spent a lot of time in cafés because one could thaw out a bit in the stuffiness and warmth produced by other people. Most of the time one could only get tea without milk or sugar or hard drinks, no food. In the afternoons they were jam-packed with soldiers, sometimes fair ones like Jan that I watched wistfully. There were hardly any cigarettes (we had brought some with us) and matches were almost unobtainable. People with petrol lighters could not always get petrol for them and the soldiers had the kind that strikes a spark and has a long rope of yellow wick. A similar type is used by workmen in France and is very good in a high wind. I used to sit in the café until I saw someone strike a light and then borrow it. The Madrid match factory was at Carabanchel and it had recently fallen into the hands of the enemy. Once or twice we saw queues outside the tobacconists and waited in them hoping for cigarettes and only got a ration of two boxes of matches per person.

As all the population was supposed to be having military training or digging fortifications for part of each day, some shops, such as tobacconists and food shops, were only open in the morning or the afternoon. The resulting queues were endless, for everything including coal. Everything shut very early and I do not think the latest café was open after eight o'clock. Then the long, dark, cold night set in, listening to the artillery and the stray rifle shots of patrols fired as warnings at unshuttered windows.

Most shop windows were boarded up, having been broken in air raids or as a precaution, so they were semi-dark inside. They had been great stores, like Selfridges, but only luxury articles were left now in most of them, costly editions of books, elegant porcelain dinner services, English imported men's wear. These things seemed cheap because of the fall in the peseta.

We moved to rooms over a newspaper office, at least over the printing presses. We used to eat in a cellar at a long table with the employees, who were a merry crowd. At first I did not know why hungry people did not empty their plates but soon the food was nauseous to me too. The newspaper had adopted an old tramp, who could no longer live by begging or foraging in rubbish bins as no one threw anything edible away any more. For his keep he waited at table, his grimy thumb well submerged in each plate of soup, while people shouted at him, 'Hurry up you fascist!' The truck drivers were usually in a hurry. There was also a dwarfish girl they teased, but who always had a sharp answer. We called her Nell Gwynn because she came round after each meal distributing small, sour oranges from a basket.

When Humphrey went to the front he always got good food with the officers and he used to grab, and bring back for me in his pocket, Lucky Strike cigarettes and lumps of goat cheese. I do not know what went into the bread, possibly rice flour, but it was only just possible to eat it when fresh; within a few hours it became stone-like and would have made a dangerous missile or a solid barricade.

Madrid was full of barricades. Outside the General Post Office, gutted by fire, there were mail bags. I wondered wistfully whether they were stuffed with all the mail never dispatched or received. We were barricaded with unsold newspapers between small evergreen trees in pots such as one sees outside Paris pavement restaurants.

Most places of business had subterranean dining rooms established for their workers, as individually it was impossible to procure food – ours brought supplies daily from Valencia, sometimes very odd supplies such as a load of small squid. The Gran Vía Hotel was almost empty of residents as it was opposite the Telefónica, a sky-scraper which drew shell fire, but the journalists, who mostly lived in their respective embassies, often ate there all sitting at a long table like a school treat. There, for a price, we had meat and beans in the basement.

One of the most oppressive things about Madrid, which was grey and icy cold throughout most of my stay, was the darkness. The nights were so long in December, interiors were dimly lit and outside it was black and full of pitfalls from débris. I was always afraid of losing my way as I did not know the streets by name, only their appearance. I could only find my way between my lodgings, the Telefónica and the Puerta del Sol where there were stalls selling what soldiers might need, Cossack caps made of imitation fur, and bootlaces and knives sold by Chinese.

At night we sometimes went to a building where the Ministry of War then was, with a dark patio and guards sleeping on cots. Otherwise, we went to the censorship department at the Telefónica where the personnel also camped out. The head there was a plump, moustached, Austrian woman, later disgraced for some political reason but powerful then.[39] There was another such woman in charge of radio UGT. We distinguished between them by saying that the Telefónica one wore corsets while the UGT one did not. I think many of these central Europeans, who had good jobs during the war, were fired afterwards for Trotskyism; Selke[40] in Valencia was fired by a Republican who had not the least idea what Trotskyism was but found it a convenient excuse.

I had a strange feeling in the Telefónica because it was a modern, American building, the exact counterpart of many I had seen in the States with a number of smoothly running lifts with a lighted indicator to show which floor they were on.

There were three cafés where we used to go. The cafés that were not jammed full of people were only empty because they had nothing to offer but tea. There was the Molinero where one could get coffee and hard liquor, the Aquarium – very crowded, and the one that stayed open the latest, the Miami. The Miami had modernistic decorations and had been elegant and was still expensive. One crept into it through a half-closed door, like a speakeasy, and it had whisky and a bar. Here one found journalists, commercial aviators and whores still clean and fairly smart, though the ones with bleach-blond hair were becoming piebald for lack of peroxide. It was all at the hospitals and plenty of nurses had blond hair.

Superimposed over the modern decorations were posters warning against spies – figures with enormous ears, entitled 'Vigilancia en la Retaguardia', and posters showing bottles of milk, eggs, hens and cows, saying 'Do not slaughter the livestock

84

– food for today means hunger for tomorrow.' The atmosphere of this café was horrible, the atmosphere of war, feverish and demoralised. Only once we saw there a party of German soldiers, all middle-aged, with short-cropped, greying hair. They were drunk and singing terribly sad songs, marching songs.

When the time came to return to barracks, their leader rose, followed by them all with perfect discipline and they drank a farewell toast. '*Rot Front, Rot Front,*' they shouted in deep bass voices.

'We need more like them,' said Humphrey.

Once again Humphrey went to the front. He said he was going to see the Edgar André Battalion, so many English confounded this with the Franco-Belge because of the name, vaguely reminiscent of Edgar Quinet.[41] Actually, the battalion was named after a German revolutionary hero who had been executed.

As usual he returned late, after dark. He said he had found some English but several were absent as they had been wounded a few days before and we set off immediately for the hospital to visit them as one was a friend of Humphrey. There were guards at the door and we had some parley to get inside. Humphrey looked at the register in the porter's lodge and I looked over his shoulder, with hope and dread that I should find there the name I was seeking. If he were slightly wounded then at least he would be safe for a bit, but it might be something dreadful, he might be mutilated or disfigured, or dying.

The name Humphrey was seeking was there but we were told it was only a scratch and he had already been discharged. Then we asked to see any English-speaking patients. It was an immense building, with many courtyards, iron fire escapes and wings connected by long corridors. We wandered a considerable distance until at last we entered a vast, dimly-lit ward. Near the door a blond boy was on his feet, convalescent. He looked at us eagerly. He was German but led us, limping, down the ward between the double row of beds until we came to an American. He shouted to us in welcome and recognised me before I recognised him. He was a cheery, boastful, very young boy with thick, square-lensed spectacles. I had met him in Barcelona where he had arrived with the intention of being an aviator.

'I found I hadn't enough experience as a pilot, only a few hours in the air,' he said, 'and my eyesight was a disadvantage. So when I got to Albacete they shoved me in the Thaelmann and those German guys are swell and we get on fine. The other night I led a raid on a little red hen-house in no-man's land where there were some fascists and I took a couple of Jugoslavs with me. We couldn't understand a word each other said but we managed all right and we stormed the hen-house but I got one in the knee, but I'll soon be all right.'

'Yes, I heard about it,' said Humphrey, giving him a couple of cigarettes, Luckies. We wanted to move on but the boy detained us as long as he could. He was so glad to have someone to talk to. We got away by promising to come again (though we never did) and he pointed out an old Australian further down on the other side.

The Australian was pretty tough, though he seemed less lively than the boy, but he was glad to see us too. We gave him some smokes and asked him what unit he came from and if there were any English in it. 'Yes,' he said, giving several names, 'and there is that quiet German chap, Jan.' He went on to describe him and I had no further doubts; the search had ended. He told us the name and number of the unit; Jan was in a machine-gun section of the Commune de Paris (Dumont) Battalion. He said he had not been in hospital long and he thought the battalion was still resting at a certain barracks if we wanted to find them. I surreptitiously noted down the name on the corner of a magazine I was carrying. Humphrey did not want to find them and was in a very bad humour at my excitement.

We went from there to another hospital, the San Carlos, to see another friend of Humphrey. This did not look so much like a real hospital as the first one and made a dismal impression on me. It was perhaps an old monastery. There were thick stone walls and arches and the walls were caked with the dirt of ages.

'This isn't as good as the other hospital,' I remarked. 'Why does your friend stay here?'

'It's better in a way,' said Humphrey. 'The other has been a good hospital but it's much nearer the front than this so the wounded don't feel so safe there. They're very nervous of air raids when they're lying helpless, or that the fascists will get in and slaughter them in their beds as they did in Toledo.'

We found the youth, Donald, near the door. He was a well-educated, pleasant boy, with a fresh face. He was rather thin and overgrown and did not look a day over eighteen. He was just such a son as must be the pride and joy of many an English, suburban, middle class home. It seemed strange to see him tossing with fever in his soiled bedclothes in these surroundings. He was a modest boy and most annoyed that his mother had taken to writing and telegraphing to the British Embassy to try to get news of him.[42]

Humphrey told me that Donald had enlisted in the very beginning hoping to be an aviator. Like the American, he had not enough experience and so went into the Fifth Regiment as the International Brigades had not then been formed. The Fifth Regiment was organised by the Spanish Communists for the defence of Madrid. It was well disciplined and was the nucleus of the later People's Army. It was largely manned by the JSU including many students, and several painters and sculptors of note were killed in it. Its losses were very heavy. In Donald's section he was the only foreigner though the regiment contained a sprinkling of German émigrés who found themselves in Spain at the outbreak of war.

He was happy with the Spanish comrades and had recently rendered a signal service in capturing an enemy machine-gun at a time when the Republicans were desperately short of weapons; for this he was promoted to sergeant and then he was wounded. It was only a slight wound in the wrist but it had gone bad, his whole arm was swollen and, from his chart, his temperature was very high. He looked very ill with deep lines under his grey eyes and flushed cheeks. He did not know how bad he was, for he was not very clear in his mind, but he was a bit worried and wanted to get out of Madrid if he could as his wound had not been dressed for a couple of weeks and hurt him a great deal, and he could tell it was not healing as it should.

That night we went round to talk to some people of the Scottish Medical Aid to try to get Donald evacuated to the coast. We argued and argued. We said he would not take up much room in an ambulance as he could sit up. The ambulances were being used to evacuate people from the British Embassy – Spaniards who had some claim to be British, Gibraltarians and such, and in a day or two they were going to Alicante. From there it would be possible for Donald to get a plane to France. Humphrey knew people in Alicante who, he said, would look after Donald until he could get away but we were not sure if he had enough money to take the plane. We were as eloquent as we could be as Humphrey was convinced that Donald would die unless he got to a decent hospital, and I kept imagining Jan in a similar situation and how grateful I would be if people helped him.

The next morning we went to the Embassy and tried to persuade the officials there to help. Humphrey was in a filthy temper because he said he was wasting his time being humanitarian instead of writing articles and he would be fired. On the way I saw an old woman feeding a goat on a strip of ornamental shrubbery that ran up the boulevard and another collecting sticks in the park for firewood. There were one or two ancient horse-cabs with horses as stark as Don Quixote's Rocinante.

At the Embassy they knew about Donald who, I think, had his passport with him, but they said he had forfeited all rights as a British subject in joining the Spanish army.

In the afternoon I went with Gabriel to fetch Donald from the hospital and take him for a drive. Donald was helped out wrapped in a blanket and it was only when I saw him trying to walk that I realised how weak he was. The nurses had sprinkled him liberally with eau-de-cologne. 'Because my arm smells so,' he explained with the blush of miserable embarrassment of the nicely brought up boy. It did. It was rotting and stinking. Of course I pretended not to notice it but was torn between his wish to keep the window open to avoid offence and my anxiety lest he should catch cold. His arm gave off the sickly odour of the grave which, combined with the cheap eau-de-cologne, made me feel quite faint.

It was one of the few sunny afternoons but he was in no state to enjoy a chat or a change of air and scene. He seemed more apathetic than before and sometimes dozed off as I saw his small, narrow head nodding above the blanket. Our way was often blocked by barricades and guards and we had to turn back several times. Not being a *madrileño,* Gabriel only knew the direction of the front and kept well away from that. All the roads were very bad and I told him to be careful because of the bumps and to go slowly, but the little Ford was not very comfortable for an invalid. We went on the Guadalajara road, past fine houses in the suburbs, all closed and deserted, and then bare, rolling hills, blue and red in the sunset, until we came to a signpost to Zaragoza. The signpost gave me an eery feeling, leading on to the dry, white, open, unbarred road to enemy territory.

When we were back in Madrid, Donald suddenly showed signs of animation and pulled a couple of crumpled pound notes from an inside pocket. 'Let me stop at the bank and change them for pesetas,' he said. 'I shall need them for my journey.' We were in fact passing a bank and I jumped out to humour him. It was barred and surrounded with sandbags and bore a sign to say it was no longer functioning. In any case, all foreign currency exchange was strictly controlled by then. I soothed him as best I could. He made me keep the notes and promise to change them for him. He became increasingly peevish and had to be carried back into the hospital.

I gave Humphrey an account of the afternoon and we went again to the Embassy to press the matter, as we were certain now it was a question of life and death. This time we were successful and Donald was evacuated and reached Paris, where he recovered his health and did not even lose his arm, as I had expected.

It was two days before Humphrey went to the front again. People may think I was very lacking in initiative not to have gone to the barracks to enquire for Jan. As a woman, I had small chance of being allowed near a barracks and as a foreigner, I did not know my way about and rarely went out alone. I did not know how to get to places by tram and had no command of Gabriel or the car. Moreover, it was a perpetual struggle to obtain petrol for our immediate needs and cars left parked outside cafés or elsewhere were liable to be requisitioned. I was in Humphrey's employ and he kept me busy typing and translating though in an agony of impatience.

It was a frozen, iron-grey day. There was no hope that the room might be slightly warmed by a few short hours of sun through the window. I gazed out most of the afternoon and obtained a very bird's eye view of the blind alley in which we lived as the houses in Madrid were several storeys high and we were near the top. I saw a camouflaged car draw up, it was the first I had seen. It must have come from the front for above the camouflage of paint was a more effective one of mud. It had been painted in a red-brown, the colour of dried blood, by someone who usually devoted his skill to producing imitation marble patterning on shop fronts. I could see that from the design, and the effect was striking. I saw a big rat running along the gutter, in broad daylight, no doubt driven out into the open by starvation for there was no longer enough garbage to support the rats.

Night fell and I waited, carefully nursing the remaining cigarettes and matches. At last the Ford drove up. I had become preternaturally quick at recognising its sound. I went down by the stairs, for I could not work the heavy lift meant for freight, but I watched for it as I groped my way so that Humphrey should not pass me on the way up. We met in the dark porch.

'Well, I have seen Jan,' he said drily, 'and I suppose you want to hear how it was.'

We sat down on a huge drum or barrel.

'It was in a building in University City where the machine-gunners were. The others crowded round when they saw me but he stood apart until they called him.'

'How was he looking?'

'Dressed in navy blue. Thin but well. I gave him your message and told him where you were. He sent his love.'

I poured out questions, wanted more detailed description, but did not get anything and we both fell silent. I had realised at length that Humphrey was jealous of the soldiers. It sounds an odd thing to say but he envied them their heroism. I must add, to be fair, that he later joined up himself, being dissatisfied with a passive role in the war, and acquitted himself creditably.

The next afternoon, at about three, when we were working, I with wandering thoughts, there was a tramping of heavy boots and a commotion in the passage, and suddenly Jan burst in followed by two other men. Before we had even looked at each other, we had hugged each other. The man from below, Menéndez, brought in some bottled beer for a treat. Humphrey forced himself to be genial.

Jan should have looked tough; his face was very thin, red and weather-beaten, his eyes strained and tired. He had great hobnailed boots, a scarf and dirty trench coat, the navy blue jersey I had sent him to Paris, and blue ski trousers with a rent in the knee. On his head he wore a little khaki, Spanish forage cap. His beard was half grown. His cheek was fresh and cold like that of someone always in the open. Somehow he looked much more young, tender and vulnerable than ever before.

We all went to a café and ordered buns and drinks as they had made a rendez-vous with some other comrades there. They ate voraciously and the waiters treated them with indulgence. There was a man with curly hair, evidently an undergraduate, who talked about his dysentery, an older, working-class man, who asked where he could get books and maps, informative ones on Spain. There was John Cornford, big and dark and handsome, with a white bandage round his head making him look like a Moor, who asked after friends in the British Medical Aid and others.[43] Jan and I went and sat at a table by ourselves and drank gin and lime because we wanted to remember sitting in the Load of Hay on Haverstock Hill and he talked nostalgically of Camden Town and how one could buy chocolate bars and go to the movies there.

He told me that by some miracle he had received a letter sent as a forlorn hope to Albacete. It was delivered to him in the front line and all the English were very excited, especially the man it was addressed in care of, and he was very disappointed when he found it was really for Jan. None of the English had received any letters from home though the French had done so. Mine only reached him because it was sent from within Spain. After he received it, he gave my name and address in Barcelona to the Commandant in case he should be killed or wounded, as nearest of kin to be informed.

I asked why he had not answered. He said his life now was too different from anything I could imagine. He did not want to see girls or maintain any links with what to him was another world. He talked as if he were already dead. At one time, he said, he had formed a plan to get leave, perhaps at Christmas, and come to Barcelona to surprise me, but the Internationals never got any leave. They were now having *descanso* (rest) in barracks and had to be back every night. There they had lectures on poison gas and politics, and sometimes saw Russian films.

He said that they were in the Philosophy and Arts building at University City and that many fine books had been left there. They made barricades of them but read them too. He had read Dickens and some poetry that he liked very much but he could not remember the author. The scholars read old books in Greek and Latin, for several of the English were from Oxford and Cambridge. He had never been in Barcelona. At six o'clock it was time for him to return to barracks.

The next day, Jan appeared again in the morning, though not early as it took an hour or so to come from the barracks in the lorry. Humphrey insisted on taking us to lunch at the Gran Vía, the only place we could go where, in the perpetual artificial light of the half-empty basement, we consumed an old vintage wine for which we were grossly overcharged. It was an unhappy day, somehow taken up with practical trifles. Most of the afternoon was spent going round various places trying to get some clothes for Jan as he was quite inadequately clad for sleeping out there on those freezing nights or on a stone floor in barracks. At the headquarters of the Brigade they made a lot of red tape as there was a German in charge who said Jan's own battalion should give him clothes. At that time, none of the men had uniforms and most had bought their own boots and revolvers in France. One of the boys had a fine khaki overcoat that he had pinched off a dead fascist officer.

Gabriel and I waited a long time outside the *Socorro Rojo* (Red Cross aid station) while Miguel, Humphrey and Jan went in and negotiated. There was an air battle going on in the distance. Jan was pleased with what he got: warm underwear, a brindled woollen jacket, black corduroy peasant trousers – stiff and too big for him. He said the socks I had sent were very good.

We went back to my room and talked for a while. I am afraid I cried and argued and then was ashamed of myself for disturbing his few hours of peace and rest. At nightfall Gabriel had leave to drive the two of us back to the barracks. We went silently, holding hands, and I watched him go in at the big gates as if he was entering a prison.

Humphrey got very drunk that night and was ill and I had to help him to bed. In Madrid there was no way to be happily drunk. Perhaps because the drink or food was bad, one always became miserable and had a hangover the next day as we did in prohibition America. Yet one was driven to drink because it produced a little warmth.

The next afternoon, just as we were setting to work, Humphrey said, 'One can't get settled any more. Every day now I expect to hear those cursed Internationals tramping down the passage.' Sure enough one of them came and Humphrey said he was busy and sent me out to amuse the man, George. George said that Jan was ill with a feverish cold and was lying in the infirmary. I took George to a big store to try to buy a pocket knife but they only had table cutlery in stock. I left him in a café while I went to get a new glass for Jan's watch. There was a queue of people waiting in a little room underground for clocks and watches to be mended, but at last I got the glass. I sent George back with it and a note for Jan and some out-of-date American magazines which were still available on the news stands.

That night I was the one to get drunk and be ill. Jan had said, just as the Poles had done in Valencia, that I should not have come to Spain, that I should not be mixed up in a war, that if I insisted on remaining at least I should get a 'safe' job in Barcelona or on the coast and not stay in Madrid. I knew also that Humphrey did not really need me and had only brought me so that I might perhaps find other work. I had promised not to stay in Madrid, but I wanted to stay to be near Jan in case anything happened to him.

For two days I could not get up for I had a fearful cold or flu. The Spanish people there, a hard-faced woman in an apron and a blousy one with tangled hair and a kimono, were kind. They pottered in the neighbouring kitchen, where the gas was turned on for only a few hours a day, and made me tea from a packet I had brought with me. Once, Humphrey brought me a cup of hot milk which was almost unobtainable in Madrid.

While I was ill, Humphrey bought me a couple of books to read, in one of the grand bookstores in Madrid, *Moby Dick* and one of William Faulkner's. In Madrid's shops things were much more the same as before the war than in Barcelona. In Barcelona there had been time for more 'revolution' before war threatened. Everything had been changed; a new era had been launched. The Ritz was called '*Gastronómico no. 1*', everything was requisitioned, new publications and posters poured in an avalanche off the presses; schools and maternity clinics were installed in fine, deserted villas. Later in the war all this regressed.

In Valencia, not so much had been done. The orange-growers of the Levant had been annoyed by the anarchists' early efforts at forcible collectivisation and regarded the Minister of Agriculture, Uribe, a communist, as their protector. He had finally arranged to sell the entire crop to Russia, which amused Manolo: 'I can see those snow-bound Russians saying to themselves, "Aha, we shall have oranges this winter".'

The women tended to be more conservative than the men and scenes took place like that described to me by an Irish volunteer: 'The men were making a bonfire of the confessional boxes and other tawdry rubbish out of the church while their wives stood wailing with their aprons over their heads.'

* * * * *

On the Sunday, there was a gleam of sun and I thought I would creep out in the afternoon to warm up in a café. I bundled myself up in all the clothes I possessed, woollen stockings with socks over them, gloves, and a scarf over my head. Humphrey and I were walking up the Gran Vía when we met Jan by chance, shaved and smart, with his muffler round his neck and his little cap on the back of his head. I left Humphrey and ran up to him. I must admit that I treated Humphrey with abominable rudeness. He was considered an attractive and popular young man and was not accustomed to such treatment, but Jan seemed a visitant from another world and every moment I could spend with him was of the utmost value.

Jan and I turned into a café where we spent several hours. We obtained toast and he had a fancy for jam. The waiter produced a horrible, gluey, spinach green concoction out of a tin, that looked truly poisonous. By six o'clock we were fairly drunk and cheerful and it was time for him to leave. I tried to persuade him to stay. He said that he had never once disobeyed orders or been in any trouble since he joined up and was a model soldier. He added that many of his battalion had behaved badly at the base, so much so that now the Government locked them up and he was very anxious to avoid the Internationals getting a bad reputation with the Spanish population. Eventually he said that he would go to Cuatro Caminos and if the lorry was there he would go and if it was not he would stay.

We went down into the metro, the only time I ever travelled on it. Jan did not buy tickets, he just said '*Columna Internacional*' and everyone smiled and patted him on the back and sponta- neously gave him things. The Internationals were the heroes of the populace in those days since everyone believed they were saving Madrid. On the platform, a number of poor refugee families were camping and Jan gave them all his small change because, he said, money was no use to him. The train was crowded and we had to stand.

All was dark at Cuatro Caminos and at first we saw no truck, but after walking round the crossroads for a short time, when we were just about to give up, we saw it standing a little way off. We stood and watched it. There were some men in it and they shouted, '*Tu viens avec nous?*'

'No,' Jan suddenly shouted, and they drove off. We turned away quickly and hurried back into the metro as Jan was afraid the military police would come and get him. We went back to the Gran Vía Hotel, which was the only place I could think of. At first they did not want to let us have a room but at last the manager agreed and we did not ask the price. They made it very expensive because they knew we wanted it and probably suspected that Jan did not have leave, and were snobbish because he was not even an officer. I left him in the Miami bar and went to fetch my night things, which I brought in a bundle like a refugee.

We had dinner in an alcove in the basement, some sort of stew and some wine. Jan said it tasted very good but it disagreed with both of us. There was a fat, drunken old French officer who knew Jan from Albacete and rushed up and embraced him. We went upstairs and I tried to get Jan a hot bath but all the water was cold; I do not think there were any hot baths in Madrid then except at the British Embassy. Our room had thick curtains but was like a tomb. We shivered in bed and could not sleep. Jan said it was a long time since he had had his boots off and still longer since he had slept in a bed. He was so unaccustomed to it that he nearly had to get out and sleep on the floor. The wind must have been blowing our way for we heard the guns firing so loudly that we had to shut the window to deaden the noise. Jan kept worrying that there might be an attack and that when he got back to barracks his battalion might have moved and he would be unable to find them.

In the morning, shivering and dead tired, we went to a café for breakfast. Then I took Jan into the press department in the Telefónica and begged some old copies of the *News Chronicle* for him to take back with him as his comrades were very glad of papers they could read. Jan gave me some English money he had brought from home because he said he did not need it and I might. We were sitting in the half-empty café drinking port when some men came in that he knew. They had come into town to fetch supplies and said they would take him back with them. The last I saw of him he was sitting on the back of the truck with a grin fixed on his face and his fist raised in the People's Front salute. I stood in the street with my fist up too, waving at him until he disappeared and then I crawled back to my room.

The next evening Humphrey had decided to leave Madrid. In the meantime Miguel had deserted him on some pretext, really because he was afraid to stay, but he still had the driver, Gabriel. Humphrey said he did not need me any more and I got in touch with the Austrian woman who worked at the Telefónica, who said she might have work for me speaking in English on the radio or work in the Telefónica. This was not a very enviable workplace as it was always being shelled, as the tall white skyscraper was the best target in Madrid.

I decided I could not stay in Madrid then as I felt ill and my own money was almost gone. I had pooled most of it with Humphrey's resources to help pay for repairs to the car. I told her that if I came back I must have some place arranged where I could eat as it was impossible to obtain food in Madrid. I promised to be back in a week or two, but it was longer than that before I saw Madrid again.

It was nearly Christmas and I spent the remaining hours trying to get together some little gifts for Jan. I bought him some elegant leather gloves in a smart store as I had seen he had none. Then I scoured the chemist shops for aspirin, the only remedy he had any use for. Most of the aspirin in Spain was made by Bayer and after the war started of course it was no longer imported from Germany and stocks had run out. I was obliged to content myself with a Spanish substitute. Then I put together a handy little mending kit (which my mother had given me) which Jan said he needed. I did this odd collection up in a parcel with a letter.

I then found my way by tram to see a friend of Jan's, Walter.[44] I knew he would be sure to see him if he was in Madrid again. I had understood that some sort of celebration was to be provided for the Internationals in Madrid – either at Christmas or New Year, called the *Cena de la Victoria*. I did not know Walter at all – he had known Jan long before I met him. He was now employed in a newspaper office. When I got there I was embarrassed to discover that he did not speak English or French and we were obliged to converse in Spanish, a language foreign to both of us. I was rather feverish and hysterical. The frost had broken and wet weather had set in. The rain poured down like passionate tears. I charged Walter with a lot of messages for Jan. I had wanted to meet him too because he made one more contact in Madrid; I meant to return there and it was so hard to get along without knowing anyone.

Chapter 6
Retreat

We left that night but almost had to turn back at Vallecas because we did not know the password when we came to the armed post there. Every day the *consigna* was changed and whoever invented it had a poetical turn of mind. When we had entered Madrid the answer was 'Cossacks' but I forget the question. One time it was 'where are you going?' and the answer was 'to victory'. After an argument, they let us pass.

The night was as black as a pocket and towards Valencia we ran into fog, but I was glad enough to descend from the plateau as the air was sensibly warmer and my hands and feet began to burn and ache as they thawed. At Utiel we stopped in a great café papered with old, once brightly-coloured but now faded posters for bull-fights with the war-time slogans superimposed, and had coffee for the asking. It seemed like a miracle and still more so when in Valencia, which seemed a land flowing with milk and honey in comparison to what we had left, we had fried eggs in another café. By great good luck there were still rooms to be had in the place where we had stayed before.

I spent most of the day sleeping. Humphrey wrote me a reference in French, this was very necessary as anyone discharged without due reason might be suspected of not being politically valid. Had this happened, I might have been arrested or, being English, more probably expelled from Spain.

I was obsessed with the idea that Jan might be wounded and then he would be put in the San Carlos Hospital or one of those dreadful places where people had their legs and arms chopped off unnecessarily or got blood poisoning like Donald. I determined to make a quick trip to England, write some articles, raise some money any way I could and return with enough foreign currency on me to get Jan out of Spain by air if necessary. It was permitted to bring money in if one declared it and had the amount written in one's passport. It did not occur to me that I should be up against any official red tape in getting Jan out of

Spain as Donald had just left without hindrance. This must have been either because Donald belonged to a Spanish regiment or because things were tightened up later. Though the Fifth Regiment was the most disciplined of Spanish troops it was not as strict as the International Brigades by any means. The latter were kept in puritanical strictness and seclusion.

The next morning at eight there was supposed to be a train for Barcelona and Gabriel and I were waiting at the station but the train did not come until midday. It was called the train from Seville because it had always been called that but actually it came from Aranjuez, the nearest station to Madrid remaining to us. It was crowded with refugees. The evacuation of the civil population of Madrid by road had been slowed down by lack of petrol but they still came by train.

I found a corner in a third-class carriage which was cluttered up with a mattress and a very awkward sack of something knobbly that barred the doorway. The carriage contained an old man, several children and a respectable old lady in black. She talked to me of the dangers of a young woman travelling alone and counselled me to speak to nobody. Just after the train started a little boy, of about ten, was found howling up and down the corridor. His mother and a small sister had got out at Valencia to try to find some food and the train had gone without them. Other people fed and soothed the boy, telling him he only had to sleep the night in the waiting room at Barcelona and his mother would come by the next train and find him.

As I was very tired, I wandered down the train to try to find a more comfortable seat and found a cushioned first-class carriage with three anarchist militiamen in it. Whenever I travelled, I always met anarchists who seemed to be the only people who ever got leave. I talked with them for a while. One was tall, thin and dark with an aquiline profile, a typical handsome Spaniard, in a long *capote manta* which hung in folds about him and gave him great dignity. He was a 'thinking' man. He asked if I were Russian and, though disappointed at my reply, said, 'Never mind, all foreigners who are antifascists are our brothers.' He said that he thought women should have more freedom and independence and lamented the influence of the Catholic Church over them. He wanted to hear what a foreigner thought of the war and the prospects of Spain.

'Why don't the English help us?' he asked.

I answered this, ashamed, but as best I could, by saying that many English people were for the Spaniards but their rulers were against them.

He was from the south and spoke with an accent I found hard to follow. The other two were small with bristly chins and were much jollier and less austere than the tall one.

They went to the restaurant car and bought sandwiches, some of which they gave me, and then they tore the bill into small pieces and trampled on it. One kept trying to make me drink from a leather wine-bottle which they passed round. The tall one had some garlic sausage and a linen bag containing dried figs from his home town, prepared with aniseed, which he said were especially good and he pressed them on me though I dislike aniseed very much. They were all so very friendly, not flirtatious, that I did not wish to hurt their feelings.

One took off a rather greasy neckerchief and unfolded its creases with an air of reverence. Then he showed it to me. 'Durruti,' he said, since I looked blank. It was in black and red artificial silk and on it was printed the tough face with out-thrust jaw of the dead leader, and over it was written 'the hero of the people'. He admitted it was not a very good portrait. I later saw a similar one with Lenin's portrait on it – one of the Internationals gave it to me knotted round a lump of *turrón* (something like nougat) and, I am sorry to say, Lenin looked quite as greasy as Durruti.

My companions fell asleep and the shortest one began to snore loudly, the carriage grew stuffy, some sort of insects emerged from the upholstery and began to bite me, so I returned to my original compartment. The old lady in black gave me a reproachful look for leaving her safe chaperonage. I wondered what she would have said if she had seen me fraternising with the anarchists.

At ten that night we reached Barcelona, where I was astonished to find the streets brightly lighted and quite an air of animation.

I returned to London as quickly as I could. At Port Vendres I had to borrow francs from an acquaintance so I could go on to Paris. In Paris, I had to telegram London for the necessary to pay my fare to England.

As soon as I got back I telephoned some friends of Jan to tell them that I had seen him and he was well. These friends invited me to lunch at a grand restaurant, to make up for the privations in Spain. They were in the newspaper business and they had news for me.

'Our correspondent in Madrid tells us that Jan has been wounded in the legs,' said Plummer.[45]

'It is not possible,' I gasped. 'It is only a week since I saw him and he was well.'

'Well, one of the papers published it, with his name, though slightly garbled,' said Plummer. 'Of course they may have mixed him up with someone else, people have been wrongly reported dead.'

'But I saw George, a comrade of his, in Barcelona, and he said he had left him well,' I protested.

'It might have happened just after you both had left,' said Plummer.

I was dreadfully upset, and I determined to go back as soon as I could. I remembered those hospitals in Madrid and was horrified. I began to describe them all too vividly to Mrs Plummer and her husband told me to shut up as his wife was very sensitive to such things and I should not upset her. I rather despised that kind of inactive sensibility. I am sure I felt it more deeply than she did but I did not banish it from my mind.

Everyone seemed to think it very brave of me to have gone to Spain and to be going back there, which surprised me. On Christmas Day, I was taken to a fancy dress dance where most of the people were dressed as pirates and looked for all the world like anarchists and I felt very strange and out of place. I spent most of my time not in the ballroom but the buffet where there was cold tongue and goose and Roquefort cheese and more abundance of good things than I had seen in a great while.

I wrote two articles and got them published through V.S. Pritchett who also gave me an introduction to the *Christian*

Science Monitor and I became a correspondent for this paper. A friend gave me an opportune cash Christmas present. Mr Plummer gave me directions to get in touch with their *Daily Express* correspondent in Madrid and to tell him to add a message about Jan on to his daily telephone call to the paper, and he gave me a card of introduction.

I went to see a lady connected with the Medical Aid and told her I had been working in Spain and was about to return and offering to carry parcels or letters back with me. She was very cool, entrusted me with nothing, and merely said, 'I thought I knew all the English people working in Spain.'

I took my mother to see a film of the International Brigade, a very bad, foggy film, with no Jan in it, but a close-up of the German hero Hans Beimler who had been killed just as I got to Madrid.[46] A lady made a speech asking for subscriptions to buy boots for the Internationals. I cried when I saw the film, as bad as it was it brought it all back to me.

When I left, Mr Plummer had additional intelligence to give me. He said that their correspondent had seen Jan and that he had been evacuated to some hospital outside Madrid. This was untrue but gave me some ease of mind. I kept wondering if the wound were slight, in which case Jan might be back in the line before I could return, or if something dreadful would happen like a leg being amputated before I could stop it. I collected together what was portable and what I thought he would like, chocolate bars, Woodbine cigarettes, some *New Yorkers* and *Times*, bought in Paris, and I set off again just before new English regulations concerning Non-Intervention were about to come into force which would have made my journey more difficult.

American and English rules varied in this matter. Both were chiefly afraid of allowing young men to go to Republican Spain who might join the International Brigades (and often did) but tried to discourage everyone. The Americans threatened their commercial aviators, serving in Spain, with deprivation of citizenship. All American passports that Washington could get hold of were stamped 'not good for Spain' regardless of the mission of the owners who had terrible difficulties, sometimes being obliged to cable Washington to get this prohibition removed. The French police supported the American regulations and would not give the necessary visas.

In January 1937, the English made it necessary for British passports to be specially endorsed by the Foreign Office for Spain. The persons who were to be allowed to go were those who were vouched for by a humanitarian organisation, such as Medical Aid or the National Joint Committee, (the Americans made no allowance even for doctors and nurses), or on the permanent staff of a newspaper. Freelance journalism was not good enough but the Americans were more indulgent to writers and journalists. The only other acceptable reason for going was if one had business or property to be looked after. The English, characteristically, thought this was the best reason of all.

I slipped through before these regulations came into force and while the French Popular Front still had some strength to show its sympathy for Republican Spain. It might annoy the British Consuls very much to have the responsibility for British subjects and they might be always warning them that they stayed at their own risk, or be urging them to leave on the next battleship but, as the Consul in Valencia told me, they were really obliged to take care of them whether they liked it or not.

In Paris, I again stayed with Jan's friends, Monsieur and Madame Pozner, who were as kind as possible in trying to allay my anxiety, and I spent an afternoon with little Madame Pozner looking through old photographs taken in Jan's early youth, and she wrote a long letter for me to carry to him.[47]

On the train, I saw four women in dark blue clothes with unbecoming caps, rucksacks and mackintoshes, and was sure they were nurses going to Spain but I did not speak to them until the next morning. There was also an English businessman, very neatly dressed, with a moustache and a rolled umbrella, who looked like Anthony Eden. We all started talking the next day as we approached the border. One of the women was middle-aged and had been in Russia doing social work just after the revolution. She was a member of the Labour Party and said she had given up a good job in a nursing home, where Lord Dawson of Penn attended, to come to Spain. She said the Medical Aid were too choosy about their nurses. 'Nurses are not political,' she said, 'and it is no use expecting them to be.'

This conversation took place while we were all walking by the sea at Port Bou. We had arrived there quite early in the morning and the train did not leave for Barcelona until three in the afternoon. This older nurse – who was not, I believe, trusted by the Medical Aid but sent to stagnate on the Aragón front – said that there were plenty of nurses who would go to Spain for the experience and for humanitarian reasons but the Medical Aid was very particular, more so about their politics than their other qualifications. One of the other women was a trained nurse so I suppose she was politically conscious. She was the one referred to in a dispatch by the Reuters correspondent as 'Nurse Sharp Bolster', her real name, 'formerly of the Contact Bookshop, Bloomsbury.' She was not young and had a tremendous nose. The other two were proper nurses, quite young, one rosy, with a large bosom and long, lank hair, who was Scottish though afterwards well-known as 'English Penny'.[48] She got typhoid, and finally was badly wounded in a bombardment. The fourth was a pale, silent girl with black eyebrows who looked too frail to stand the strain of nursing. These two had never been abroad before, spoke no language but their own and were very excited by everything they saw.

The businessman took us all under his wing and arranged with the anarchist committee in charge at Port Bou to let the nurses travel free. Beyond this he was busy arranging to take with him from France sundry parcels of eggs and other dainties for his friends in Barcelona and his former servants. He said all the English colony now lived at the club. I asked why they did since I found Barcelona quite normal enough to live in a hotel. He said it was because their wives and families had left so they were all grass widowers for the time being and could not be bothered with housekeeping and it was jollier to be all together. He said most of the women had left Spain but he knew of one old lady who remained in Majorca because she was much attached to her dogs and would not leave them and she could not take them to England on account of quarantine regulations.

It was a warm sunny day, though one of the first in January, and we sat outside the restaurant and, with the sun and the red wine, the nurses unbent and took off their unbecoming caps with the turned-back ear flaps. They were liberally sprinkled with red crosses and small Union Jacks which protections soon disappeared after they entered Spain for the former were unnecessary and the latter rather regarded as a badge of fascism.

Someone had been sent to meet the nurses in Barcelona. While I was taking a friendly leave of them and they were thanking me for my help on the journey she, with the uneasy austerity which I learned to regard as characteristic of the English Communist, ignored my existence and showed impatience to be gone.

The businessman hired a horse-drawn wagonette, the only vehicle available, and in this we rumbled off. He dropped me at my usual destination giving me some packets of Bisonte cigarettes which he had been fortunate enough to obtain on the train and evidently unaware that he would not be able to get more and would regret giving them away. These cigarettes, an imitation Lucky Strike in a rather similar packet, were fabricated by the millionaire Juan March, a Majorcan Jew and supporter of Franco, who had been exiled by the Republic. They continued to be available on the other side of course, as I was told by a prisoner from Salamanca.

The businessman, who was engaged in investigating the possibilities of setting up some social relief for the Spanish civilian population, showed me the notepaper of the then newly formed Joint Committee for Aid to Spain, with many distinguished names at the top besides that of the Duchess of Atholl. He invited me very cordially to call at the club but I never did.

The next morning, I met the nurses again at the Department of Foreigners, which had moved from the Colón to a building in the Diagonal, one of those created by Gaudí, with a hall like a grotto full of artificial stalactites and stalagmites. They were filling in the usual forms in an English section which had just been created in a dingy back room which was piled with parcels, cigarettes, *Daily Workers*, and letters which did not look as if they would ever reach their destinations. The nurses were already more reserved and distant in manner, probably having been told to be by the monitor who had met them at the station.

I found there a Medical Aid man I had met before and asked

him if he knew any hospital in which Jan might be but, though he mentioned one or two English wounded, he only knew the Barcelona and the Aragón front. I told him I wanted to go to Albacete where I was sure I could be useful but he put on a grave face and said no one could go there without special permission from the military authorities. I then said I wanted to go to Valencia and he seemed glad at the prospect of getting rid of me.

Unluckily, my old friend the German had left but the Englishman took me in to see the supreme authority of the department, an Italian with a pretty secretary, who was not at all busy. The Englishman was rather annoyed that our conversation was in French too rapid for him to follow though he tried to appear in command of the situation still as he had evidently been made responsible for all the English who passed through there. One had to have a permit to go from one town to another and that I obtained without difficulty.

I went next to the Spanish hospital headquarters and they told me that some Internationals were in Montjuich hospital. I took the tram up there and hoped very much that Jan had been lucky enough to get there as it was a fine modern hospital, fresh and airy and quite as clean and efficient as if it had been American. In most respects Catalunya is the most advanced part of Spain. On looking at the register in the hall I saw the only non-Spanish names were Polish or something. While still in Barcelona, I obtained the address of an information department in Valencia called *Enlace de hospitales* and was naïvely assured that they would know the exact whereabouts of every casualty in Republican Spain.

In the evening I met Zachary at a café. He said that he had an excellent interpreter now, the young man I had so envied for speaking Russian, but had sent him home for Christmas and could still find a job for me if I wanted it. I temporised as I did not know what I might want. Peggy, a friend of mine, came in.[49] It looked rather incongruous to see a stout girl on crutches and someone warned her that alcohol was bad for wounds healing as she ordered a drink. I asked her how long she had been incapacitated, thinking of Jan, as she was nearly well again. She said that she neglected to stay in bed at first and therefore had been slow to get better, but could have accomplished it in a month if she had gone into hospital at once. I reckoned I had been away three weeks and felt I must hurry to catch Jan before he went back to the front.

* * * * *

There was only one train to Valencia now and it left at night. I was warned to be at the station an hour beforehand, which was just as well or I should not have got a seat. The train was a very long one carrying freight as well as passengers, made innumerable stops, and we were all gradually blackened by smoke from the engine. It seemed an age before we reached Tortosa which I knew was quite close to Barcelona. I brightened up in the morning when we reached Castellón, but we meandered on stopping at small halts where I bought pretty bunches of oranges with the stems and leaves still on them. Some women in the train laughed at me and told me I had paid too much for them.

In Valencia, the sky was grey but it was not actually raining. I left my bags at the station and went to find a room. I tried every place I could think of but all were full. At last, worn out, dishevelled and dirty, I dropped into the Wodka café wondering if it was worthwhile to pursue the advice that one *pensión* had given me of a brother-in-law or someone who might have a room to let. I had no idea how to find the address or how far away it was. Suddenly, in came Kitty and waved to me animatedly.

Kitty was a petite and vivacious American girl, a freelance journalist I knew only slightly.[50] I explained my predicament. She took me round to several hotels but no room could be found. A number were reserved for certain categories of people, officers, or Russian Embassy officials, and were not available to the general public at all. There were a great many hotels for the size of the town. At last she said I had better have a mattress on the floor of her room until we could find something better. I remained her room mate for a considerable time though she had only a small room and we could barely find space to unroll the mattress at night. For this accommodation I paid full *pensión* at the hotel which was by no means cheap. The hotel porter accompanied me to the station to fetch my bags on the tram as there was no vehicle to be had.

As soon as I had had some sleep I went off to the *Enlace de hospitales*. It was off the Plaza del Temple, a small square with a statue of a poet in it, in one of the many old narrow streets near the river Turia which was fairly full of dirty yellow water at that time of year. Inside, there was the usual windowless hall with many chairs round the walls and an air of bygone splendour. The tearful anxious women waiting there did not augur well. I saw an official who was all that was polite and sympathetic, he took down the particulars and said he would enquire. I gave him my permanent address in Barcelona where, of course, I had never been informed that Jan had been wounded. I had written to him several times, once just before leaving Spain and once from Paris as I thought these letters might reach him whereas from England they would not, but he never received anything after he was wounded. The official never betrayed a doubt that I should soon receive information; I called there often enough to jog his memory.

I soon found, in the course of conversation, that Kitty had gone to Madrid just after I had left. She said she had a terrible time, took the train to Aranjuez, then could not get transportation beyond there, arrived after dark and slept in a cot in the Telefónica. If it had not been for the *Mujeres Antifascistas* (a women's organisation like the YWCA) that apparently looked after her, she would not have known what to do. She had returned on an evacuation bus. She told me she had seen Jan at Christmas in the Palace Hotel which had been turned into a hospital. He was badly wounded and in great pain. She did not know if there was any question of taking his leg off but knew it was planned to move him as soon as possible. It was useless to bolt off to Madrid until I knew he was still there but I hated my inability to do anything immediately.

Meanwhile I prosecuted my enquiries and renewed acquaintance with everyone I had met even once, as one never knows who will be in a position to help, and in war time everything is complicated by counterespionage and defence regulations.

I was also at once swept into the whirl of Kitty's life and always in a rush, hardly alone for a moment day or night. Kitty was also separated from her boyfriend, Tom Wintringham, and only remained in Spain for the chance of seeing him when he could get away from his military duties. She was afraid even to go back to Paris to fetch her clothes lest she should be unable to enter Spain again.

Her anxiety was not so acute as mine, she knew he was at a training centre out of danger and was well. He wrote to her frequently but she fretted a good deal nevertheless and 'distraction' is the precise word to describe her methods of passing the time.

She was a typical American, or rather New Yorker. Her conscience troubled her if she was not always busy and active, she was energetic, capable, sociable and nothing floored her. On the debit side she talked a great deal, imperceptibly organised all her acquaintances into cooperating with her plans and I found it very fatiguing. As I am inclined to solitary moping it was probably much better for me to be with her than alone.

Despite lack of Spanish, Kitty had already made an immense number of contacts in Valencia. She knew quite a number of Spaniards with whom she got along in bad French, and she knew several newspapermen to whom she introduced me. There were quite a few English and American commercial aviators staying in the hotel, with whom she carried on lively and harmless flirtations, inviting them up to the room for brandies. She was very popular and I must have seemed a sad wet blanket as I took no trouble with my appearance and never wanted to see anyone. So we hardly ever ate a meal alone together and I could not go to bed until late at night and then she was still talking, although I am the worst of confidantes.

There was a telephone beside the bed and, first thing in the morning, we would start telephoning while we were eating breakfast and sending the buttons out on errands – to buy a newspaper or some complicated remedy from the chemist. I say *we* did these things as I was pressed into service to help with the Spanish parts. Kitty got various ailments, a sore throat which made her lose her voice completely and for which a throat spray was necessary, and a swollen eye, but these did not deter her from her usual bustling activity. She banged away on her typewriter constantly and I had to translate bits out of the newspapers which she could not quite make out, bright as she was at guessing, long homilies about things like the gold of the Bank of Spain were rather beyond her and, indeed, beyond me, but neither of us liked to admit it.

Another feature of life at the Hotel Inglés was protracted wrestling with the weekly bills. Ours was made out as one bill under the room number, but since we often ate with the aviators who were billeted in the hotel there was the question of who we had invited to dinner or who had invited us, and whose account the wine should go on, and so on. This meant long arguments with the fat hotel manager, a very pre-war figure, in French. He undoubtedly tried to charge twice over for everything and, though I usually forced him to take something off, the bills were still formidable. As neither of us were earning anything at first we had to husband our resources. I would like to think it was that manager who was killed in the subsequent bombardment but unfortunately it was the innocent buttons who was blown to bits as he sat in his wicker chair in the doorway watching the passers-by, as was his habit.

One of the first days I was there, we went to one of the mediaeval towers and saw the art treasures, or rather the packing cases which contained them, which had just been brought from the Prado for safe-keeping. Kitty, with all her linguistic and other disadvantages, had ferreted out the director of the Fine Art Protection Board and we took the representative of the *Toronto Star* with us. Articles were duly written about them (this was January 1937, before people had even begun to ask questions about what had become of them) for the *Toronto Star*, and by Kitty for the *Manchester Guardian*.

It was a clear sunny afternoon and the best part for me was climbing on top of the tower, ostensibly to see how many layers of earth and sandbags there were, but really to admire the view and get a breath of fresh air, as our room overlooked a narrow side street and smelled of the kitchen. After that we also 'took in' an exhibition of the Duke of Alba's works, rescued from the burning Liria Palace by the Fifth Regiment. They were in a large patio and cloister. I remember particularly the Goya portrait of the Duchess in white with a red sash and a little dog. I knew this picture well from reproductions but had never had a chance of seeing it before; it was a strange chance in the end. The others were keener on journalism than art and I had to tell Norman Griffin[51] that Velazquez's *Las Meninas* was an important picture to mention in his 'story'.

Kitty also got an interview with Oliver, the anarchist then Minister of Justice,[52] who spoke French as he had been exiled in France and had qualified for his post by doing fourteen years in jail sentences. He lived in our hotel and was a small, high-coloured, youngish man with bright blue eyes. Altogether, Kitty did very well considering her lack of political pull.

I was too nervous for interviews though the bartender from Ibiza, Selke, who also wrote for some central European paper and could not get away from the press and censorship office where he was employed, commissioned me to get some interviews for him and paid me in advance (I still owe him the money). I went one dark evening, losing my way half a dozen times, to the Ministry of War, where I saw a very polite officer, after going through splendid tapestried rooms and up marble staircases, who told me absolutely nothing.

However, Selke did try to do me a good turn. He telephoned every evening to the Telefónica in Madrid and I persuaded him to add an enquiry as to whether Jan was still at the Palace Hotel. I knew the number of the room he had been in from Kitty. It was after midnight and we were both in bed when our phone rang. Kitty thought it was for her and called me rather crossly and sleepily. It was Selke. He had just spoken to Madrid; the girl in the Telefónica knew all about it, there was a Swedish nurse she said who took a great interest in Jan (I felt a jealous pang).[53] The nurse said he had been very bad but had taken a turn for the better and was still at the hotel.

I was grateful to Selke for letting me know at once what he had heard. He ended his message: 'Now, goodnight and perhaps you will sleep well.' For once I kept Kitty awake, talking and planning, as I was too impatient to asleep. My course was now clear. I would go to Madrid with all speed.

This was easier said than done; it would never do to get on the train and be stranded at Aranjuez like Kitty; I must get on some sort of vehicle. I obtained the address of the editor of the Spanish newspaper with which Humphrey had been connected. I went to see him and poured out my story so incoherently that he did not follow me and looked alarmed. At last he said with relief, 'Ah, you want to go to Madrid – well go by all means, I thought you wanted *me* to go! And I have no intention of doing so.'

Kate's press pass.

I had to say I wanted to see Humphrey on business as that sounded a plausible excuse. I showed him my safe-conduct, made out by the Ministry of War in December. Very fortunately for me, it had on it the blessed words '*sin plazo*'. This meant there was no date for its expiry and it was still valid – they no longer made out papers in this way, but only for single journeys.

I went to the Ministry of War and they said it was still good but made me out another also. They then asked how I was going to travel. I said I did not know and they filled in 'by what means she sees fit'.

Then I went to the newspaper office and asked them if I could go in one of their cars and told them the editor had said I could. They held up their hands and said, 'He doesn't know anything. You might as well be asking for the moon, we have cars laid up in the garage for lack of petrol.'

I went down to the garage where I found the big gangster I already knew, who had arranged to take Humphrey to Madrid once. He was very friendly, but said it was true enough, there was a fierce petrol shortage in Valencia, an expected Russian tanker had not come in, probably sunk, and they had no cars going to Madrid.

I went to the *Seguridad* which had been recommended at the Ministry of War. They said they had cars going but they were all full. They took my name and address and said they would let me know when there was a seat available. Needless to say they never did; but Spaniards are always polite enough to raise one's hopes.

Very discouraged I returned to the gangster and he gave me a good tip. I said I did not mind going in a lorry as long as I got there and he sent me to the *Comité de Abastos* (Food Supply Committee) as he knew they had lorries going up every day. Before this, I had tried the Evacuation Committee but their activities were all held up for lack of petrol. I also went to the UGT Transport but their offices were deserted. At the *Comité de Abastos* they were charming and friendly as only anarchists can be. They said that, unfortunately, their lorries for that day had gone.

By then it was late afternoon of the second day that I had been wandering all over Valencia on foot and waiting for hours in offices. It had taken me the whole of the first morning to get my papers in order. I was frantic and quite worn out but too preoccupied to notice fatigue.

The *Comité de Abastos* took pity on me and telephoned the *petroleros* of the CAMPSA petrol storage tanks. If no one else had petrol they would have it and they went up to Madrid every day with supplies for the city. This was going to the fountainhead and well-spring of all transport indeed.

I heard the question, 'Is it a *compañero?*' and the reply, 'No, a *compañera.*'

They demurred because I was a woman but the man at my end of the phone persuaded them. There were then no regulations in force, as there were later, against taking women to Madrid. People showed a great reluctance to leave Madrid and would stop at nothing to get back there if they had left. Later, when the Basque Catholic Irujo superseded the anarchist Oliver as Minister of Justice and forbade women to enter the city, they smuggled themselves in in empty wine-barrels.

At last it was all arranged. I was to go the next morning to the Grau, the port district, where the petrol storage tanks were located, and the *petroleros* would take me. The man typed me an authorisation, which I still have: 'I hope that what you said on the telephone may be a reality as this comrade is going to Madrid on an important mission and moreover she goes well documented by the Ministry of War – Yours and of the Revolution . . .'

I bought myself a rucksack and stowed into it all the little things I had collected and saved for Jan. I informed Selke, for whom I had been doing some work, that I could not continue as I was going to Madrid. He was very curious to know how I had managed it and wished that all misfortune would befall me for letting him down.

Early the next morning I boarded a number 2 tram for the Grau. At first I could not find the petrol headquarters but a lorry picked me up and I split my skirt climbing into it. Soon I was sitting before a roaring fire (the petrol boys seemed to have a corner on coal as well) in the office waiting to start the journey. I was treated with the utmost courtesy but the *responsable* was evidently displeased at having a woman in his charge, and not even a working-class one, though I did my best to fraternise. The boys behaved rather as if they were sailors and a woman would bring them ill-luck on their voyage.

I found that I was to ride very comfortably in a car with the *responsable* but that we had to go slowly as we had to convoy the caravan of tankers, of which there were twenty-one, and as far as possible we kept together. We would have made a fine target for an enemy plane. Before we got fully under way there were so many farewells and preparations to make, so many messages given and parcels of food and tobacco stowed in the car for friends, that I felt as if I were part of a real caravan about to cross the Arabian desert. It was, of course, prohibited to bring in food without handing it to the Supply Committee and dire penalties were risked.

At about three, we stopped at a *posada* where we were expected and where the woman had prepared a fine meal such as I never had at the Inglés. We saw several cars stopped on the road for lack of petrol and their drivers waved to us imploringly, and men with dry petrol pumps in villages also did their best to corrupt us, but the gasoline caravan was adamant and continued on its way. In the afternoon, heavy rain set in and we had a collision with another car which, as I was dozing with my head on my elbow, shook me up badly but luckily did not break the glass next to my face.

It was dusk, the road very slippery with wet and visibility very bad, when we pulled up to discover the meaning of a scene taking place in the middle of the road just ahead of us. One of the lorries had stopped and a big fat man, in floods of tears, was being embraced fervently by his mate, so small his arms would hardly go round the other's middle.

'He had a wife and children probably just like me,' blubbered the fat man incoherently; he had been drinking but was not drunk. Suddenly, on the black shiny road I saw a little black shiny Ford, right under my wheels, I couldn't stop and what chance did a little car like that have against my great Ruso.'

What chance indeed? There were many heavy Russian trucks. The Ford lay crumpled up in the ditch like an old sardine tin and was, as they said, *completamente deshecho* – totally undone. As the big man was in hysterics and calling himself a murderer he was not allowed to see his victim who had been hurried off in another truck to the nearest village and doctor. His little friend kept assuring the big man that there were only slight injuries while privately informing the *responsable* that it was very unlikely the occupant of the Ford would reach a doctor alive.

The *responsable* swore at Jaime, the big man, but Jaime's nerves were so broken that there was nothing else to do but leave his truck by the roadside to be fetched on the morrow and take Jaime into our car. We were going to leave him at the next village to hitch a ride back to Valencia. We refused his requests to be taken to the same village as his victim as we did not want him to be howling with vain remorse over the corpse. A little later the death was confirmed by telephone, however we assured Jaime that the man was doing very well and would recover. There was something very touching about the efforts of Jaime's little friend to comfort him though; if one had not the tragic cause, it would have looked very droll.

Jaime sat next to me with his head in his hands, his fat face distorted with grief, and cried all the way. The *responsable* in front was very sour and sarcastic.

'I'm not fit to drive a truck,' wailed Jaime.

'You won't get a chance to drive one again, don't you worry,' was the response.

'I'd rather be a peasant and work on the land where I can't hurt anybody.'

'Indeed, that's about all you're fit for.'

'He too had a wife and children.' Repeated over and over again.

We were very glad to be rid of Jaime at the next stop, where his little friend tenderly consigned him to the care of the inn-keeper and we all had some black coffee and brandy to pull us together again.

I did not much like our *responsable*, a tall, thin, very dark man with sunken eyes, a blue chin and a big beret overhanging his brow like a cinema villain. He wore a suit with a pretence to elegance and tried to play the gentleman with me and to keep me apart from the overalled drivers. The drivers were much nicer, with that charming Spanish gesture of rolling one a cigarette and then holding out the open paper for one to lick it together oneself.

At that time, a certain kind of navy-blue peaked cap was sweeping Spain like wildfire. It was the mode among soldiers, who thought it made them look like the Red Army, and among the more urban working men. The drivers sported such caps and wore on the front whatever badges took their fancy, a red five-pointed star, UGT or CNT. One dashing young man, a lanky youth, with the white skin, big bones and grey eyes with long black lashes that make some Spaniards look Irish, said, 'I wear Popeye the Sailor, just to be different.' Sure enough, he had a little image of the famous spinach hero in his cap, complete with pipe and exaggerated biceps.

'Popayer' as they call him is quite the most popular screen character in Spain, overshadowing Mickey Mouse, and a Popeye programme is sure to be crowded with adults. Popeye, with his always successful struggles against fearful odds, always overcoming the dastardly plots of the great brute with the whiskers, has a special appeal.

The *responsable* had to reprove the Popeye driver for taking too much *coñac* and then we went on.

A fog came up and we did not want any more accidents that day so we stopped fairly early at the most desolate *posada* I had ever set eyes on. The lorries were ranged under cover in a great cobbled courtyard and we entered a room, vast like a barn, where an old witch-like woman, with wisps of white hair, was crouching over a great hearth where a few sticks were burning on a pile of ashes.

She threw up her hands when we asked for supper for twenty-three people but eventually she was persuaded to produce some eggs and make us a tortilla, liberally sprinkled with ash though the light was too dim to notice it, and of this we each received a fragment on a piece of bread. Two trucks had arrived ahead of us and their drivers had bagged the only beds in the house, but one of them yielded his up to a lady and solemnly handed over to me the key of the room.

It was as well I had a key as I had to lock the door to keep out a goat which was wandering up and down the stairs all night. The room had no window except for a small hole giving onto the next room, from which the loud rhythmic snores of a driver kept me awake for some time. It was, however, icy cold and the sheets were wringing wet, so I lay down fully dressed on top of the bed.

At five o'clock in the morning the *responsable* awoke me with thunderous knocking and I crept down and found a chair inside the immense chimney. It was still dark and round about, on piles of straw, wrapped in blankets, many of the men were still sleeping. We saw the goat and therefore were able to insist that the old woman should give us milk with our coffee.

'I suppose it's the war that makes food scarce?' asked the *responsable* politely.

'Oh no,' replied the old hag grimly, 'it was always like this here – *en Castilla la Vieja siempre una miseria*[54]!'

She seemed quite unaware of the present time, as if she might have sat there through the Napoleonic wars and seen armies come and go.

When dawn broke we set off, going cautiously because of the white mist.

They set me down at the Palace Hotel with my rucksack.

It was only eight in the morning and there were very few people about, which was just as well. The sudden transition from the mediaeval *posada* to the centre of the city was quite bewildering. I was travel-stained and had my luggage on my back. With a wild and wistful idea of not making too bad an impression on Jan, I tried, standing in the street, to powder my dusty, tired face and comb my straggling hair, with the aid of a pocket mirror.

The Palace, though now a hospital, had retained some of the appearance and staff of a hotel. I stepped into the lobby and was greeted with a flourish by a magnificent, uniformed hall porter. When I gave him the name and room number he began to turn over the pages of a book in the porter's lodge quite as if he were looking for a guest rather than a patient, and while I waited I fumbled anxiously in my bag to make sure of the whereabouts of the letters and other things I was bringing for Jan.

At last he turned his dignified, whiskered face.

'The *señor* left two days ago.'

'It's not possible!' I cried aghast. 'Where was he taken?'

This the hall porter could not answer, being quite unconnected with the hospital services. He thought it might have been Valencia.

I was completely exhausted but nervous energy had kept me going somehow. Now the reaction was dreadful; I hung there quite helpless and undecided. I had never dreamt of such a contingency. If he had been travelling to Valencia while I was coming to Madrid perhaps we had passed each other on the way. It seemed altogether too hard a disappointment to bear. From being able-bodied and eager I suddenly felt such weakness come over me that I almost sank to the floor. I had not the faintest idea what to do next. Suddenly I recollected that Humphrey was staying here. I had not seen or communicated with him for some time and we had not parted on the best of terms but, absolutely friendless as I was, I could only think to ask for him. The porter telephoned to his room and told me I was to go up. He showed me the way.

When I entered his room, Humphrey was in bed having breakfast. I burst out into something about Jan having gone away and then dissolved into tears. Humphrey made me sit down, for I was trembling all over, and ordered more coffee and bread and jam. I found I was starving and ate while he retired to the bathroom to dress.

When he came back, I found he did not need much explanation. He had been living for some time at the hotel and had seen Kitty there at Christmas. He had frequently visited Jan whose room was near his own. He said that Jan suffered terribly and was amazingly brave about it and that he liked and admired him since he had got to know him better. He felt a bit jealous because, he said, all the women, old and young, took a fancy to Jan and he had not lacked visitors or people to fuss over him. So Humphrey talked while I tried to pull myself together, and gave him, grudgingly, one or two of the delicacies I had been keeping for Jan, one or two chocolate bars and cigarettes to mitigate the hardships of Madrid.

I was quite broken down but Humphrey was very practical and he had soon prepared a plan of action. Fortunately, he was not busy that day as all was very quiet on the Madrid front and air raids had ceased, though the city was still shelled sometimes. He said it was deadly dull and he was quite pleased to see me. He did not know where Jan had been taken but proposed to take steps to find out and then get me back to Valencia with all speed. He was rather irritated at my lack of foresight in not providing for the return journey. I had only the vaguest idea about where to find the gasoline caravan. It was Sunday and one of the men had said he was going to spend it with a relative in Vallecas, where the others were to pick him up.

Gabriel and the car were summoned and we went first to the headquarters of the International Brigade, Calle Velázquez. Humphrey sent me in alone. They looked up the name for me but refused to say where he had been sent, but did suggest that it was probably Murcia. When I told Humphrey this he said Jan had probably been sent to Albacete but, as that was only a clearing station, he was unlikely to remain there. They would not mention Albacete to me because I should not be allowed to go there as it was still a closed town.

At the Palace Hotel we discovered that a certain nurse, who Humphrey knew, had accompanied Jan and was expected back. Humphrey said he would ask her about it when she got back and let me know. He also said we had better mention it to anyone else who knew Jan, giving my name and address in Valencia so that information could be sent to me.

We then went to see the girl at the Telefónica. She was staying at the Gran Vía and we had a vermouth with her there. She said she was anxious to see me as she had just received a message from Valencia to say I was wanted there for a job in the Press and Propaganda office. This I put down to the efforts of Selke. She said she would have offered me work in Madrid but, naturally, all desire to stay in Madrid had evaporated. After we left her Humphrey advised me not to tie myself up in a job if I could help it until I had located Jan, as it might prove inconvenient, but I was unable to follow this advice.

We returned to the Palace for lunch, served on a tray in

Humphrey's room as there was no other place we could eat.

'This is the best food in Madrid,' he said, doing the honours to a mysterious tinned meat with pride. 'Being a hospital, you know, and the Russians staying here, we get the best of everything, the only milk in town, and they keep chickens on the roof. It is great sport to watch them lassoing one when they want it and all the rest cackling and screaming.'

The habit of keeping fowls on the roof is common in Spain and stood them in good stead in the war.

'I like living here,' he said. 'I like the blood-stained corridors and the revolvers parked in the cloakroom.' He carried a revolver himself.

I found the smell of anaesthetic and disinfectant nauseating.

Humphrey was as sympathetic as he knew how.

'Cheer up,' he said, 'your troubles are really over. A man in hospital is really pretty immobile. Now he has been evacuated from Madrid he is sure to stay put for some time. You are bound to catch up with him soon. He is not likely to die and with that leg of his he can never go to the front again. When he is well enough to travel you only have to take him home. You really couldn't wish for anything better. It is getting increasingly difficult for foreigners to stay here. The authorities know that none of them are hanging about now that Spain is getting so uncomfortable without some very good reason. But soon everyone will know that your reason is Jan and be satisfied and not suspicious of you.'

It turned very rainy in the afternoon and at dusk we set out for Vallecas bridge. When we got there, I could not see any of the lorries and could not remember the name of the *responsable*. After one or two enquiries in cafés it became obvious that it was pretty hopeless to try to find the gasoline caravan. Some people thought they remembered the trucks passing through and others thought they had not gone by yet. After hanging about a bit, we turned back, after going through all the business of passwords and guards, in a very bad humour. I was now in just as great a hurry to get back to Valencia as I had been to get away from it, and Humphrey thought me an incompetent fool not to have fixed up a meeting with the caravan.

We went to the centre for gasoline supplies and they telephoned the depot and found that the caravan had left, but another one would go the next day from the bull-ring. We left a message that a passenger would join it. There was nothing for it but to take a room for the night. After that we tried to get into a cinema but it was full so we sat in a café. I had dinner at the Palace with Humphrey and then he walked me back to the Gran Vía through the pitch dark. Madrid seemed emptier and sadder.

The next morning, I wandered from my cold room to the kitchen of my hotel, lamentably empty of food, and borrowed a needle and cotton, to do some mending, from an old Argentinian woman who wailed about the war. I asked her why she did not leave Madrid and she said that she would not leave her house and furniture or she might never see them again, which was the feeling of many of the older inhabitants.

Gabriel and Humphrey picked me up and we drove out to the bull-ring. The sun was shining but there was a sea of mud and we wandered about for some time amongst the puddles behind the seats in the arena before we found the office. They left me there in front of a good fire and I waited some hours before the new *responsable* turned up. I think it was four in the afternoon before we left, but I dozed.

The journey back was not so cheerful as the journey out. All my excitement had died down and I felt only fatigue. The new *responsable* was a rough, red-faced, bullet-headed man, much nicer than the other but, at first, he did not much like taking me either. My papers said nothing about a return journey, but he could hardly refuse and Humphrey, who wanted to be rid of me, persuaded him.

He was very angry at the behaviour of the other *responsable* in the matter of the accident. He said he should not have left the truck on the road all night and that he should not have stopped for the fog, making the caravan late in arriving.

We took a different and less frequented route and, in one village, saw a fleet of ambulances standing in the muddy street. My thoughts flew to Jan but it was impossible to get out and insist on looking inside them. Besides, he must have arrived somewhere long since.

I saw a signpost to the forbidden land – Albacete, and so hushed up was that town then, as if the very Spaniards themselves had no right to be there, that I was almost surprised to see the name openly on a signpost!

In the evening we came to a *posada* where they were expecting us and gave us a great welcome. We all sat round a long table and ate a magnificent *arroz* with chicken and the men were much merrier than the ones going up to Madrid.

We then sat round the stove for what seemed an age. Though the room was bright lit and the men's talk very noisy, and I was in a hard, straight-backed chair, I kept falling asleep and nearly toppling onto the floor. The men thought this a great joke and kept waking me up again.

At last the *responsable* came and shook me awake and I was shown to a very neat, clean but bare little room in a cottage across the road, where I found I was to share a double bed with the owner's wife. I felt bad about turning her husband out but she said it did not matter for once. As far as I remember, she did not undress but only took off her corsets with a great crackling and rattling.

The next morning as we sat round waiting for coffee, she admired my sheepskin coat and asked if I were Russian – with the natural association of Russians with fur – and began to meditate whether her husband could not make her such a coat. She took me into a barn to show me some rough skins hanging there but they were quite stiff. I told her that officers did wear short coats made of sheepskin but usually with the leather outside and the wool inside.

There was a young woman sitting there, with two chubby little boys, who wanted to go to Valencia and had been hitching rides for days. It was agreed that she should go in the front of one of the trucks. She was a rosy brunette who looked taller than she was because she carried herself so erect. She was bare-headed, as Spanish women always are, with long hair in a knot behind. She was a lovely girl but wore a stern, sad expression on her handsome, aquiline face.

'Ah, you're travelling with the two little ones and their father is probably at the front,' said one of the drivers sympathetically.

His supposition was correct; she showed us a photo of the father in militiaman's dress, which she wore in a locket round her neck. She came from quite a different part of the country and her husband was a peasant, but she could not manage the land alone. The boys were two and four; we all admired them, they were fine boys – almost too fat and heavy for her to carry. She was going to relatives in Valencia until the war was over. She climbed onto the truck, the children were hoisted up after her, a battered cardboard suitcase after them, and we started off.

In the end, I was quite good friends with the *responsable* and he said that any time I wanted I could ride with the caravan if I did not mind such a slow method of travel, but I was not to tell other people they would take passengers or they would have too many requests. On both journeys the men were kindness itself. They dropped me in the Calle de la Paz, near my hotel.

All through the war, one had a wonderful feeling of freedom from the responsibility and individual worries of ordinary life. Once I got used to it, I never worried any more about possessions, or money, or when I would get anywhere, or where the next meal was coming from. Possessions did not seem to matter; I had very few with me but nothing I clung to except my typewriter.

Chapter 7
The Rearguard is also a Front

When I got back to the Inglés, I wanted to go on with my enquiries instantly. I did manage to look at a map of Spain to see where Murcia was, it looked a long way off, far away in the south. Alicante would have been much better, that was where the aviators went to convalesce but I knew they were a privileged class. They always are in modern warfare. Compared to infantry these technicians are pampered and spoiled and allowed a great deal of freedom. Trained pilots are not easily replaced and when they are wounded their comrades can fetch them by plane to a good hospital – if they survive, for the risks are, of course, undeniable. Pilots were the favourite exchange prisoners and we were prepared to hand over two or three Spanish grandees for one aviator.

Kitty swept me up at once. I must immediately go to another hotel to see her friend Liston Oak.[55] I was wanted at once to start on a job at the press office. What had I been doing running around for days in Madrid? The situation would admit of no delay.

It was only a job as secretary and translator, so Kitty could not take it herself, but she had expected to get work assisting in the English section of the press office, which was just being set up, and another woman had been hired which annoyed her very much. She got over this quickly, but initially she gave me a very unfavourable account of Milly, the other woman, so that I was rather in dread of meeting her.[56]

Liston Oak, like most of the people Kitty introduced me to, was not really a friend of hers. She probably did not know him any better than she knew me. I went round to his hotel which was a gloomy one in an echoing arcade. The rooms had heavy, carved beds and crimson hangings which were rather dusty. It was not at all like the Inglés which was light and cheerful. This seemed to suit Liston who was rather pompous and habitually melancholy.

He was a tall, distinguished-looking, middle-aged American with glasses and curling grey hair which he wore rather long at the back. He generally wore a large-size floppy beret. Some Spanish ambassador abroad had decided that, to get the right kind of publicity in English, an American was the thing needed, and Liston Oak had impressed him.

Liston was a chameleon kind of character. I always felt he was unreal and a faker though I did not know until afterwards what he was up to. Milly told me later that he had been an actor and a schoolmaster and an organiser for some charitable society and that he was really an all-round failure. He was not bad to work for, except when he had fits of thinking he had to be business-like in the American style. Then he would hurry everyone up and scold and pretend to be strong-minded.

He was subject to headaches, insomnia and spells of rheumatism. His illnesses were largely neurotic. We did not know about his politics though I thought he took rather an interest in FAI and POUM, but he said he did it to be fair. When I discovered his second wife had left him, I assumed that he had come to Spain to forget about it. Many of the odd people who turned up had some such reason.

He had a letter of introduction to Kellt, the former head of the foreign department at the Hotel Colón, which gave me confidence in him politically.[57] I do not know how he got it as Kellt was certainly one hundred per cent politically sound. I ran into Kellt one morning at the police station, where I was having my passport stamped, and he shook me by the hand and was very friendly. He lived quietly in Valencia engaged on some important work for a long time but I never saw him, no one did. When I told Selke I knew him and could get a reference from him Selke said, 'That's not his real name; it's a *nom de guerre*,' but he seemed impressed and said a reference from him would be very good, though he seemed rather afraid of him himself.

I took Liston Oak's letter of introduction round to Kellt and told him I was going to work in the press office as he had told me to report to him what I was doing. He laughed and said, 'Very good. I hope they pay you well. Keep your eyes and ears open about what is going on in there.' Then he came with me in a car to Liston's hotel and we found Liston in bed with the curtains drawn suffering from something or other. I had to be there to translate from Spanish as Liston did not speak German nor Kellt English. Kellt warned Liston about the people at the press office.

'They are very bad people,' he said.

'Rubio, the head, is very clever,' said Liston.[58]

'*Sí, sí, muy listo, demasiado,*' said Kellt. 'A bit too clever. And beware of Selke. He's not to be trusted.'

I never liked Selke but Liston was very thick with him and said he found him a very pleasant, helpful little fellow. I felt very important being present at this interview. It seemed rather odd afterwards as the person we all should have been warned against was neither Rubio nor Selke but Liston himself.

Liston said, 'I suppose you'll be satisfied with what we all get, which is six hundred pesetas a month?'

I agreed. He was getting eight hundred himself as head of the department; this was typical. The most unworthy person got most money. After he left, subsequent heads of department only got six.

He took me round to the office to introduce me. He said, 'Don't you mind Milly. She's just a hard-boiled newspaper-woman. Rather crotchety because she's not a beauty.'

I felt more scared than ever. We had a bare room, very cold in winter, very hot in summer, and very noisy as it gave onto the main street. There were not enough desks, chairs or typewriters so Milly and I used our own except for stencils as the office typewriters were Spanish with a different set of keys.

Milly, who wore thick glasses and was very near-sighted, was bent double poking at a typewriter in a fury of haste. She always worked like this. She had thick, tousled black hair, she constantly ran her fingers through it, and prominent teeth. She was about forty and rather battered.

There was also Carmen, a Mexican, stout and yellow, with a flat Indian face and a chilli pepper temper. Liston said she had been given to him as an interpreter as she spoke English well. She had been a school-teacher but she had no idea about politics so I should be more useful. Her husband was a distinguished writer who had therefore been evacuated from Madrid along with other learned men who had been saved, like the Prado art treasures, as part of the national heritage. They lived, at Government expense, in a kind of zoo for intellectuals called the *Casa de Cultura*. Later this establishment was found to be rather a racket and the inmates were made to pay board. Although Carmen was drawing a salary, she was enraged by this and took her husband, a mild, elderly man, back to Madrid.

'This is Kate, come to help us with translations,' said Liston in his most suave manner.

'Good,' said Milly, without looking up from her typewriter which she was banging furiously. 'I'm going nuts here.'

'We don't need 'er,' said Carmen, giving me a cold look from her little, black, snake-like eyes. 'I am 'ere for the interpreter and the boy can do translations.'

'Rubio telephoned Madrid for her to come here,' said Liston firmly, 'and we're only just beginning. There'll be plenty of work for everybody.'

'This is Coco Robles,' said Liston, indicating the boy.[59] He got up and shook hands and gave me a shy smile. I hoped he would not think I had come to cut him out as I liked him at once.

Coco was a lanky boy of sixteen with dark skin, big white teeth and clear grey eyes with long lashes. He had a lock of hair which fell over his forehead and he wore navy-blue overalls. He was shy but not in the least awkward as an English boy of that age would have been. He was extremely intelligent, much more so than Carmen, and spoke good English as he had been to school in America. He grew fond of Liston but Milly, with her impulsive behaviour and free flow of lurid language, embarrassed him. He was, however, very loyal to all of us. He taught himself to use a typewriter, make stencils, use the duplicating machine, which was an awful broken-down thing that needed a lot of coaxing, and took a pride in our work and was generally invaluable. He stayed with us until he was old enough to go and fight. At seventeen, he volunteered to join the Youth Battalions when Aragón was attacked and I do not know what became of him.

In the very beginning, however, we only made carbon copies, then for a while we had our stencils run off in another part of the office. Carmen took offence at my arrival and, within a few days, she had too much to do producing propaganda for South American countries and moved her desk into another room and left us.

Liston said he wanted to learn Spanish and would take a lesson every day but, of course, he never did and Milly never learned it either, though she talked of going to the Berlitz school. She was not a person with a talent for languages anyway.

The first day I had to accompany Milly somewhere to interpret, I discovered she was quite different from Kitty's description. She had scraps with Carmen, I gathered, because Carmen laughed at her for wearing a little cap on the back of her head and Milly was extremely sensitive to teasing.

At first I thought she might have a grudge against younger women because she was single but I soon found she took a great and most sympathetic interest in romances. I put this down as living vicariously but I was wrong again. Milly was exceedingly popular with men and never without a romance of her own – probably because she was warm-hearted, such a genuine good sort, and also very amusing company.

She was a first-rate newspaperwoman and quite well known as such and if it had not been for her Left sympathies (though she belonged to no political party) she would have been earning very good money. She had done so in the past. Only her Left views and her love affairs, which made her rather a rolling stone, stood in her way. She had been everywhere, Honolulu, Shanghai and Moscow and never lacked a job as she was very competent. I discovered she used to visit Jan in the hospital in Madrid and thought him 'such a nice boy' and she was very sympathetic.

Liston and Milly assumed that I knew all about journalism and propaganda so I very soon learned. When a lot is expected, one does all sorts of things one never thought possible.

In the mornings, we had to go through all the newspapers and magazines, Coco and I, and pick out bits suitable for translation. We had not the faintest idea what to pick out but used to read things aloud in English to give Milly an idea of what the articles were about and she would seize upon something and say, 'That could make a good story, translate that.' We would do that and then she would edit it, but soon she let me write my own stories and she re-wrote Coco's. She did not know about politics, only about news value, but all our stuff was censored anyway. Later, they trusted us and we sent out stuff almost without censorship and, occasionally, got into trouble afterwards.

I liked the mornings as Liston did not come in because of his insomnia. He used to come into the office at night and send off cables all by himself. He tried to make me come at night to help him but I refused. As it was, we worked from ten to two and four to eight, including Saturdays and Sundays, and sometimes longer if something had to be finished. I often came back at three to work alone when I had a long speech or anything else to do. La Pasionaria, Uribe, Hernández and José Diaz made a lot of fine, long speeches.

Besides the newspapers, we had the Febus sheets. *Las hojas de Febus* were a great trouble to us. Sometimes none came, sometimes some were missing and sometimes the newspaper-men stole our copies. Also, Liston was incapable of pronouncing *hoja* and his efforts annoyed Carmen who would bounce in from the next room and stand over him repeating, '*Hoja, hoja, hoja;* say it; no, that's not right, say it again,' which made us laugh and her angrier.

Febus was an official news agency and they sent out sheets several times a day. They were carbon copies on very thin paper, terribly faint and difficult to read. Liston was able to guess what they were about well enough to mark paragraphs for translation. On my first evening, I did a very simple piece – I think it was: 'There are now 500,000 beehives in Republican Spain and it is intended to increase them to one million to guard against sugar shortage.' Milly was delighted. 'If all the translations come as clean as this we have no more worries,' she said.

* * * * *

I had only been working there a couple of days when Liston suddenly appeared at my hotel while I was eating lunch and said I was to go with him to a reception for President Azaña,[60] the first since the war had broken out, to take down the speech in shorthand from Spanish into English as he wanted it immediately. This seemed rather a tall order but I put a notebook in my pocket and followed him.

'You want a much bigger notebook than that,' he said, being in a fussy mood.

President Azaña had been living in seclusion for some time, in the monastery at Montserrat outside Barcelona, as he was a moderate man and was afraid, at the beginning of the war, that the anarchists would bump him off. Now that the Government had come to Valencia, he had been persuaded to make a public appearance to demonstrate the continuance of the Republic.

When we got to the venue there was a crowd and a lot of guards in uniform and I had some difficulty getting in as I had no invitation card. Azaña drove up and, as he got out of the car, a baker or a miller in the crowd slapped him on the back and left a floury mark on his immaculate dark suit. He waved and gave a sickly smile but in such a way that one could see that he did not like quite such democratic behaviour. Azaña was a short, fat man with a bald head, receding forehead, wire-rimmed spectacles and a large mole on his chin.

We went up the carpeted stairs and there were guards in white gloves and everything was very grand. There were two big salons with crystal chandeliers and a long buffet with a white cloth, glasses of wine and plates of *petits fours* such as I had not seen in a long time, so I ate as many as I could. There were old generals with sashes round their paunches, ribbons across their chests and gold *épaulettes*, very colourful. I whispered to Liston, 'It seems odd for a revolution.'

'I don't like it either,' he said, 'but they do this sort of pageantry in Russia too.'

There were diplomatic representatives there, of course, who looked very young and out of place and I was introduced to a lot of people. For the first time since I had come to Spain, I wished I had been better dressed.

I could not see Azaña because of the crowd of people round him shaking his hand. A very tall American journalist lifted me up so I could see over all the heads. Edward Knoblaugh, the American, was a friend of Milly's and often used to take us out for a beer or invite us to cocktails at his flat. When he left Spain, he wrote a pro-Franco book in which he said Milly was a red agent sent straight from the Comintern and we laughed a lot about it, but perhaps some people believed it.[61]

Then we went into a small auditorium with blue velvet seats. Liston and I sat high up and a long way from the speakers; I strained my ears and scribbled and scribbled. While Azaña spoke, Largo Caballero sat on the platform and regarded him with a cynical look. Largo Caballero was an old, wrinkled man with pale, shifty blue eyes.[62] Liston liked him and whispered, 'A typical old style trade unionist.'

We went back to the office and I transcribed my notes. Azaña had appeared very ill at ease and had started by saying that his heart bled for the sufferings of Spain and then, rather strangely, 'I don't like my position, no one would envy it,' which was probably just what he felt. He was afraid of doing the wrong thing and did not really want to go on with the war. He was a liberal and would have given up sooner if he had dared.

All my work was quite useless in the end, for though Liston wrote a cable, the censor would not allow him to send anything until the official version of the speech was published, which was days later.

As soon as I could get a few minutes off from the office, one evening at about eight, I got Kitty to take me to the then head-quarters of the International Brigades in Valencia, a great, old stone monastery with stone arches. The address was sedulously guarded from the general public but of course Kitty had found it out.

The official language of the Brigades was French, as there were more French than any other nationality in them and many of those who were already political refugees, Poles, Italians, Germans and others, had been living in France.

The man in charge at the headquarters was a nice, ugly German, with his arm in a sling, and a floppy, artistic-looking, khaki beret that accorded very ill with his worn, red face. There was also a homely German girl with a pasty face, mousy hair and a Sunday-school manner. They were both very kind but did not know anything.

As usual, there was a pile of dusty letters, addressed to

soldiers, lying on the desk which was not very encouraging.

'I know just how you feel,' said the man, wringing my hand with his good one. 'We are starting a wonderful new convalescent hospital for the Brigade at Benicasim, perhaps he has gone there. It is a beautiful place, it used to be a leisure resort. There is a lovely beach.'

There was a map on the wall and I could see Benicasim, way up the coast. I quickly calculated that it was too far for weekends with the train service as it was, even if I had had free weekends, which I did not.

They gave me the address of Oscar Telge, Head of the *Service Sanitaire* in Albacete, and I wrote to him in French.[63] How scared I was then of this legendary man, of whom I heard afterwards, in Paris, as a broken-down refugee with barely half a lung left.

They also gave me the names of all the towns where the Internationals were sent to hospitals. I noted them all down; Valencia was not among them.

I went to the Post Office, always crowded with soldiers and soldiers' relatives who were allowed to send telegrams free of charge. There I sent telegrams to Jan addressed to the military hospitals at Murcia, Benicasim, Cuenca and half a dozen other places, begging him to answer if he was there. Kitty still thought he would have been sent to Alicante.

Whenever I could get out, I went to the *Correos* where there were always queues waiting while semi-literate people, who could never have afforded anything so new-fangled as a telegram before, spoilt form after form with the scratchy pens and watery ink provided.

Women with shawls over their heads struggled to express their thoughts in brief while trying to keep their babies quiet. Militiamen pondered with furrowed brow, wielding the pens like weapons in their clumsy fists.

Then one joined the queue at the window, inside which was a disheartening pile of blue envelopes for there were not only letters but also telegrams *restante*. I once got the clerk to shuffle through them in case someone had sent me news there instead of to the hotel which I had given as my address.

Nothing happened and I had not much time for worrying as I was putting all my energy into holding onto my job. I knew I was not very competent and was terrified of being fired. I need not have worried about this as, at the time, I was irreplaceable. There was no one else available who knew both Spanish and English and could type. Fortunately, Liston and Milly had both taken a fancy to me. Selke was still friendly also and thrust on me articles to translate from French until Milly threw him out saying I had no time for extra work. He wrote a very sentimental piece that we called *The Rape of the Olives* about Nazi Germans cutting down olive trees in Andalusia.

* * * * *

Before starting work at the press office, I had committed myself to accompanying a Canadian newspaperman as interpreter when he needed me and Liston always made a fuss about letting me go.

One morning I accompanied Griffin, the *Toronto Star* correspondent, to the People's Court. The Minister of Justice being an anarchist meant everything was free and easy – none of the 'lips sealed' business that communists go for – so we could go where we pleased, but it was terribly difficult to find out where or when a case would be tried.

There was nothing important on; we had just missed the trial of a priest the day before. He had been acquitted and had shouted, very naturally, '*Viva la República*'. There were, however, some farmers and peasants being tried for disaffection to the régime. There were no ordinary criminal cases being tried.

There were three judges, or magistrates. There was a young, too-clever lawyer to advise on legal points, with a dark yellow complexion. There was a representative of the CNT and another of the UGT, both looking rather solemn and stupid. The UGT man was a metallurgical worker and looked slightly brighter than the other, who belonged to the Wood Branch. He was a carpenter, and had a face like an old, gnarled tree stump. A man got up who was accused of belonging to a Catholic trade union. He was an old peasant, bald, in a black, sateen smock. He held his cap in his hands and gabbled incomprehensibly.

'Speak Castilian!' shouted the lawyer. He started off again but soon got excited and relapsed into the Valencian dialect. I and my notebook were completely lost. If I could have heard what he said I could not have followed it. Even if he had spoken Spanish I would not have been able to keep up as he talked so fast. A further impediment was that we all faced the judges and Griffin and I were behind him. I watched the dry, leathery wrinkles in the back of his tortoise-like neck and Griffin kept nudging me and whispering, 'What is he saying?' I did not dare relax my attention from the proceedings even to answer him lest I should miss something that would give a clue to the case.

The old man was very nervous and seemed to expect the worst. Fortunately, I was able to gather, from the testimony of the witnesses, that the defence was that the accused was a candle maker. It was no use being a candle maker if one did not keep in with the Church; how could one make a living? Therefore, he was obliged to join the Catholic union for business reasons. Two people from his village spoke in his favour, saying he was generally liked and had a son in the militia.

He got away with a fine of 500 pesetas, which seemed quite heavy to me, and went out waving his hands and protesting that he could not pay it. I pieced all this together with the help of the doorkeeper and then told Griffin what it was all about.

The other cases were similar and when the session was over the doorkeeper took us up to the platform to shake hands with the judges. The sinister young lawyer, who sat in the middle flanked by the two trade union judges, gave us a fluent explanation of the way the court worked.

'We fine everybody heavily, on principle,' he said. 'All these farmers have plenty of money really, and why shouldn't they pay? We don't put them in prison but some of them are watched and some deprived of civil rights.'

I went back to the office and told Coco about it as he always knew everything and everybody. He said the young lawyer was a Portuguese and a bad hat. I thought his fine speeches were a bit slick myself.

Though I was now out all day, the rest of my life at the Inglés was more *mouvementé* than ever. There was a bunch of English and American commercial aviators staying at the hotel, some not bad fellows, others awful braggarts, and most of them would not go up because they were not satisfied with their contracts. They grumbled about the rotten old crates they had to fly and were indignant that the Government had stopped paying their whisky bills. As it was, they got free supplies of Lucky Strike cigarettes and were paid large sums in gold.

In the end, the Government sent most of them home. A few stayed and some were used to train Spanish pilots. One, who we called Texas, had his wife come out to join him.[64] She was an actress and looked like Jean Harlow. She wore fashionable satin gowns, jewellery and sprays of orchids. She had impossibly long eyelashes that she flapped at people, and created quite a sensation in the hotel and at the Café Wodka.

We were friendly with two of the boys who had a room with a bath which we used. Kitty had engineered this arrangement. We had no bathroom and the other bathrooms in the hotel were all turned into bedrooms as it was so crowded.

One day, greatly to my inconvenience, Kitty's boyfriend, Tom Wintringham, got leave and turned up so, of course, I could not sleep in her room. We tried to get hold of a rather decent aviator we knew who slept in the barber shop but there was no extra bed in it. I had to take to the spare bed in a room occupied by a handsome young pilot with a toothbrush moustache. This was a bore as, of course, he thought it was up to him to try to seduce me and he needed quite a lot of convincing that I only wanted to be left in peace. Fortunately, it was only for one night but it created a scandal in the hotel as no Spaniard could ever have believed the truth of it.

One night after dark, I ran into Jan's photographer friend Walter. He had come down from Madrid for a Youth Conference. I told him all about the Jan situation and begged him to try to find out where Jan had been sent on his return to Madrid. He promised he would. By this time I did not put much faith in such promises, only I still went doggedly on pestering everyone. One lunchtime, Kitty turned up with a mischievous sparkle in her eyes, which I knew boded no good, and said in a low voice, glancing round the dining room to ensure no one was listening, 'What do you think? I am going to Albacete to see Tom.'

'You can't possibly,' I said. 'You know women and journalists are particularly forbidden there, and you are both.'

'I've got a pass,' she retorted.

'How did you get it?'

'Never you mind. It's okay and I'm going.'

I could see she was in one of those moods of triumphant obstinacy when I could do nothing with her but still I ventured to say, 'Please don't go, Kitty – you will only get into some scrape.'

She was as elated as a schoolgirl breaking bounds and, though I begged her to be careful and keep out of trouble, I knew I was wasting my breath. She only made fun of me. I went with her to the station that night, after we had had an early supper together and left her, with her rucksack on her back, dancing up and down in the crowd, irrepressibly gay. I had sworn not to tell a soul where she had gone. If anyone asked, I was to say she had gone to Barcelona to fetch some clothes she had left there.

She said she would only be absent a day or two and I did not expect anyone would ask about her except Griffin, to whom I handed her version of the trip the next day. To my surprise, however, the next morning, when I was enjoying the unusual luxury of a bed after so many nights on the hard and draughty floor, there came a knock on the door.

I got up and answered it to find a stout, pale, short, learned-looking Jewish-American stranger standing there in a pepper and salt suit. He asked for Miss Kitty Bowler, saying he was a friend of hers. I thought he was probably just a chance acquaintance like so many of her friends and said she was away.

'Oh, where has she gone?'

'Barcelona,' I lied glibly.

'What a pity I missed her. I have just come from there. When will she be back?'

'In a few days, I expect.'

'I particularly wanted to see her, can I write to her?'

'I don't know where she is staying,' I said, beginning to flounder a bit in the face of such persistence. He was quick to find something fishy in this last statement and plied me with questions. He stepped inside the room and peered round in a way I did not like, but I got rid of him eventually.

The next morning, stranger still, there was another knock on the door. I bounced out of bed, rather cross and ready to repel intruders, and opened the door. In the corridor stood a young girl, tearful and agitated. I had seen her before, in the dining room, with the stranger who had called the previous day.

'Come in,' I said. 'Sit down and have some coffee.'

She came in, closing the door behind her, looking round in an alarmed way, rubbing her red eyes and pretending she was not crying, though her bosom still heaved obviously.

"He's gone out somewhere so I took the opportunity to come and see you,' she began. 'Of course, you don't know me.'

'No,' I said, beginning to dress. 'Hurry up and tell me as I have to get to the office.'

'I expect you've seen me with Professor Borkenau?'[65]

'Yes, who is he?'

'He's writing a book and I'm his secretary. My name's Micky.'

'You don't like Professor Borkenau?'

'No,' she said. 'He's a very bad man and it will be a very bad book. He ought to be stopped from writing it.'

'I don't see how one can do that except by hiring an assassin.'

'He might be turned out of Spain. He knows I know now he's writing a fascist book so he won't dictate to me, but he writes notes and hides them or tears them up. He's an awfully suspicious person.'

'There's nothing to be done about it. His book is in his head and when he leaves Spain he will write it and no censor can stop him. What on earth did you come here with him for?'

'It seemed like such an adventure to come to Spain and he bought me new clothes, an entire outfit, and offered to take me. But now it seems he is a psychoanalyst and he says I am a mass of complexes and he wants to cure me – you know what I mean – he's just a dirty old man, really.'

'Well, what on earth did you expect coming away alone with a man?'

I thought she was an awful ass but of course she was very young, a university student, not more than twenty.

'He gets very angry with me now,' she said, 'and doesn't like my being an expense to him any more now that he realises he won't get anything in return. I've had such a dreadful time and I don't know what to do. He says he'll abandon me here with no money and I don't know a word of Spanish.'

It turned out that she had stayed a few days in Barcelona where she had met people I knew who had given her my name. She also had a letter to Liston Oak.

They had arrived in Valencia late at night, in pitch darkness, and had spent the remainder of that night sitting in the railway station. The situation had been aggravated since their arrival at the Inglés as the only room available happened to be a large one with two beds which she was forced to share with the professor who was personally greasy and unattractive. I confess I should not have relished his attentions either.

I told her I did not know when Kitty would be back but that she could sleep on my floor for a night or two if she was desperate. I took her round to see Liston, who was ill in bed as usual. What she really wanted was another job in order to escape from dependence on Professor Borkenau. I did not see how she could get one without knowing Spanish.

She took to spending her days at our office giving unpaid help, either cutting newspapers or typing. Milly got very cross with her as she was a lousy typist being very short-sighted and too vain to wear glasses.

'I always have said voluntary workers are no damn good and I always shall say it,' said Milly.

Micky also became very friendly with Selke, who transferred to her his fancy for me, and she picked up several young Spaniards who were supposed to be teaching her Spanish in exchange for English.

Naturally, I only heard Micky's side of the story. She had worked herself up into a state of distress, but may have imagined or invented half of it. Professor Borkenau taught history at one of the smaller American universities and was a widower. He had some views that the Spanish Government would have objected to and to Micky's simple mind that was indistinguishable from fascism. He was an extremely nervous and ill-balanced man and

139

dabbling in psychoanalysis had made things worse. He may have been angry with Micky because he thought she knew beforehand the terms he expected to be on, and she was just making use of him. A man of that age, he was at least fifty, is very sensitive to rebuffs and very deeply piqued at finding himself repugnant to a blooming young girl.

He undoubtedly had persecution mania and was also one of those people who saw the hand of Moscow everywhere in the Civil War, even in the most unlikely corner. It was difficult to know how the Spanish Republic should have treated such people. If banned from Spain, they said the country would not bear investigation. If, as sometimes happened, these Moscow obsessives were arrested and deported it only gave them material for more lurid tales about the Spanish GPU when they did get out.

Kitty's absence was prolonged and I heard nothing of her though she had said she would contrive to put a telephone call through from Albacete. Naturally, as she was going to the headquarters of the Internationals I had charged her with going to see Oscar Telge at the *Service Sanitaire* to find out if Jan was there and, if not, where he had been sent. I had also sent with her a note and various messages to Ilse, the German girl I had met in Barcelona. She was still working in the administration at Albacete and I knew she must have facilities for finding out the whereabouts of men and letting me know. I still trusted both Ilse and Kitty to help me – Kitty anyway was energetic and I knew she would do her best. So, not only for her own sake but for mine too, I was eager for her return and grew uneasy when day after day passed and there was no sign from her.

* * * * *

As I was the only English person in the office, I was the only one who found the long afternoons unendurable without a break for a cup of tea, so I usually went out alone to the café and Liston had to put up with this habit. I generally took Spanish papers out with me to read so he could not say I was wasting time.

I was sitting in the Wodka one day, the lights were on so it must have been about five, when I saw a young man at a neighbouring table, also alone, drinking tea and writing notes. He was fair, with short, straight, untidy hair without a parting and out straight across the front. He wore a rough, loose, tweedy suit and a collegiate air. He looked very young. I was sure he was English and supposed he was an ambulance driver from the Medical Aid. This was the poet W.H. Auden but I did not know him by sight.[66]

Assuming he might be feeling lonely and lost, after staring at him for a bit, I went over and said, 'Are you English?' He said he was and suggested I join him. He asked me what I was doing in Spain and I told him. He said I might be able to help him as he did not know Spanish.

He told me his name and said he had just arrived and was writing his impressions of Valencia. He told me the Spanish Embassy in London had said that he might perhaps make propaganda for England. He was keen to arrange English broadcasts as well as cultural Spanish ones from Valencia.

'Do you belong to the Communist Party?' he asked.

'No,' I said.

'Neither do I,' he said, a bit regretfully.

'I'm just an anti-fascist,' I said.

He agreed but added rather dreamily, 'but I suppose it would be a help, here and now, to belong to something.'

I said I thought belonging to a political party was a help as it was a guarantee of good faith and that an individualist in a civil war was liable to be rather a fish out of water. He sighed.

'Have you seen a man called Cornford in the Brigade?' he asked.

'Yes, I saw him in Madrid, but he is dead now.'

'Are you sure?'

'Quite sure.'

Auden started and twitched nervously. 'He was a brilliant mind, one of the most brilliant at Cambridge,' he said. 'I had hoped to meet him here.'

I went back to the office and did my best to impress on everyone that Auden was a famous poet and they had better go out of their way to oblige him as he had a lot of influence in England. I knew this was necessary as he was so unassuming in manner. The Press Office was always making a fuss over people who were of no real importance. As Auden had a letter from the ambassador, Rubio was bound to be polite and offer him some facilities.

Unfortunately, Liston took up a violently hostile attitude. He did not want him working with us, not even in the same room, he always raised objections to lending me or Coco, and the more I told him Auden was a great man the more jealous he grew of this propaganda rival. Milly judged him as a newspaperman, not as a poet, so her view too was unfavourable. According to her standards he was vague and unbusinesslike and took too long over everything.

At a later date, under the reign of Constancia, who had a much more proper sense of things, he would have had either Coco or me, full time, at his disposal. At the time, Constancia had only just joined the staff.[67] The place had only been going for a month and was not properly organised, and Auden was often left to struggle with Febus and the papers unaided. He would come into our room with his dictionary and timidly ask for an explanation of a paragraph only to be snapped at by Liston.

One night I went out with Auden to see the man in charge of Radio. Of course, he kept us waiting ages in the outer office. He was a fat, pompous little man with a grand desk and armchairs. We were treated like a couple of applicants for jobs as office boys. It emerged that the radio station which would carry to England was not built yet and I got entangled in a lot of technical translation about wave-lengths.

To keep Auden quiet Rubio gave him Azaña's speech, which was very long, to write in good English! He did it as meekly as a lamb and made a speech much better than Azaña was capable of. It was duplicated in a great hurry and then produced as a pamphlet; Rubio had fits of being in a great hurry. Micky and I made the stencils, working one Sunday until midnight, with Auden dictating from his long-hand. He displayed admirable good temper and patience through the long and trying day. Micky was so thrilled to be actually in the same room with him that she held her breath while she was typing. She had been in some amateur performance of *The Dog Beneath the Skin* and she, at least, did not need any telling to think Auden a great man. I think that day was the high spot in her Spanish visit.

We were further irritated by there being only one bottle of red correcting fluid which Myra, Selke's little sister, kept stealing from us when we were out at meals. Myra was simultaneously engaged in stencilling the speech in French and we had violent battles of words over which was the most important or the most urgent. I had to speak to her in French and always became inarticulate in a foreign language when in a rage, especially when I had to switch abruptly from one language to another. There was already a shortage of stationery supplies in Valencia; they had to come from Paris by air, and we hoarded as much as we could. Carmen was a fearful hoarder and used to sit over a whole box of stencils like a broody hen.

Sometimes the newspapermen used to borrow my typewriter at night and I would find it in the morning with the ribbon all tangled up as if the hobgoblin had been enjoying some office Walpurgis Night. I did not feel communal about this and took to locking it up, leaving it with a skull and crossbones PRIVATE PROPERTY sign on it.

In the end, Auden got fed up with the politics and intrigues in Valencia and went to the front as a stretcher-bearer and one could not blame him.

* * * * *

One night I went back to the office in the evening after dinner. I was beginning to feel a bit lonely and to miss Kitty. I always hated eating alone. So I went back with Liston to read him the ten o'clock military communiqué. It was very quiet as not many journalists happened to be in Valencia.

Rubio was away on one of his periodic trips to Paris or Geneva and Selke was left in charge of censorship, a state of things which always made him rather uppish as he was not used to authority. Generally, Rubio was as much a night bird as Liston himself. He never came to the office until the afternoon and stayed there until the small hours and had his supper and trays of black coffee taken into his private room. Rubio was pallid and bald and looked rather sinister as he had weak eyes and always wore dark glasses. His private room was always half dark in the daytime and illumined by a very much shaded desk lamp at night.

From this dim sanctum Selke beckoned me, with the air of someone with a significant communication to impart.

'Are you expecting your friend back?'

'What do you mean?' I stammered.

'You know who I mean – Miss Kitty Bowler, as she calls herself,' he said in accusing tones, as if even her name were suspect.

'Of course, she left all her things at the hotel.'

'She won't have long to stay there. I doubt if the police will let her stop to pick up her belongings.'

'What on earth do you mean?' I said, wondering what he had found out and how, and thinking how angry Kitty would be if she jumped to the conclusion that I had betrayed her secret destination, which I had not.

'You know what I mean. You know she went where she should not. Whoever gave her that pass is in for trouble, and she is going out of Spain so fast you won't have time to say goodbye to her. You didn't pick a friend very wisely.'

Kitty was not a particular friend of mine except by chance but she was my room mate and I felt angry at this unprovoked attack and defended her with some heat.

Selke could be very nasty when he chose and he had got his knife into Kitty and me too. I do not know why but some personal animosity would suddenly break out like this when, another day, he would be as sweet as pie. I never forgot such scenes and knew him for the treacherous enemy he was, though he used to try to smooth things over afterwards.

It was useless to pretend Kitty had not gone to Albacete as he had obviously nosed it out somehow, so the best thing was to give the simple, true explanation that she had simply gone to see Tom, that women would fall in love, but there was no harm in it. I said all this but Selke evidently intended to make it all as black as possible.

I excused myself and went home very cross and anxious, feeling that all my worst forebodings were coming true. The next day dragged by with me imagining all sorts of horrible things.

I was extremely relieved when, while I was eating dinner, Kitty marched in with her pack on her back and no one stared, though I fancied by this time that everyone would know she was some sort of criminal and that I should not see her again except under guard and in handcuffs. She looked extremely tired and tousled as if she had been pulled through a hedge backwards.

'Where have you been, I thought you were never coming back,' I gasped.

'Hush, I've been in the jug,' she said, but her eyes danced merrily as usual.

She would not tell me any more then so we bolted our food and went up to the room. I introduced her to Micky and then turned Micky out because we wanted a private chat.

'I had great fun at first,' she said, 'and I saw Tom quite a lot which is something. All the Internationals wear uniforms and berets now. I suppose it's easy to make them here, and the more important they are, the bigger and more overhanging the beret and they wear them in the most individual ways. I was quizzed by André Marty, the Commander-in-Chief, and his is like a pagoda.'[68]

'Did you find out about Jan?'

'No. I did try, truly. We saw Ilse one evening but we couldn't get any sense out of her. She has got swelled headed because she is practically the only woman in Albacete except for Spanish whores, so she has lots of admirers. And she has fallen in love again, with a political commissar and you know how sentimental she is, she wouldn't do anything but burble on about him and about how she wanted to get away from Albacete. To think of all the trouble we had with her in Barcelona when she wanted to go there!'

I told her about Selke's strange behaviour and how he had threatened and hinted the worst things. Neither of us could guess how he had found out.

'I got arrested almost immediately, unluckily, which rather cramped my style,' she said, 'and the rest of the time I was being cross-questioned, really third-degreed, which quite wore me out. They were furious because I didn't break down and weep as they expected a woman would. But they couldn't prove anything against me, of course, so they let me go. It'll all blow over.'

'I hope so,' I said. 'And are you really free now? No police surveillance or anything?'

'No,' she said, but she was looking through a drawer where she kept her papers and suddenly turned to me with an annoyed flush on her face. 'Have you been using this drawer?'

'Of course not,' I said. In fact I was never able to unpack in that room as there was no place to put my things.

'The beasts,' she said, and began to cry. 'They've searched my room while I was away and you at the office, I suppose. They took some copies of articles I wrote – much good may it do them! You know they went through my letters to Tom and wouldn't believe they weren't in code. They think I'm Mata Hari the second or something.'

She subsided on the bed. The fact was she was all in; she had not had much sleep and I gave her some brandy and made her go to bed. Kitty liked to create a stir but this time the notoriety was hardly the kind she liked.

'What about this girl, Micky?' she asked.

I told her Micky had been sleeping in the room but I was sure she was okay, and told her all about Micky and Professor Borkenau and she laughed again.

Of course the most innocent were always liable to be arrested with the war and Micky was always being arrested but this was because she carried a camera. She had got a permit for taking photographs but, nevertheless, everything she tried to take, the beach or the town hall, always turned out to be of military importance and her films were all confiscated. Sullivan, a rather stupid American photographer, was hardly ever out of hot water. The American consul used to go round to the prison every morning to see if any of his fellow citizens were there and he nearly always found Sullivan and had to get him out. I never attempted to use a camera in Spain as it was a certain passport to jail.

I was badly cast down by the result of Kitty's visit to Albacete. I felt pretty disillusioned about Ilse, who I had really thought of as a German idealist who would think of other people's troubles as intensely as she did of her own. Really one did better to rely on the apparently hard-boiled Americans in the long run. Kitty was dependable enough, she made demands on one, but she was ready to repay with interest. Of course, she could not do much when she was locked up and I had been expecting her to solve the whole problem.

Chapter 8
Hospitales de Sangre

I felt it was particularly ironic when, one morning soon after Kitty's return, I received some mail from the outside world. The letters had been re-forwarded, opened and stuck down again by the censor, and were very out of date. One was from my friends in Paris telling me to cheer up and be of good heart for I was sure to find Jan soon. One was a brief note from Jan himself, written from Madrid to London, to say he was wounded. One was a notification, sent to Barcelona, from the *Enlace de Hospitales* in Valencia saying that Jan was in the Hotel Palace in Madrid and was going on well! I folded up the letters, stuck them in my pocket, and went mournfully to the office to bury myself in work. I had had no replies to any of my telegrams and did not know what move to make next.

I read and re-read Jan's letter. It was evident he had received none of those I had written, because I had sent them to his battalion and, being wounded, he had left it.

I was feeling very tired and left for lunch a bit early. As I got into the room the telephone was ringing and I was just in time to stop the man at the desk downstairs from cutting off the call because he thought we were both out. At first I could not make out who was calling, or where from. It was long-distance and a strange female voice with a foreign accent.

'Jan is in hospital here,' said the voice, 'bed number 365, ward eight.'

'Where is here?' I cried.

'Murcia,' said the voice. 'He has just been operated on. He is very ill and in great pain and should see someone he knows. Can you come as soon as possible?'

'Who are you?' I asked.

'I am Madame Frieda Richter, a Danish journalist. I knew him in Madrid. I came here for my work and found him here. He's very low. Come as soon as you can and ask for me at the Hotel Victoria.'

The call was cut off. My brain was in a muddle and I rushed here and there aimlessly. I hurried back to the office to find Liston and Milly but they had gone to lunch. I hurried back to the hotel. Kitty was out. I ate something. I went back to the office impatiently. At last the others came back. I broached the subject to Liston.

'Yes, I know,' he said, 'I have heard the whole story.'

He did not want to let me go as we were so busy. Milly put in a good word for me, then took me aside.

'Take my advice,' she said, 'go by the next train. If I were in your place that is what I would do. In a woman's life, the man she cares about is much more important than any job. In any case Liston may be disagreeable but he won't fire you as he can't get on without you, none of us can.'

We found out that there was a train that night and I told Liston I was getting it. He made me promise to be back in two days. I said I believed Jan to be very bad, perhaps dying, but I would get back as soon as I reasonably could. Milly invited me to have some coffee at her hotel, before the train left, and bought a bottle of expensive English gin for me to take to Jan as, she said, she knew that in Madrid he liked to have a drink to dull the pain.

She insisted on doing this as she said that Jan was on her conscience as, when she left, he had given her some letters to take out with her to post in France and she had forgotten to post them.

I went round to the *Correos* and sent a telegram to him to say I was coming, and I asked Constancia if I needed a pass to go to Murcia. She looked at my papers and said I did not. In the afternoon I received a letter from the mysterious Frieda, sent a day or two before, again asking me to come and to bring little comforts, if I could, for Jan. I wondered if he had asked her to send for me or if, after she had seen him, she had just used her own judgement about the matter. I think the latter, as he was too ill to care much about anything then.

I went early for the train, which was as well, as trains were hell in those days. A young woman let me share her seat and there I remained wedged all night. It was an 'omnibus' coach and there were militiamen in it who talked, sang, danced and played guitars all night and no one seemed to think of trying to sleep. They sang *The Internationale, Hijo del Pueblo* and *La Cucaracha*, the last with obscene variations. There was one wounded man in the coach. At first he sat in a corner, only complaining of the noise which made his head ache. As the hours wore on he grew tired and his wounds hurt him and he lay down on the floor and groaned. The floor was very dirty, with people spitting on it, and men kept walking over him.

At dawn, I had to change at Chinchón junction, and people made jokes about it and said it was full of *chinches* (bed-bugs). It was up in the mountains and an icy cold place. After I had waited on the station for some time, I got on the train from Aranjuez which was full of refugees from Madrid. The train began to creep down from the heights into a landscape full of blue mountains and orange groves, stopping constantly for long spells.

I sat opposite an old woman, big and unwieldy in a black shawl, who was deaf and nearly blind and was trying to be sick out of the window. She was very agitated. At the stops she would get up and look out to try to see where she was and then lose some of her bundles or forget where she had been sitting. When the train started again with a jerk, she would be nearly thrown off her feet and a very handsome young soldier, who sat with her, would help her back again.

I began to eat a chocolate bar and offered her some but she would not eat anything. She was weeping all the time, tears trickling down her leathery old face out of her little red eyes and the young man comforted her. She kept up a continuous lamentation. She said she was eighty-five and it was terrible being uprooted; she was being evacuated to some relations she did not know well, who probably would not want the burden of her when she was so helpless, and she would never live to see her dear Madrid again. The lack of food did not matter at her age but change was awful.

All the time the young soldier kept talking to her and telling her everything would be all right. When she reached her station he put her and her bundles out and found her relatives in the crowd. I had thought he must be her grandson, he was so thoughtful and gentle with her, but the other soldiers teased him about his 'girlfriend' and it turned out he was a complete stranger who had just taken pity on her.

It was about midday when we reached Murcia and I was so tired I was just in a waking dream. I did not know the town. It had been raining and the streets were full of yellow mud. Many had been dug up as a start had been made on air raid shelters, and the holes were full of water.

A militiaman carried my rucksack and walked with me to the hotel to show me the way. I offered him money and cigarettes which he good-naturedly refused, saying he was only doing his duty. The hotel was different to the Valencian ones, built in a southern style with rooms and galleries opening off in a central patio with a glass roof. In the patio some wounded Internationals were at a table drinking. One very pale one had a bandage round his head. I took a room and asked if Madame Richter were staying there. I was told she was. I had a wash and some coffee and asked where the hospital was. I was told it was just across the street. Luckily, this was the right hospital; there were several in Murcia.

I met Madame Richter at lunch. She was not young, stout with child-like blue eyes, sensible and kind. She told me Jan usually slept in the afternoon or, at least, rested, so I decided to do likewise as I felt a wreck. I was so relieved to have arrived that I slept like a top for some hours and woke much refreshed.

At about five I set out for the hospital. It was in a secondary school, across the plaza and past the flower market which was under an arcade. Opposite there was a public park with some trees and a few roundabouts. The land sloped down to a river-bed but I could not see any water. It was very windy so I bought myself a beret.

I went into the hospital which was also built around a stone courtyard and found the office on the ground floor. In the office there was a soldier, I think Italian, and he had no hands, only stumps. He was very sharp with me and said the wounded were allowed no visits. Actually, the Internationals, being mostly foreigners, had no one who could visit them apart from foreign journalists. The authorities tried to prevent the journalists seeing them and getting lurid and inaccurate stories out of them.

I got into a panic that they would not let me in and hauled out all my papers to demonstrate that I was a 'person of confidence'. I finally said I was Jan's wife and another soldier, a Frenchman who was there, interrupted and said he would show me the way. While he was taking me up stairs and along corridors he told me not to mind the other man. 'Don't you pay any attention to him,' he said. 'He's always in a bad temper poor bugger because he lost his hands.' My guide limped.

It was dusk. I entered a ward with a wooden floor that was always dusty though they sprinkled it with water. There, facing the window, was Jan in a very hard and narrow folding cot which would have been uncomfortable even for a well person.

He kissed me and really seemed glad to see me but I was so pleased and excited that I talked too much at once and did not see how weak and easily tired he was. I tumbled all the treasures out of my rucksack thinking he would be pleased and would exclaim over them but he could not take much interest though he pretended to so as not to disappoint me.

When I showed him the chocolate he said he had no appetite any more, and he did not seem to care much for smoking either. However, he liked to have chocolate and cigarettes to give other men in the ward who did little things for him. He read the letters but put the magazines aside as if it were too much of an effort to look at them but said he would look at them later on. He greedily smelled some violets I had bought and seemed most pleased to see and touch them. He liked the gin and made me hide it in a cupboard beside the bed so the doctor would not see it.

Most of the time, I stood there awkwardly as the bed was too narrow to sit on without running the risk of bumping his leg. Eventually, someone brought me one of the few chairs. We hardly knew what to say to each other after so long and so much had happened. I sat silent until the man with the bandage round his head came in. He was a tall, young Irishman with bad teeth. He looked ghostly pale; it was the first time he had been out. He came and told Jan what it was like in the town and offered some caramels he had bought.

'I used to belong to the IRA until I saw there was more to Socialism,' he said. He was a very nice, friendly fellow. They all were, and it was wonderful in the midst of such sordidness and suffering to see how unselfish they all were and how good to one another. No Christians could have been better than those boys, and since then I have often missed that spirit and that familiar, *tú, camarada* that made me feel that I too had been adopted into a fraternity.

Jan was anxious to know how he really was as the doctor did not speak much English, so I promised to come when the doctor made his rounds and ask him. Jan was tired and so I left him for the time being. I cried bitterly at the hotel at finding him so feeble and impossible to move but I pulled myself together again to be able to present him with a cheerful face.

In the hall of the hotel was a young Russian, probably a mechanic, in a plain suit and a beret. He looked just like what one sees in Soviet films as representative of post-revolution youth. He was healthy and well-grown, with a rosy Mogul face, bright, small, black eyes, and a frank, engaging smile. He looked as if he had never been snubbed or oppressed in his life and yet was not at all bumptious. Apparently quite fearless of any possible rebuff, he came up and attempted to explain something he wanted. I tried all the languages I knew but we did not get anywhere. At last, I made out that he wanted to go to the cinema. I explained this to the girl cashier and she said she was just leaving work for the night and would show him the way, so off they went together. She was a bit thin and sallow but not a bad looking girl, mostly dressed in black.

The next morning she called me over to her desk.

'You know that young *Ruso*,' she said. 'Of course he doesn't know our customs, but I had some trouble with him.'

'I'm sorry to hear that,' I said.

'Yes, when we got to the door of the cinema, do you know what he wanted? He wanted me to accompany him to the show. He was most insistent, he took my arm and tried to pull me in. Of course one can't blame him; he doesn't know any better. He didn't mean any harm but it was hard work persuading him that I was not going with him.'

'I suppose you'd only go to the cinema with your fiancé,' I said.

'Oh, no, I wouldn't go with my fiancé,' she said, shocked, 'only with my family.'

When I got back, the hospital had a more cheerful air because the electric light was on and the Spanish girls, always laughing, chattering and singing, were rattling plates giving out the supper.

Jan, like all the very sick ones, could ask for eggs if he did not like the food and he had a big jug of boiled milk by his bed. The Irishman came and talked with us and also an old Spanish woman, fat and comfortable, really a cleaner, called Concepción.

'All the boys like me, ' she said, sitting down on an empty cot and folding her work-worn hands in her apron. 'I'm a mother to all of them. The poor boys,' she sighed, 'they all ask for Mother Concepción when they come out from their operations. I sit with them and hold their hands and give them wine,' she went on reflectively, 'and some of them die but, poor boys, they die happy.'

'Have you children of your own?' I asked.

'No. It's a great pity. I had many but I lost them all and now it's too late. I'm too old. But I love these boys as if they were my own children.'

'See, the doctor is coming,' said Jan, nervously, raising himself on one elbow and looking towards the door with a flushed face.

I saw a young, thick-set, rosy man, with a dark, curly head and low forehead like a young bull. All the soldiers suspended eating and looked towards him. He started on the farther side of the ward and slowly progressed round the room, addressing a few cheerful and encouraging words to each man in French, German or English, though he only knew a few phrases in the last two. The matron, tall, elderly and sour, with a clean white kerchief on her head, followed him attentive for orders respecting the patients.

'He's a great doctor,' said the Irishman. 'I've got a hole in my skull but he'll fix me up fine, you'll see. He's going to operate on me again soon to straighten out these bent fingers; my head doesn't bother me.'

'You couldn't be any crazier than you were before,' said Jan. The Irishman grinned.

'There's nothing that fellow can't do,' he said. 'I'd trust him to take my brains out, polish them and put them back again. What a worker! Always cutting people up, day and night, a regular butcher,' he said admiringly. 'I wouldn't trust a Spanish doctor, but this fellow can do anything. He's only a young chap, with no experience of war surgery before he came here.'

'He's very decent,' said Jan, 'always telling us that we're going to be good as new or even better. You would think, to hear him talk, that a man was better off with an artificial leg than with his own. But I don't believe all he says, that's the worst of it. I think he just talks like that to keep up morale.'

The doctor, who was a Belgian, came up to us.

'*Tu manges?*' he enquired of Jan, who shook his head sadly.

'*Il faut manger* – you must eat and get strong,' he said, and shook his finger at Jan. I followed him out into the corridor.

'I want to know more about my husband's condition,' I began timidly, for he was obviously very busy. He turned at once and gave me his attention.

'*Vous savez c'est grave,*' he said kindly. 'It's serious. He didn't come here soon enough. He should have had an operation much sooner. I did what I could. His leg and foot had shrunk. I pulled them out as much as I could and then set it in plaster.'

He gave a technical explanation of what he had done.

'But will he walk?'

'Sure, he will walk, but he may limp. One leg may be too short. I can make him an apparatus so he can move his foot. He can have a built-up boot. We can't really tell if the operation has succeeded for a couple of weeks, not until he's out of plaster. You must keep up his spirits; he mustn't get ill from staying in bed so long. He's naturally very healthy. *Salud, camarada.*' And he hurried off as the matron was calling him.

I felt pretty gloomy at this account but I tried not to show it when I went back to Jan. I told him the doctor had promised faithfully that he would walk and I was sure he was speaking the truth. I told him the doctor had pulled his leg out, like torturing someone on the rack in ancient times, so it would be as long as the other.

'It feels like a Chinese torture,' said Jan. We had a bit of gin together and then I had to go for my own dinner at the hotel. I promised to come again early in the morning. I said I hoped he would sleep but he only sighed, and he gave a bitter smile when I hauled out of my bag a lot of aspirin I had brought.

'It doesn't have any effect any more,' he said, 'and here they won't give me morphine like I had in Madrid. I can't sleep now without morphine or something strong like that.'

I had also brought with me a bottle of Alonel which Milly had brought from France for headaches and given to me to take to him. He hid it in his cupboard and said he would try it later.

When I got back to the hotel, I felt very sad that Jan could not eat or sleep and I did not see how he was to keep his strength up. The doctor had said it would be a long time before he was better.

I had a wonderful dinner at the hotel, with good wine, lots of courses and grapes. I wished Jan had been well enough to have got across the square as I was sure that the food would have tempted him. I decided to try to get some grapes the next day, as he had plenty of oranges and was tired of them.

The next morning, I asked the hotel manager for some grapes but he said there were no more as they came from Almería and, with the offensive on Málaga, the transport was not very good. The people at the hotel and in the town were really all fascists. It was a rich place and the people stuffed themselves like pigs as if there were no war on, while the wounded in the hospital could hardly get anything fit to eat.

I went into the town. It had narrow, shady streets with high, old buildings, rather oriental, and shops with painted fans in the windows. I bought Jan a bottle of eau-de-cologne, some fine handkerchiefs, a packet of cornflakes and some grape juice which is very refreshing. It was hot and sunny, hot enough to sit outside cafés, and I saw that spring had come here already. In the plaza were parked a lot of buses that went to different towns round about. The market was full of flowers, and I bought some freesias.

When I reached the ward Jan was sleeping, his face flushed, a lock of hair hanging over his forehead on which a vein was standing out. He frowned as if he were in pain. He looked very uncomfortable, with his head hanging down over the side of the bed and one hand clutching the iron rail above him. He breathed heavily and flies were sitting on him.

I suddenly felt a wave of despair. How was he ever to get out of this squalid place, with the soiled bed clothes and used bed pans under the beds? The flies, the dusty floor, the smell of very ill people, it all looked more sordid still in the brilliant sunshine.

I went over to the French window where a nurse was standing on the balcony with her back to me. She turned and I saw that it was English Penny, with whom I had travelled from Paris. I told her how I had come to visit Jan.

'Don't disturb him,' she said. 'He had a very bad night and he must get some sleep when he can. He's always in pain.'

'They *must* give him drugs,' I said.

'The drugs are all locked up or I would give them,' she said. 'As a matter of fact we're short of drugs and waiting for more from France just now. Time and again I've almost been on my knees to matron begging her to give me something for him, he suffers so much I can't bear to see it. They only give him aspirin and phenobarbital – that's very bad stuff, it's bad for your stomach and your brain. They give it to epileptics.'

I looked down on to the sunny street, hopelessly.

'I can't do any good here,' Penny said. It was clear she was terribly upset.

'I don't understand anybody or they me.'

'Are you the only English person here?'

'No, there's one other, the pale girl who was travelling with us. But it isn't so bad for her because she is in the operating theatre and she knows her work so well she can guess what the doctor wants handed to him. I am on the wards, that is different, and between that old matron screaming at me in French and the Spanish girls, who have no training and don't even know that they must dip a thermometer in alcohol between patients, I am nearly going dotty.'

'Why don't they keep the English together?'

'Oh, I don't know, it is some political idea of the International Brigades to mix everyone up, so it is like Babel, or more like Bedlam I should say.'

We were silent for a while. I thought perhaps she had just made some mistake and been scolded and was upset about that.

'I wish I could go to the front or somewhere where I could do some good,' she said.

'Is the hospital badly run?' I asked.

'They do the best they can,' she said, 'but this building was never meant for a hospital: no running water, nothing, and the girls in the kitchen have no more idea of hygiene than a fly. There's my pneumonia patient here.' She pointed to an unconscious man who lay next to the window. 'I'm sure I'll lose him and it's so unnecessary,' she went on fretfully. 'The French and Spanish are always closing the windows when he must have fresh air. And there seems no way of laying the dust from these wooden floors. They are washed every day but it's always the same. And they've got all sorts of cases in this ward that should never be together: tuberculosis, venereal, dysentery and I don't know what. I can't do any good here. I must get away.'

'I wish you'd stay and keep an eye on Jan,' I said. 'I think I'll go now and come back later as he is sleeping. I'll leave these parcels with you.'

* * * * *

Outside the hotel stood a car with which a chauffeur was tinkering. In the large, shady hall stood a traveller with his bag, impatient to start. I had met this man, Claud Cockburn, somewhere previously, and he asked me to have a vermouth with him. I was depressed which made me feel extremely irritated with the outside world in general. Claud Cockburn was a communist of a kind I did not like. I suspected that he had 'seen the light' politically at a recent date – though I may be wrong about this – as he had, in a marked degree, all the typical communist failings, which are usually mellowed by years of persecution. He was then writing for the *Daily Worker* under the name of Frank Pitcairn. He was always sour and irritable and I thought he might have an ulcer as well as no sense of humour.[69]

'Something wrong with your car,' I enquired. 'These Spanish chauffeurs don't seem to be very good mechanics. Humphrey Slater was always having trouble.'

'Oh, Humphrey,' he said, with the utmost scorn. '*His* car, *his* chauffeur. Mine is very different, a good Party Member,' as if this were complete insurance against flat tyres or other motoring trials. I did not ask whether it was the car or the driver who was a good Party Member or whether both were.

'Humphrey has a specious sort of charm,' Claud went on with a sneer, 'and you fell for it at once, as they all do.'

I was nettled by these personal remarks on so scant an acquaintance. His judgement was so far from the mark, however, that I laughed.

'One can hardly fall for someone one has known half one's life. Humphrey and I were at the Slade together.'

A very distinguished German émigré stepped out of the dining room in conversation with another, who was in the uniform of the International Brigade. Claud left me and barged into the conversation. When speaking, Claud tried to combine the appearance of a confidential chat with a voice loud enough to hear that he was talking fluent German with a correct accent. It was like watching an actor giving an aside. The German, who could speak excellent French and English, smiled politely but evidently wanted to get away.

'I just wanted to have a word with Emil,' said Claud, looking at me to see whether I was impressed, as he sat down again. I was meanly determined not to pander to his snobbery so I changed the subject.

'What do you think about Málaga?' I asked. 'Mussolini stated months ago that it was the next place he was going to take.'

'Oh, Málaga is fine. It won't fall, of course not. It will be another Madrid. I am going to look it over, ' Claud said, with rather the air of one in charge of the defences.

'I hope you are right,' I said, 'but in Valencia we know so little about it. We only see censored news and we don't know whether they have tanks or aeroplanes, or whether they have good commanding officers and troops, or whether they have made second line trenches, or whether the navy is helping out or anything.'

'Do you want to go there?' Claud suddenly asked sharply, 'because I can't take you. I make a point of never giving people lifts in my car.' It was, of course, not his; both the car and the driver were only lent to him.

'I'm going the opposite way,' I said, 'and had no idea of cadging a ride. But I hope you are right about Málaga.'

I had my doubts. Communists always displayed this exaggerated optimism, I don't know whether it was to kid themselves or other people. They always talked, too, as if they had Soviet Russia in their pockets, and gave mysterious hints about the help that would come at the right moment as if they had inside information. Most of them had not the faintest idea of the situation in Spain itself, let alone the intentions of Moscow, but apparently it is painful and disgraceful for a communist ever to admit that he is not omniscient. Neither will they ever admit they are, or have been, wrong. If I had talked to Claud a month or so later he would probably have said that, of course, he knew Málaga was doomed, any intelligent person would have known, but it was not expedient to give his views to a lay person like me. Then he would add that the fall of Málaga was quite unimportant, but that some other town, such as Bilbao, would never fall.

Their attitude to Russia irritated me intensely. Russia could do no wrong and if one was critical, one was a criminal Trotskyist and, in fact, a fascist, as it was the same thing. Whatever Russia did or omitted to do was explained afterwards by the communists as being the best and wisest course. I do not know how they explain away the Spanish debacle now; I feel too bitter about it to ask them. At the time, they interpreted the Soviet Union like priests interpreting the will of the Almighty. God moves in a mysterious way, and so does the Soviet Union.

If help came late, or not at all, we were told that Russia, like a school teacher angered by unruly children, would let them get on with it as best they could and learn from their mistakes and then, when things were desperate, of course she would throw in her weight and tip the scales. Those bad children with their Popular Front, which included Left Republicans and, worse still, anarchists, must learn their bitter lesson first. Russia had suffered in her civil war and Spain must suffer too.

Communism is international, but it is very different in different countries. French, English and American communists were untempered by suffering, and they showed an intolerable kind of snobbishness about Russia. To them Russians were the new aristocrats. The summit of their social climbing was admission to the Russian Embassy circle. The attitude was that the meanest communist was worth two of anybody else and the meanest Russian was worth four of anybody else.

Claud made a few remarks to this effect which angered me as such remarks always did. He then turned his attention to another favourite communist pastime: spy hunting. How they expect, when they worship discretion beyond anything and keep their mouths so tightly buttoned about their own affairs, that any but the most ingenuous and, therefore, least dangerous people will freely answer their questions, I do not know.

'Murcia suddenly seems to have become quite a centre,' began Claud, looking me in the eye portentously. 'One meets everyone here. A little while ago it was Albacete and now it is here.'

For a few minutes, Claud persevered in trying to elicit from me what I was doing in Spain, what I was doing in Valencia and, finally, what I was doing in Murcia, but I gave him no satisfaction. Eventually, I lost patience. 'In a civil war, lots of strange types come to the surface; people you would never come across in normal circumstances; I'm one of them.'

Claud's party line had not entirely obliterated his sense of humour and he was forced to laugh.

'Do you think I'm a spy?' I asked.

'All women are potential spies,' he said.

The laughter had relaxed the tension of our annoyance slightly and I began to wonder how influential Claud really was (he evidently considered himself extremely important) and whether he could be induced to visit Jan and take an interest in improving his lot. I quickly dismissed this idea as Claud appeared selfish and had shown himself disobliging over the car. My feeling that he might be useful if he chose, but would not choose, set me off on the attack again.

'If you really want to know, it's quite simple. I came to see my husband who is in the hospital across the road, badly wounded. I'm staying in Spain to help him, if I can, to get well and get home some day. Why don't you go over to the hospital and visit the boys? Some of them would be glad of a visit from someone who could talk English to them and tell them the news. You could take them drink and cigarettes and you would be doing more good for the cause, believe me, than nosing around for spies.'

'I haven't time,' said Claud, uncomfortably, getting up and going to the door to see if his car was ready and chivvying the driver.

'You can go anywhere,' I said, 'you're a privileged person. Why don't you go to the hospital and find out what those boys need and then go to Albacete and raise hell until they get it? You'd be doing more good than in Málaga. The only people who are doing any good here are the people who are fighting and risking their lives and limbs. You political observers make me sick.'

'They have the proper channels, if they want to make complaints,' said Claud primly. 'They have their political commissar.'

'Political commissar be damned,' I said. 'He never comes near them, or if he does, he only gives a pep talk about morale.'

Claud went out and sat in his car, which was not ready, and I went in to lunch. When I came out he was gone.

Frieda was already at table.

'I shall have to go back tomorrow,' I said. 'There is not much to be done for Jan, anyway, until he is out of plaster. You will go to see him, won't you?'

'Of course. I'll go as often as I can. I didn't go while you were here as I thought one visitor was enough.'

She saw that I was absorbed in worries and tried to take my mind off them by talking.

'You know the Thaelmann Battalion is here?'

'Yes, I believe I saw some of their officers in the hotel this morning.'

'They have come here to reorganise, after very heavy losses.'

'They always have the heaviest losses.'

'But, you know, it has been wonderful for them, this Spanish war. Those boys who were hanging around in Paris with no hope or aim; it has given them a new lease of life, put new heart into them. They felt they had bungled and failed with the Movement in Germany, where it had been so strong and so near success.

Now, at last, they feel they have a chance to fight fascism and strike a blow at Hitler. It's their first real fight with weapons in their hands; not the best or most up-to-date weapons, perhaps, but still, some sort of weapons. And what they lack in armaments they make up for in spirit. It's a fine thing for those boys. I've seen some of them change completely. Men who were pacifists in the last war are fighting now they feel they have something to fight for.'

'Someone should write the story of the Thaelmann Brigade. They've made that name famous as it never was before. I'm ashamed to say I'd never heard of Thaelmann until I came to Spain.'

'After the war it can be written – not now. They are very secretive about all their affairs, even the names of their leaders. I was almost turned out of this town because they thought I intended to write about them. Of course, I wouldn't now. One can't blame them at present. If our side wins this war, and it *must*, that will be the end of Hitler and Mussolini. Even if it isn't the end of them, those of the boys who survive will be entitled to Spanish citizenship and a new start here. This country has plenty of room, and it will be a free country.'

Frieda's eyes shone and she was animated by this rosy dream. I have thought of this talk since, when I read of the remainder of the Thaelmanns rotting in French concentration camps after the disastrous end of the Spanish war.

'I went for a drive this morning,' said Frieda, 'to see a collective farm.'

'How was it and what were they growing?'

'Oranges.'

'This looks like a very rich country.'

'With very poor people in it.'

Frieda looked meditatively in front of her as if she were seeing something a long way off. Then she spoke quickly.

'There is a lot that needs changing here. Near the orange grove I saw a wretched little cabin. I asked my guides to drop me there as I wanted to visit the inhabitants, talk with them, see how they lived. My guides, who had proudly been showing me their beautiful, well-grown orange crops, and telling me how it was sprayed against disease, didn't want me to go into the cabin. They told me it was of no interest, but I insisted. It was dark and dirty and primitive beyond belief. There was only one room and no window. The people were illiterate; one was an idiot and the others so dull they seemed sub-normal. They were a large family and were all ill with something or other. The small children had some skin complaint; one had trachoma. There was one small bed; in it were two of the older children, one dying of tuberculosis, the other had a broken leg which had never been set. My husband is a doctor and I know a little about medicine. I saw the girl's leg and found she had been lying there for weeks. With great difficulty, I persuaded the family to let her go and brought her back in the car and left her at a hospital in town. My guides were very apologetic, said this family was a backward relic, that the new generation would be different. Still, it was only one family that I saw, quite by chance; there may be many like them. I told them to take the child with trachoma to a clinic for treatment; but, of course, they won't, and couldn't even if they wanted to as it is some miles away and there is no transport to town.'

'I've seen posters about trachoma,' I said. '*Trachoma and smallpox, the signs of a backward people,* that was it. A horrifying poster with a bloodshot eye and a baby's face covered in spots, very realistic.'

'The Minister of Health is Federica Montseny. It sounded good to have a woman minister, and I'm a feminist as far as that goes, but she's one of those up-in-the-clouds anarchists, which means fine posters and no action I'm afraid.'

'The Government is doing a lot of good work considering how they are hampered by the war.'

'Oh, I quite agree. Such families are relics of the bad old days; only I was shocked. It must be completely different some day. It is so strange after Denmark where such things couldn't exist. I am fond of children and it upsets me to see them ill and crippled. Have some coffee with me?'

We went out into the hall. There were one or two Internationals there, including the Irishman, and she asked them to join us and was very jolly with them. I was fidgety and soon left them to go to the hospital.

*   *   *   *   *

The ward was very hot and still. All the patients who could crawl out had done so. Penny was not on duty. Jan looked very worn out. I poured some eau-de-cologne on a handkerchief and dabbed it on his forehead and wrists and he said it was refreshing. He asked me to go over to the window so he could see me. I went and stood on the balcony. A young German in glasses and striped pyjamas was also standing there. Another German, on the balcony below, shouted up, 'Who is that girl?'

'She's English,' replied my neighbour and the other lost interest.

A Spanish girl, I suppose she may have been a probationer, anyway she was helping in the hospital, came after my neighbour with loud cries of '*a la cama*' and bustled him back to bed.

I went back to Jan.

'Go and talk to the Frenchman three beds down,' he said. 'You can speak French; I think he's dying and it would be a kindness.'

I went and sat beside the man he indicated. He looked like a waxwork with glass eyes. His face was smooth, oily, yellow, his black hair lay on his forehead in plastered locks. His eyes were enormous and very bright with big dark circles round them. They looked as if brimming with tears and I felt he could not see.

'What is your name?'

'André.'

'Where do you come from?'

'Nice. I am half Italian.'

'Where were you wounded?'

'Low down in the spine – it has gone bad, it hurts very much, I shan't be here long. My brother and I were always together, and in the war too. When he said goodbye to me, when they took me away on the lorry, he said he knew he would never see me again. We were never separated before; now it's goodbye.'

He rambled in his speech, was a bit delirious, but I saw he liked to have someone there to listen, so I stayed. Jan had told me his wound should not have been serious but had turned

165

tubercular.

'Angelita!' he drawled out. 'Angelita,' like a cat wailing. '*Agua.*'

A girl brought him a glass of water. She moved and spoke softly. She was not more than eighteen but looked older because her face was fixed in a tragic mask like Our Lady of Sorrow or Our Lady of Pity. She seemed like the Madonna with the seven swords sticking in her heart but still with sympathy to spare for the suffering around her, and as though the sufferings of the whole world were part of her and made her knit her brows.

'Everybody is always calling Angelita,' said André with the ghost of a roguish grin, 'and she always comes; she is always kind, she always has patience, she is our angel. She is never too tired to take care of us.'

Angelita gave a sweet, sad smile and went over to another bed where the patient was clamouring to have his pillows re-arranged.

'Is she a local girl?' I asked Jan.

'Yes. She must have got some shocks coming here when she never had anything to do with men before. I like to watch her; she is so graceful and beautiful. She is like a symbol of tragic Spain itself.'

On my second visit to Murcia, I found Angelita gone. She had advanced pulmonary tuberculosis herself and had been obliged to give up work. André, on the other hand, had miraculously recovered and had got fat, with a face like a full moon, though still unhealthy looking. His character proved disagreeable and he stumped about with a stick making a noise and disturbing the very ill ones and yet pretending he was not fit for duty at the front.

I sat down beside Jan. Further up the ward, a wretched man, nothing but skin and bone, who had dysentery, was sitting up, in his shirt, on a bed pan. I tried to ignore him. He looked as if he were frightened of his illness, with staring eyes and lips pulled back from his teeth like a dog snarling. Everybody hated him for he was a nasty man with a nasty complaint and they made rude jeers when the poor wretch had to sit on his bed pan.

A *responsable* came round.

'*Voulez-vous donner quelque chose por la couronne. Un*

camarade dans la salle sept vient de mourir.'[70]

'All my pay goes on wreaths,' said Jan, fishing out five pesetas.

'It seems too bad that the wounded should be reminded of the dead by this collecting for wreaths,' I said. 'Does it happen often?'

'Nearly every day,' said Jan. 'They are nearly all serious cases here, operation cases you know, and people are always dying. As long as it is in some other ward than mine I don't mind so much.'

He shifted wearily, or rather made a vain effort to do so.

'If only I could lie on my side for a change, it would be heaven,' he said. There was a pause. 'I'm afraid I'm feeling rotten this afternoon,' he said at last. 'You'd better go, I can't even talk.'

'Is there anything I can do?'

'No. I'm afraid I'm going to be sick.'

He raised himself uncomfortably in bed, on his elbow, and started retching over the side. He was so weak that the effort made drops of perspiration break out. I was distracted and called Angelita in a loud wail. She came running with a basin and held his head with the utmost tenderness. He retched and retched but could not produce anything and, at last, sank back exhausted. Angelita made some tea with sugar in a glass and brought some for both of us. After we had sipped it I said I would go and return later, and I went despairingly away.

'It's those foul pills they give him,' I said to myself. 'Penny said they were bad for the stomach.'

I went back to the hotel and scribbled letters to all his friends in London or Paris, telling them how deplorably ill he was and begging them to write to him and send books and magazines if possible. None of these letters ever arrived and I remembered that the English Post Office refused to accept parcels for Spain and instructed the English friends to send them to a Paris address from which they would be forwarded. All the time I was writing, tears kept falling so, when I had finished, I went up to my room and had a good cry; a thorough cry from which I emerged quite damp. The effort of doing something, even though it turned out to be futile, and the flood of tears had done something to relieve me.

In the hall, I met Frieda. She looked at my face but was too tactful to say a word, even to comfort me – she would certainly have started me off again. I was reproaching myself for being unable to remain at the hospital or bear that atmosphere for more than an hour at a time.

'What must it be like for people who have to be there all the time for months?' I asked myself. 'Do they get used to it? How could anybody get used to it?'

I went to the *Correos* and sent my letters and a telegram to Liston to calm him down in my absence. Then I set out to find transportation back to Valencia, as I had decided the train took impossibly long. I went to a transport office where I was very rudely treated and told I could get the bus as they would not give me a lift in a car. I found the bus office and bought a ticket to Alicante, where I had to change, for the next morning.

I went back to the hospital. It was supper time again. I took some cornflakes and milk in a bowl and tried to coax Jan to eat by feeding him with a spoon. He tried, to please me, but it was no use.

The doctor did not appear but the matron came in. She came up and asked me to find out what a cockney soldier wanted. He was demanding something and they could not understand each other.

'For God's sake tell the old buzzard I'm constipated and want some salts,' said the soldier. 'I've tried the Spanish nurses and they don't understand either.' In Spanish *constipado* means one has a cold so his reiteration of 'constipated' had led to confusion. I explained the problem to the matron and took the opportunity to ask her to let Jan have an injection that night.

'Speak to me when I have done my rounds,' she said.

When she had gone round the ward, she went straight out of the door and I headed after her. I called and ran. She did not turn round but kept walking rapidly away from me. At last I ran her to earth in the linen closet and she turned at bay, her mouth tight shut, already determined to refuse what I asked.

'He is in great pain and must have an injection.'

'He gets a sleeping pill.'

'It's not strong enough. In Madrid he had injections.'

'Yes, too many,' she snapped. 'He will be an addict. He gets no more narcotics here – *des calmants,*' she said.

'It's ridiculous,' I said. 'When he's well, of course he won't need it any more or be an addict.'

'He's always asking for drugs. It shows they've got a hold on him.'

'Nonsense, he's in pain,' I said. 'Anyway, you can't cut off the morphine suddenly like this, you ought to taper it off, not stop it all at once.'

I protested and pleaded but she went off and shut herself into some private sanctum.

I went back, crestfallen, and told Jan it was no go; they would not give him an injection. I did not know what to say to cheer him up. I was only there two nights and during both I was in agony at the thought of him lying awake through the long hours, but there were all the nights when I was not there as well. I promised to come in the morning and went back to the hotel.

I dined alone. I felt irritated by the good food and the black-coated, polite waiter. In pre-war days, I could never have afforded a first-class hotel like this. In the hall, Penny and the other English nurse were with some other people having coffee and I joined them.

'I am writing a letter to Albacete to ask to be transferred to another hospital,' said Penny. 'You don't think that is a breach of discipline do you? I really can't bear it any longer.'

'Is your friend going too?' I asked, indicating the other nurse.

'No, I don't want to,' said the other girl. 'You see, I'm in the operating theatre and the surgeon is first-rate and I love my work. It's hard but I love it.'

'I'm glad,' I said.

We talked a bit and advised Penny about the wording of her letter. One of the men she was with was going to carry it by hand to Albacete and see it got to the proper office.

The next day, the sun was dazzling on the white buildings and in the dusty plaza I wished I had dark glasses. I got up early and, on my way to the bus office, I saw a lovely old baroque church and well-dressed women in black, with veils over their heads, were coming out of it. It was Sunday and for one wild moment I thought they were coming out of Mass, it looked so like it. There was a sentry at the door and I asked him what was going on.

'The church is used as a prison and Sunday is visiting day for the relatives,' he said.

Some of the Thaelmann Battalion were drilling in the road as I passed.

I bought a mass of flowers, narcissi and other kinds, in the market and went to see Jan who was awake and seemed a little brighter. I told him about the church, how the town looked and anything else I could think of to amuse him. I told him to be brave and patient and in two weeks the plaster would be taken off and I would come back and we would see about moving him to Valencia. I could not stay long as I had to catch the bus.

* * * * *

When I arrived in Alicante I rushed to the bus office to try to get on the next bus but they were all full up until the next morning. There was nothing for it, Liston would have to wait. There was a cold wind blowing in the palm trees on the waterfront, the sea was rough, there had been a recent bombardment and most of the windows of the hotels were boarded up and their fronts pitted with shell fragments. I suddenly felt ill and at a loss. A respectable-looking, middle-aged Spaniard in a beret and ulster, carrying a briefcase, also wanted to go to Valencia.

'I think we are both in the same boat,' he said as he saw me standing there.

'Better take tickets for the bus at six tomorrow.'

I did so and followed him to a small and unpretentious hotel where he took two rooms and then explained, embarrassed, that we were not related, that I was a foreigner so he was helping me out. We had lunch and I went to bed. The fat old chambermaid brought me newspapers and tea and stayed to talk to me.

'Oh, this terrible war,' she said. 'If only they would get it over. Food is getting scarce and I have two boys fighting. Neither of them has been hurt yet, thank God, but it drags on so long.'

I crept down to dinner and my new friend did not intrude at all, but he could see I was feeling helpless and he gave instructions that we were both to be called early.

It was still dark when we left. The bus was crammed full of people. Just as we were leaving Alicante a fat, well-to-do woman in a fur hurried up, very out of breath. For half an hour beforehand an undersized little servant girl, not more than twelve years old, had been waiting there, guarding a huge pile of suitcases and hat boxes. She had dragged them to the bus office by herself though some were bigger than this diminutive little creature. The bus driver said the bus was full. The fat woman was indignant and tried to push her way on. Then she set on the little servant and scolded her roundly for not keeping a place. The driver bawled at the woman to hold her tongue as it was not the girl's fault that all the tickets had been sold the day before. The woman flew into a fury and screamed at him like a regular termagant but he would not let her or her luggage on and she was left behind.

Later on, he stopped several times and piled in poor women with parcels and girls with hens under their arms, with the utmost good nature, until he had scarcely elbow room to steer the bus. I was pleased by this practical example of 'the first shall be last and the last shall be first'. Alicante the Red – the last place to hold out against Franco.

There was a beautiful pink sunrise. The road ran between the blue sea and the blossoming almond trees. I saw lovely old villages and sandy beaches, Benidorm, Altea where Jan and I had meant to go for a holiday last summer. I imagined taking him to convalesce at some such fishing village. We stopped at one place and my companion suggested we stretch our legs and have some coffee. The occupants of the bus crowded round the bar at the *fonda* but he, regarding me as a lady, made them bring our coffee upstairs to an empty dining room. We also had some omelette sandwiches. He told me he was a librarian at Valencia university and was also worried about being late back to work.

On arrival, I went straight to the office. There was so much work to be done that Liston had no time to be angry.

Chapter 9
Valencia

I was back in Valencia before lunch and Milly, who was with Knoblaugh, dragged me out to a café to give her the news. We went into the Wodka to look for someone else and I saw Auden at the far end of the café with a group of people. He got up and tried to talk to me, suggesting the British Embassy might help to get Jan back to England. It was a useless suggestion but he meant it very kindly; he was really sympathetic and tried to shout to me above the noise of the crowd. We were some distance apart, Knoblaugh was waiting outside, Milly was tugging at my elbow to get me to leave. I was unwillingly pulled away and that was the last I saw of Auden. I always regretted the stupid obtuseness people showed him.

I found that Professor Borkenau had gone back to Madrid, leaving Micky behind, and Kitty, with her usual genius for arranging other people's affairs, had decreed that I should sleep in the spare bed in Micky's room for the present. As there was never any space in any of the various hotel rooms I occupied for me to unpack or settle down, it did not much matter to me where I slept, though I was rather in dread of the professor returning unexpectedly, after I had gone to bed, for instance, and I very much disliked his belongings lying about. They all smelled rather heavily of shaving lotion and I was always falling over several pairs of elastic-sided boots.

Just after I got back, the first American Medical Mission arrived. They came late one evening and they came with a splash of publicity that the English Medical Aid had not enjoyed. The State Department in Washington held them up, stamping all their passports 'Not Good For Spain' and it took them some time to circumvent this proviso. At last, they landed in France through which they made a slow and triumphal progress, being entertained at various towns by Popular Front committees. They travelled in ambulances painted in large letters: 'American Democracy in Aid of Spanish Democracy'. In Catalunya they received an official welcome and were all photographed with President Companys. They spent some days there being shown the sights of the town, including the beautiful hospital and Montjuich, and must have wondered where the war was and why the Spaniards needed medical aid at all.

As they were lodged at the Inglés, where rooms had been officially reserved for them, Liston commissioned me to get an interview and then decided to come himself as well. It was late when they turned up – in Catalan cars with a handsome supply of Catalan petrol. The interview was not satisfactory. The doctors and nurses were under orders not to speak to strangers and we were referred to the *responsable,* a young woman in a fashionable hat, silk stockings and high heels. We were so unused to such a sight that we all got the impression she was some sort of 'star', which she was not.

Her name was Patricia and she was one of those tiresome people, numerous in Spain, who pretended great importance but whose lips were sealed. She had a large mouth, well rouged, which she kept tightly shut and smiled at the same time. Milly said she was a fool not to realise that the more the papers wrote about the Medical Mission the more contributions they would get in America, but she would not give anything in the way of a story.

She was nearly torn to pieces by warring newspapermen. Liston chased her upstairs leaving his defeated rival whining in the lobby. The rival was a very young, pretty, curly-headed Jewish boy, who was always fighting with Liston anyway. The real bone of contention was the cable allowance. The Spanish Government gave Liston a free cable allowance to America and, as it was expensive and they were always horrified by the monthly bills, they would not give it to Seldes as well.[71] He was also an American correspondent for a Left paper and maintained that it was no use without a cable allowance as stories mailed to America were too late to be any use as it was so far away. The Left papers never had the money to pay a cable allowance. He poured all this out to me in his complaining, nasal voice as we stood in the lobby and Liston was snatching a word with Patricia halfway up the stairs.

'Why should he get a story just because he butts in and follows that girl upstairs; I was here first,' grumbled Seldes.

Patricia left shortly for Madrid, with a select escort, to look things over and decide where they would set up their hospital. The nurses and doctors were left for some weeks kicking their heels at the Inglés. Like all medical people they were raring to go. The surgeons, mostly Jewish and some of them distinguished, were just longing to start cutting people up and the nurses were burning with impatience to be ministering again.

They all had natty uniforms, much smarter and better fitting than any Spanish officer's. The girls wore dark blue cloaks and no hats and had had anti-gas training – which they never had to put into practice. Most of the nurses were pretty and had brought with them a load of French perfume and silk underwear, unlike the English who had brought trench coats and rucksacks. They tied up their curls in ribbons and used lipstick but I felt they were reassuringly competent at the same time. There was one grotesquely fat one just for contrast.

In the mornings, they all used to gather round in an upstairs hall to have Spanish lessons with one of the doctors who was a Cuban. I used to lean over the balcony and listen to them struggling with the rudiments of the language. Of course, in the end, they were all trailed off to Albacete to be amalgamated with the rest of the *Service Sanitaire* for the Internationals. They were already afraid this was going to happen. They had been told so often by their *responsable* that Albacete was a secret that they called it Abyssinia. Lorca called it 'Albacete, the city of knives'.[72]

A day or two after their arrival, I got up feeling very strange and, when I reached the office, Milly sent me home again.

My recovery was not hastened by the sternly parental attitude of the hotel management to what they regarded as malingering. Their view was that if one was ill one did not need to eat, and if one felt faint longings for a plate of soup or an omelette one was quite well enough to go down to the dining room. In fact, they refused room service. I argued very hoarsely with them on the phone and sent Micky and Kitty as emissaries but without success. Kitty surmounted the difficulty with her usual energy by going into the kitchen and seizing dishes from the cook.

A waiter, who did come up one day, explained to me the real

reason for this. The hotel was greatly overcrowded and understaffed. Like all other catering establishments, or members of the 'gastronomic industry' they chose to be understaffed because they had a profit-sharing system and the fewer people in it the better. The waiter told me they could hardly manage to serve the clients in the restaurant and had no time to spare for running up and down the stairs. The waiter said they were afflicted with a number of clients who wished to avoid appearing in public, for diverse reasons. Some, I dare say, were under house arrest, others were well known foreign fliers who did not want to be recognised. All these people feigned illness and ordered meals in their rooms.

This situation was getting out of hand and the manager had therefore issued a general order against taking meals upstairs, as all the other 'invalids' had hearty appetites and expected five course dinners.

I prayed Professor Borkenau would not return while I was in bed in his room.

The first morning that I tottered downstairs, I ran into a tall Canadian boy I had met previously at a cocktail party in London.[73] He was driving a car for Dr Bethune and they were bound for Málaga with a load of bottled blood.[74] Dr Bethune was absolutely dedicated to blood transfusion and was, I think, in advance of his time. He looked like an orchestral conductor, he was short with a red face and long, wild, white hair. He was a Canadian and we all regarded him as a bit of a crank. The young man was an architect and what had moved him from cocktails to blood I did not enquire. I knew their route lay through Murcia and I made him promise to visit Jan. He knew Jan from Madrid where Dr Bethune had given him morphine. He said Jan was lucky not to be operated on in Madrid where no one had dared to risk it and I told him how Jan even had to wait for his operation in Murcia because they were waiting for the instruments from France.

Just after I was back on my feet again, Professor Borkenau came back. I can say nothing in defence of the subsequent proceedings. Micky, Kitty and I plotted against him and treated him abominably. He had, of course, paid for the room all the time he was away in order to ensure having a place to sleep after he got back. I am not at all sure he did not have to pay the entire *pensión* bill for me as well as Micky. No other rooms were available in the hotel; some people from the American Mission had even been stowed away in dark basements and box-rooms. I said I was ill and refused to move out; he was angry and argued with us and the hotel people but he finally took his elastic-sided boots and other paraphernalia away.

Micky said he was a Trotskyist – all she meant was that he was a dissident communist. So many of these people fell over backwards to be anti-fascist that it was easy for the simplistic to call them fascists.

At last, Liston got hold of him and they had long conferences together in a corner of the Lion d'Or. This was not a popular café; it was dark and gloomy and usually empty and, therefore, Liston liked it. It was in the arcade near his hotel and was in the style of a German beer-hall and had high wooden pews in which one was almost concealed from one's neighbours. The funny thing was that both these odd characters distrusted one another. Even Liston's Trotskyism was unconvincing. Everything about him, his rheumatism, his wife who had left him, failed to carry conviction somehow, though why he should not have had a wife and why she should not have left him I do not know. Professor Borkenau mistook Liston for a communist spy and they parted in mutual suspicion. I think the professor was deported from Spain; at all events he went away. He was an Austrian and, for some reason, no one trusted them politically.

Micky moved into a cheaper place near the station, where she lingered for some time. She made a lot of Spanish friends and became very Spanish, buying coloured celluloid combs in the market which she stuck in her hair. She was thinking of going as a nurse in a Spanish hospital, for which no training was required. I told her not to as it was a foul job and not at all romantic.

Valencia was nice and warm by now and Milly had discovered the flower market and used to bring in armfuls of flowers to beautify the office. The flower market was underneath the Plaza Castelar and one could see into it through holes in the ground; it was very cool and damp down there. A French journalist told me he had often tried in vain to find the entrance but, *'toujours, j'arrive aux lavabos.'*

The food at the Inglés got worse and worse, consisting almost every day of rice garnished with snails. These were not the proper edible snails but just any old snails that happened to be about and they were very tough and leathery.

After the American Medical Mission, the next party to descend upon us was the Bishops. They were not all as elevated as bishops but they were all clergy. They came to see the state of religion in Spain and we found them several evangelical churches that were still functioning. The only Roman Catholic Mass was celebrated *chez* the Basque representative for all the Basques. We all thought it was very plucky of the bishops to come even though they did not go so far as to appear in gaiters and hats with strings holding up the brims. There was a rush to get interviews with them. We particularly liked the Dean of Chichester and the Dean of Rochester, a combination of names with a Gilbert and Sullivan flavour.

I remember having dinner one night with Tom Wintringham (who must have been on leave) and two new arrivals, Bob Merriman[75] and Basil Murray.[76] Merriman was a fine-looking young man from the University of California, very serious. He later commanded the American part of the Brigade. Murray was clearly the *désorienté* intellectual. I think he may have come to Spain to escape some domestic trouble. He wanted to join up but Tom dissuaded him. He said, 'You can do far more good by getting your father to use his influence for the Republican cause.' His father was Professor Gilbert Murray.

Basil Murray was around forty and, I think, a bit of a failure. He wore his hair long at the back, like Lloyd George, and was very sensitive. He had bright dewy eyes like a stricken deer. He picked up a job with the International News Service but his heart was not in it.

Not long after this, Basil returned from a trip to Málaga in a hysterical state. 'It's too ghastly,' he burst out to everyone. 'That town is already lost. The bombardments are incessant and frightful. The morale of the people has broken under them. While I was there one of the refuges fell in and fifty people were buried

177

alive. There are no defences. The officers are rotten to the core and ought to be shot for treason. The cathedral is full of poor women with babies camping, who have fled from the villages. You can't imagine the horror of it. Those infernal scenes in the cathedral; I can't forget them.'

We all laughed at Basil's predictions, treating him like Cassandra. He was inclined to exaggerate and his nerves were not of the strongest. The censor crabbed his story and the rest of us paid no heed to his frantic, high-pitched warnings.

Claud had returned from Málaga at about the same time. He was level-headed and no fool. He said Málaga was safe as houses; we all believed him.

In the days which followed, the news from the Málaga front became ominously scant. The only thing the Febus sheets played up was the active role of German and Italian warships in bombarding the coast. We understood that a good part of the Republican navy was down there, however, to stave them off. Someone, supposed to be a good authority, probably Coco the office boy, whose father was very much with the Russians as interpreter, said he was sure that a field for planes had recently been established near Murcia and that there were also Russian tanks there.

An atmosphere of fear and suspense hung over the office and the Spaniards seemed very depressed but no one voiced their fears. To have spoken would have been *derrotista* (defeatist).

Then, one of the newspaper offices in Paris queried their correspondent on the fall of Málaga. He came out of the phone box and told us that the *Daily Mail* had carried headlines on the entry of Franco troops into Málaga that morning, and he asked Rubio if he could send a denial.

Rubio was in a bad temper. He snapped out, 'Yes, send a denial,' and then hurried out and did not come back to the office that day, so no one could ask him any more questions. In fact most of the big-wigs were out somewhere conferring together and the place seemed strangely empty.

Work was slack and I went to the Wodka for tea. The café was almost empty too; a few people were whispering in corners and they looked up and stared. I went into a newsreel cinema for an hour thereby risking being run in by the police as a slacker. I had a work card with the office hours on it. No police came and the cinema was half empty. The blurred reels of the *Socorro Rojo* seemed to revolve even more slowly and languidly than usual and there were no cartoons.

Suddenly it dawned on me: the town was in mourning for Málaga. I hurried back to the office. No one was there except Coco, who was in tears, and Constancia holding the fort in the inner office with a long, long face.

'It's Málaga, isn't it?' I said, in my abrupt English way, so disconcerting to Spaniards. I took Coco by the arm. 'It's gone, isn't it?'

Coco screwed up his face, a big boy ashamed of his tears, and nodded. I went in to Constancia.

'When did it go?' I asked. 'I won't tell anyone though it is obvious the whole town knows.'

'Yesterday,' she said. 'It will be in the papers tomorrow.'

'Is it still going badly?' I asked.

She gave me a despairing gesture towards some Febus sheets on her desk and I picked them up. There was a confused, unparagraphed account of thousands of refugees streaming out of Málaga and of hordes of Italians and *Boinas Rojas*[77] streaming in.

'Have you been on the telephone?' I asked. 'How far have they got?'

The newspapermen had all gone home because they had given up trying to get the censor to let them send something and Rubio was not there to authorise their messages. Some newspapers had correspondents on one side but not the other, the *Daily Mail* on the Franco side, the *News Chronicle* and the *Manchester Guardian* on the Republican side.

Constancia was crying too. She walked with me in the main *sala* where the big wall map hung. On it, the line was marked with pins and small republican flags. The line in the south had been uprooted entirely and left unmarked.

'I think there,' she said, pointing to Motril.

'But that is halfway to Almería!' I exclaimed, horrified.

'They may take Almería and keep straight on up the coast for

179

all I know,' she said, 'I don't know what is happening or who is going to stop them.'

'I can't understand it,' said poor bewildered Coco with a sob.

'But we mustn't give way like this,' I said. 'We must carry on as usual or the journalists will think the whole war is lost. We must pull ourselves together.'

Constancia said nothing. She gave me a look out of her liquid brown eyes that seemed to put me in my place as a vulgar interloper. Too many foreigners were blind to such looks. The Spaniards were always subjected to cocksure interference in their business, treated as pawns in a game, and they are proud people.

They had a saying, 'Spain is not Abyssinia' which implied not merely that the war was fought differently, but that Spaniards cannot be treated like 'natives'. One of the things that outraged them most was that Moors had been brought in against them. There was a poster on which the wording was: 'How would you feel, who lost your son in Morocco, to find your village square turned into a Moroccan souk?'

The head of the Press and Censorship Department was Rubio, a friend of del Vayo, who went abroad often, either to Paris or Geneva – vainly pleading at the League of Nations. I believe he got to Paris at the end of the war.

The second in command was Constancia de la Mora, an aristocratic, intelligent and charming young woman, surprisingly tall. She had been married off very young to a man she did not love – I think he was a Bolín and related to Franco's then publicity man. She had a daughter of eleven who had been sent to Russia. She had had a divorce and was then married to Cisneros, who was head of Republican aviation. She was *déclassé* as a result of her divorce and had been running an art and craft shop in Madrid before the war.

After the war, she escaped from Spain and went to Mexico, the only country willing to receive Spanish refugees, just as it was the first to offer help in the shape of very outmoded weapons and ammunition. In the early days of the war one often saw, on small wayside stations, banners proclaiming: *'Viva Rusia – Viva Méjico'*.

Coco's real name was Francisco Robles. All the Americans

loved his Baltimore accent. His father had been a professor in that city but during the war was working as an interpreter with the Russians. Coco was destined for the diplomatic service and was hoping to go to Russia.

There were two Austrians who dealt with the German translating who were replaced by a Spaniard later. One was Selke, who had previously been a bartender in Ibiza. He was small with fuzzy hair and had no dignity. The other, Winter, dressed in black and cadaverous-looking, was my idea of a fanatic or assassin. He commanded more respect. We used to call them Rosencrantz and Guildenstern.

*　*　*　*　*

The office was dislocated for some days, with everyone looking as if they were at a funeral. A large notice appeared on the walls of the town. It did not say that Málaga was lost but it did say that there were 30,000 starving refugees in Almería and that it had been decided to send all the bread baked in Valencia for two days to them, and the mayor was sure that the citizens would willingly make this sacrifice of going without bread for two days. There was fear of a typhus epidemic and other notices followed about not shaking bedclothes out of windows and the setting up of delousing stations.

As far as I know, the last person out of Málaga was a young Norwegian journalist called Gerda Grepp. She arrived in a state of collapse and was put in the spare bed in Milly's room at the hotel. When the fall of the town was confirmed she nearly went demented. She had gone down there with Koestler and they had seen a good deal of Sir Peter Chalmers Mitchell. The two men had stayed behind in Málaga even though, as her car was leaving, she had implored them to come with her.[78]

Both escaped subsequently, the former only after a long spell in prison, but it was a long time before we heard of their safety. We did not worry so much about Sir Peter as we felt that Franco would think twice about shooting an Englishman, but Koestler had had an interview with Queipo de Llano in which he ridiculed the radio general and Franco's supporters had sworn to have his blood if he ever fell into their hands, so most of us gave him up for dead.

'I can't stand it,' said Milly when she came to the office. 'That Norwegian girl just carries on like Strindberg. The Spaniards are bad enough but it takes a Scandinavian to keep up that degree of gloom. She cries all day. She shows me the souvenirs and costume dolls she bought for her children down there. She goes through the photos she took in Málaga, pictures of Sir Peter smiling in front of his lovely house and of Koestler and of fine old anarchists with their donkeys, and she says she knows they're all dead now. She stares at herself in the mirror and says, 'See these lines in my face; I didn't have them before I went to Málaga.' Honestly, she's getting on my nerves. I never saw anyone so inconsolable.'

* * * * *

Seldes was staying at the Victoria and his wife, Helen, had just come down from Madrid where she had been a long time working in Dr Bethune's blood-transfusion laboratory. Bethune had given up collecting blood in Madrid as the city was besieged for so long the people were too under-nourished to be donors. They were American; I found that nationality mattered much more than politics in determining people's habits. They were a fond couple, they had just received food parcels from home and it was Helen's birthday, so they gave a party in their room.

Helen was a pretty, little, dark girl who did not seem to have suffered too much in Madrid, though she did have chilblains. She was an excellent hostess, everything elegantly arranged and gifts for all the guests amongst which were miniature bottles of liqueurs.

Gerda Grepp had been invited to cheer her up and I sat down on the sofa next to her. She looked very young with rosy cheeks and big brown eyes. She wore a white shirt, like a man's with a tie. Milly said in an aside to me, 'She's quite a beginner at the newspaper game. Poor kid, this was her first big assignment.' We all tried to brighten her up but her gloom lasted impermeably throughout the evening.

182

Helen led the way to a long table at the end of the dining room, nearly all the journalists joined us, and it had been arranged where we were all to sit. The guest of honour was an old lady, a French journalist, who wore a velvet ribbon round her neck like Queen Alexandra and dangling necklaces and loose, hanging sleeves. She too was in rather a dithery state after Málaga and retired early. As her daughter whispered to me, '*Maman* is really getting a bit old for this dashing about as a war correspondent.'

Fernsworth, *The Times*' correspondent, was much in evidence with his courtly gallantry and distinguished grey hair.[79] He ordered the wine with great ceremony as he was something of a connoisseur. Milly became noisy and laughed a lot with her mouth wide open.

We all gave exclamations of joy at two dishes on the table. On one was a substantial block of salted butter and on the other was an entire Edam cheese. The waiters were eyeing these with hungry admiration and the party was almost as much in honour of the butter and cheese as of the grand old French lady.

Unluckily, this was one of Valencia's breadless days but there were a few biscuits. We drank toasts and made speeches and, after dinner, we retired to Seldes's room and capped our meal with real coffee and sugar.

We were all relaxing, Milly had been singing *Swing Low Sweet Chariot*, when we heard sounds strange to us but not to Helen, alert from months of habit. She put out the light, opened the window and leaned out. Milly felt for my hand in the dark. There were swishing sounds.

'Shells,' said Helen from the balcony. 'I know them from Madrid and they're coming quite near.'

'It must be from the sea then, ships,' said someone and we thought of those German and Italian boats that had been bombarding Málaga – they were free now to turn their attention to us. In the harbour was only one republican boat, small and old, the Lepanto. This was February 1937 and our first bombardment and, I think, the only time during my stay that the middle of the town was shelled.

We groped our way down to the lobby of the hotel which was

on the first floor and dimly lit. The waiters were buzzing about in the background like agitated bees. In the hall were two or three French airmen in their navy blue and gold braided uniforms, very excited and angry too. One was trying to telephone. They were the remnants of the Malraux squadron, most of them physically unfit. The rest had gone down to Málaga with whatever planes they could scrape together to see what they could do to stem the advance of the invaders or to cover our retreat. They were hopelessly outnumbered and hardly any returned but their fate was not then known to their comrades.

'My God,' said one of them. 'Here we are, supposed to be entrusted with the coast defence, and we can't get hold of a car to take us to the flying field. We must get up and after these buggers.'

The newspapermen went off to see what casualties there were (there were some, for the attack was totally unexpected) and to send stories, and the party broke up.

None of us knew how things were going after Málaga or how the invaders were pushing on and I began to be very worried about Jan. Murcia was too far south. If Almería fell, Murcia would be threatened or might be cut off. If there was time, hospitals would be evacuated inland to Albacete, but if time were short? The stretcher cases would be the ones left behind. I was very anxious to get him to the coast from whence he could escape by boat or plane if the worst came to the worst. The British authorities, for the tenth time at least, had published in the papers that all British subjects were to hold themselves in readiness to be evacuated on warships at an hour's notice. As a stateless refugee Jan could not have gone that way even if he were in Valencia and mobile.

After the shelling, we had a few air raids and one bomb fell right before the door of the building housing the British Embassy. After this, the diplomats began to move to villas outside the town or on board their warships. One person, a servant, was killed at our embassy and a goldfish bowl was shattered by a blast. Someone had the presence of mind to save the fish by throwing them into the lavatory pan.

The day after the party, Griffin Barry got back, looking very

184

dusty and worn. He was another middle-aged, loose-end intellectual, Irish-American who worked for one of the news agencies. He and the Reuter man shared my services to go through the Febus sheets and translate daily. This brought me some English money which I was saving for when I could get Jan out. Barry had started off to go to Málaga but had been too late to get there. He had been caught up in the retreat and delayed.[80]

He brought back a hair-raising and grotesque story. He had more literary talent than most of them and far too much for a news agency. He told of pathetic families with their donkeys loaded with household goods fleeing from the fascists and it seemed it had been a major exodus and a shocking one.

Here, it must be explained that there were two Griffins and I worked for both. As well as Griffin Barry there was Norman Griffin who was a long, lean, leathery man, the *Toronto Star* correspondent. To add to the confusion, all the foreign women seemed to be called either Ilse or Gerda. There were also two *Times* correspondents. We seldom saw the Madrid man but Fernsworth, the Barcelona man, lived in Valencia then because the government was there. He was a good friend to me. He was very natty and well groomed, with wavy grey hair and glasses, fond of comfort and very particular in his habits.

Fernsworth, who hardly ever stirred out of his routine, and Norman Griffin, who never went on trips either, were good pals and immediately formed the project of going down to Almería and getting a refugee story. I, as Griffin's interpreter, instantly decided to press my claim to go too – for the route lay through Murcia.

They had a tough time persuading Rubio to let them have a car. He was badly shaken and would not have gone down there himself for a hundred pounds. I think he did not care so much what happened to the journalists but he was afraid something would happen to the car, either it would fall into the hands of the rebels or it would be destroyed. There were only two cars available, a large one which needed repairing but there were no spare parts in Spain, and one which was too small for such an expedition.

In the glaring light of the large and dirty CNT Café Popular, opposite the office, Griffin and I ate a lot of salted nuts while we plotted how I was to go. I explained to him about Jan and he said he would love to have me along, I should be a great help and he would ask Rubio for me.

Milly aided and abetted me of course; Liston wanted to send Coco instead. Males were generally considered more suitable for trips to the front but, as I pointed out, I could write a story about it myself whereas Coco would not remember anything of vital interest.

Late that night, when Griffin and I went back to the office to conclude negotiations, Rubio came out with a veto. No woman was to go to the south. I protested indignantly. I said that I had Liston's permission and that Milly was happy for me to go.

'Ah,' said Rubio, coyly wagging his finger at me, *'tiene celos!'* For he considered her remarkably attractive, but I could see from his manner that I had won my point. I was as happy as a bird and decided to take Jan the little bottle of Kirsch that Helen had given me at the party.

Rubio gave us many warnings and instructions. He said he had no idea where the line was by this time and that we were to be careful not to blunder into the enemy by mistake and must ask frequently how far off they were. His parting shot was that it was lucky Fernsworth was not present or he might have been frightened off the trip altogether.

A day passed before we could set off. In the afternoon, Selke came out on the balcony and announced that he had got leave to go too, as official interpreter for the party. He was delighted as he said he was always mewed up in the office, and as merry as if he had been going on holiday. I felt none too pleased at this addition to the party.

I turned up at the office early in the morning but, of course, the car and driver were not ready. Selke said we did not need to take any food but Fernsworth, who did not like taking chances, took me out shopping and bought a whole box of eggs. He was most particular about the packing of them, so our journey was punctuated with hard boiled eggs. His choice was rather unfortunate as eggs turned out to be practically the only form of food obtainable on the trip.

At the last moment, when we were all ready to start, Selke suddenly produced from a back room two more people who were to go also, he said. There was some grumbling from Fernsworth, in which Griffin mildly joined, as it meant we were going to be overcrowded. They were, however, personal friends of Selke and quite determined to come. Selke introduced them as 'the photographs'. They represented *Ce Soir* and had just arrived by air from Paris. For them to find a car just setting off somewhere was an obvious godsend and any slight coolness on our part was not going to put them off.

I had never heard of them before but they were Capa[81] and his friend Gerda,[82] Hungarians. He was an extraordinarily daring war photographer, later famous, and was killed in Indochina. That day they both wore leather jackets that were the mode for the front, and Capa wore a small beret night and day, at least I never saw him without it. I got to know them very well by sight as we three sat on the back seat of the car and Capa and Gerda on the tip-up seats opposite.

They were a striking-looking couple. He was tall and thin with dead black eyes. She was a ripe beauty, with a tanned face and bright orange hair cropped like a boy's. The natural tint of her hair was copper, she had the warm brown eyes that go with it, but the sun had bleached it orange and the effect was startling. She was full-bosomed, very handsome but for her head being a bit too large for her height. She wore a little, round, Swiss cap on the back of the astonishing hair. She had small feet and was a model of Parisian *sportif chic*. She radiated sex-appeal.

As we all sat in the car in the street, Micky came up to say goodbye. She had tried hard to come too but had no excuse for going and, after the arrival of 'the photographs' Selke no longer needed her company. He kissed her hand with a flourish, however. I took a brief turn with her and she told me to look out for the photographers as such people were nearly always Trotskyists!

I squeezed myself between Fernsworth and Griffin and we were off, Selke beside the driver where his woolly hair blew in the wind. He left the pane of glass between us open and most of the time had his head turned round to talk to his friends.

Chapter 10
Almería and Murcia

Despite the disagreeable events on this journey, I shall always look back on it with pleasure. The relationship, half business and half friendly, which existed between Fernsworth, Griffin and myself, was ideal. Friends one makes accidentally, through force of circumstance, are often so much better than those one chooses oneself.

Fernsworth was a confirmed bachelor and had developed a number of little eccentricities from living alone and Griffin, who had an Irishman's sense of humour, teased him a bit in a good-natured way. Griffin was the best of employers and I never heard a cross word from him; he was exceedingly patient and adaptable.

I speedily came to the conclusion that the office of interpreter is only tolerable when one only has to deal with two people neither of whom knows any language but his own. In other circumstances, all is infernal confusion. In our party there were seven people and four languages – English, French, Spanish and German – were current, and the results were deplorable. Selke was the official organiser of the expedition and it was my lot to make known to him the wishes of Fernsworth and Griffin in French.

The party was too big and its interests too diverse for Selke to be able to please everyone. He had no tact and always became very bossy when in charge of anything. He was in a state of great exuberance which may have been a characteristic of his nationality; I had never seen anything like it before.

Fernsworth was a very courteous man and the informality of the others irritated him. He considered Capa ill-mannered because he never removed his beret and he was indignant because Selke did a little mild chiselling with the office funds entrusted to him for the expense account. The sums involved were small, it was merely a question of making on the driver's keep and a few other items, and to Griffin it was a matter of indifference if Selke emerged from the deal a few pesetas to the good. To Fernsworth, right and justice were everything and for the sake of his principles he was prepared to haggle over every *céntimo*.

At first, however, everything went smoothly. As we bowled along the straight, tree-lined avenues outside Valencia, Gerda was doing her best to make herself agreeable in broken English. She explained that they were representing a new Paris paper, and told us how many copies each French paper sold and how many it was necessary to sell in order to make a profit. Fernsworth listened politely.

The car was an unwieldy thing, somewhat resembling a London taxi cab. The driver, however, was made of very different stuff to a London taxi driver. He was a tiny, shrivelled Spaniard who could hardly get his grimy little hands round the ponderous steering wheel. He had a bristly chin and only two teeth. A toothless Spaniard is a rarity so I wondered if he had lost them in a brawl rather than from natural causes. He had wild, bloodshot, black eyes and drove like a maniac. Later, in fact, he so nearly killed Dorothy Parker and other passengers that his services were dispensed with. I was really sorry when he was fired as his personality was very *simpático*. I do not think he drank; he was just crazy.

Soon we were swooping round the sharp curves of the cliff road to Alicante in an alarming manner and the car was banging and rattling as if it were going to fall to pieces at any moment. Fernsworth and Griffin did not disguise their nervousness and began holding on to the sides of the car. At their request, I put in a plea to Selke that we might go slower and the driver reduced the speed to a crawl. Selke protested that we should never get anywhere at that pace.

We stopped for a late lunch at a *fonda* in Altea. There I had to find a ladies' lavatory for Gerda, the sort of thankless task that usually falls to the lot of a female interpreter. A fat old woman was frying in the kitchen and the food was good, though there were a lot of flies and Selke's ebullience was reaching a stupendous pitch.

'Here I sit between two red-headed women,' he said archly to me, as if this circumstance capped his felicity.

When we left Altea the people of the inn pressed cards with their name and address on us, and begged us to drop in again and tell our friends, with a melancholy naïveté. They were nice people and I hope they had many customers.

At Alicante, trouble started. Something had gone wrong with the car and we had to wait. First the chauffeur said ten minutes, then an hour, finally it was about two hours. Fernsworth, who had lived in Spain for years, spoke fluent Spanish and his ability to converse privately with our driver bothered Selke, who wanted to keep undivided control.

It proved impossible to keep the party together and, if we separated, it was difficult to assemble us all again at the appropriate time and place. We started trailing round the town, all six, like a conducted tour, but Fernsworth saw a ewe's milk cheese in a shop window and wanted to buy it, and Gerda and Capa strayed off to eat patisserie. We ended up sitting in different cafés and Fernsworth was found subsequently in yet another café all by himself in a huff.

Selke was full of himself and very bumptious; Fernsworth and he had words. Fernsworth said the expedition had been arranged for us, at our suggestion, originally, and the others should fall into line.

The party had by now divided irrevocably into two camps, German speaking and English speaking, with Selke and myself as go-betweens, and I was blamed for the sentiments I expressed on behalf of my employers.

As it was getting late, Selke proposed that we should stay the night in Alicante. He said Capa and Gerda could go to look for refugees to photograph and, as Alicante was a nice town on the sea, we could have a swim in the morning.

Capa and Gerda talked about Spain and the beautiful sunshine quite as if they were on holiday, which I thought very frivolous, but they did not neglect their work. They were always ready to leap from the car to take significantly grim pictures and were merely personally detached from their subjects. I was wrapped up, heart and mind, in the Spanish war, which for purposes of reportage is quite unnecessary, rather undesirable, in fact.

'I have no bathing suit,' I said sourly.

'The best bathing is without suits,' retorted Selke blithely.

'Not with you,' I said.

I wanted to get to Murcia and Selke knew this perfectly well. Fernsworth and Griffin also knew and showed admirable solidarity throughout the journey.

At dusk we were on our way again. There was a lovely pink sunset and Selke, who was now riding inside, became romantic and put his arm around Gerda, rested his woolly head on her shoulder, and started reciting German poetry. Afterwards, Griffin said to me, 'After all, he's quite a sentimental little fellow. When one remembers that piece he wrote, *The Rape of the Olives*, that wasn't journalism, that was purple prose.'

While in Alicante we saw a car loaded with round loaves, which I supposed was our bread on its way to Almería. It was our first reminder of the refugees.

Between Alicante and Murcia, we passed through the main street of a small town, perhaps Elche. We could hardly make our way along as the roadway was full of young people strolling up and down. It was only after repeatedly sounding our horn that we persuaded them to move leisurely aside. They walked five or six abreast, right across the road, all boys in one row, all girls, arm in arm in another, the boys chaffing the girls and the girls answering back. A few lights shone from little shops and the scene reminded me very much of evenings before the war.

In the street, apparently broken down, I saw what appeared to be an old English double-decker bus, painted green. This type of bus did not exist in Spain and, as it was rather dark, I thought afterwards that I must have been mistaken.

It was dark in Murcia. I was most anxious to get the party safely into the Victoria Hotel, which was conveniently close to the hospital. I kept shouting directions to the other driver while Selke protested that we might prefer another hotel; we were a large party, there might not be room or it might be too expensive. We managed to get in there though I had a small, mosquito-infested room at the back near a bubbling water tank.

I ran across to the hospital. Griffin wanted to come too but I wouldn't let him as I knew the authorities did not like journalists.

Jan did not seem quite so bad but was still in plaster. Frieda had left but had given him a flowering plant in a pot. When I went in there were general shouts from the Frenchmen, '*Il a de chance le bougre, d'avoir sa femme ici!*'[83]

Jan told me to take care on the trip. Dr Bethune had been in. He did not get to Málaga but he ran into the exodus and picked people up in his ambulance and bandaged them. He returned, Jan said, a changed man. The doctor's appearance was always unusual; small and dynamic, he corresponded to the popular notion of a genius. This time, Jan said, he had come back looking like a Biblical prophet, his face burned as red as a lobster by the southern sun, making his dishevelled white, wispy hair the more striking. His tale of the refugees was lurid; a story of horror and atrocity. He had bolted back to France to tell the world, all weary and worn as he was by his gruelling experiences.[84]

The Irishman with the hole in his head came and sat beside the bed. Jan was growing paler and thinner but looked less feverish and ill. He said most of the men in the war had either got better or died; only he lay there interminably. 'Don't lose heart,' said the Irishman, and to me, 'why if he don't walk soon we'll carry him out and round the town for a change.'

A gloomy, fanatical-looking figure hopped up on crutches and dropped some sour remark in German. Then he dragged himself off into the middle of the ward, where he hung on his crutches, like a flamingo on one leg, staring vacantly about him.

'He's a very cranky fellow,' said Jan, 'a Pole. But we all try to be nice to him because a few nights ago he tried to hang himself with his towel.'

He called to the man who hopped back. 'I can play football,' he said savagely, shaking the stump of his leg with the empty trouser pinned over it. The Irishman helped him to sit down, which made him groan, and he stared silently and morosely in front of him. He had a narrow head with short, bristling hair. His blue eyes, set too close together, seemed to be looking intently at some faraway scene – perhaps at himself as a healthy youth playing football. He was quite young. 'Tell him it is worse for the chap without hands,' suggested the Irishman cheerfully. Jan began to talk to him in German but he shrugged his shoulders, hauled himself up on his crutches and hopped painfully away.

I went back to the hotel for dinner, which went off amicably, if not as gaily as lunch. I had to put up with a lot of banter from Selke about how bright my eyes were now and how I looked a different creature since I had seen Jan.

I got up early and rushed over to the hospital for a brief visit as Selke threatened to bustle us off at any moment. Jan told me that Penny had obtained her transfer but the other English nurse was still there.

When I got back to the hotel, Griffin was waiting in the lobby and he told me that the others had gone off to look for refugees as we would not be able to start for an hour or so. The driver had been warned that petrol was unobtainable further south as it had all been commandeered for troops and evacuation, so he was out scouring the town for supplies. The only hope was to fill up here and, if possible, take a can along as well, though there was some law against this procedure. The driver said all the transport committees in town were fascists (that is, very unhelpful), and Selke did not back up his demands with the weight of authority as he ought. Selke was off pleasure-seeking with his friends.

Refugees were not far to seek. A truck-load of them was parked in the plaza and disputes were in progress as to where to send them as the Murcians did not want to keep them. We peered over the sides of the truck. It was jammed with filthy, ragged, bedraggled women and children with fear-stricken eyes, like wild animals. They were quite inarticulate and did not seem to know where they were or care where they went.

Fernsworth was in conversation with the hotel manager and presently came up to us and said that there was a factory nearby which made fishing-lines out of silk-worm gut and we could be shown over it if we liked. The three of us went to this establishment. It seemed curious that it was still functioning in war time. On the way, the hotel manager talked to us about the fine trade that there used to be in Murcia. He said that there were jam factories for the peaches and plums that grew in the district. He said that the fishing-lines were nearly all sold to England, as well as the flies made of feathers that were produced there but, of course, the business was languishing now.

The factory was just a big barn where women and girls were employed. They explained all the work to us, which seemed very fine and highly skilled. Griffin and Fernsworth were both interested in fishing and enjoyed the visit very much. Both bought several cards of artificial flies which were labelled in English, and which they said were very cheap compared to such articles in the States. Fernsworth was also American though modified by having lived in Europe for a long time.

We left Murcia at midday and the country began to look barer, flatter, drier and more glaringly white. Along the straight road ahead of us was some vehicle proceeding slowly in a cloud of dust. As we gained on it I saw it was the same mystery bus I had seen the night before, looking for all the world like the buses that amble about in the Home Counties. We caught up and passed it and I noticed a Union Jack was painted on the side. I remarked on this and we all thought it odd.

When we got to Lorca we stopped for lunch. As we drove across the bridge over the dry river, I saw the bus parked with a group of small boys gathered round it. While lunch was being arranged Griffin and I walked back to investigate. There were no people in the bus, only some wooden cases. On the step sat a disconsolate young man. We discovered that this and other buses had been sent out by the Duchess of Atholl's Joint Committee to evacuate women and children from danger spots. The buses had just arrived and were bound for Almería. They were always breaking down. The driver was a Canadian and Griffin perked up at this information and said it might be a story for *Toronto*. However, the young man would not give his name and was altogether uncommunicative. This was not because of lips-sealed communism, rather the reverse. He did not want his family to hear that he was driving a bus in Red Spain, and kept repeating that the venture was purely humanitarian and not political.

In Murcia, the supply of food had been normal; in Lorca, we encountered famine. The hotel where we had lunch was more pretentious than a *fonda*. Blinds shaded the windows and there was a sideboard of polished wood in the dining room. Fernsworth ordered wine – such a comfort in Spain; if one could not eat, one could at least drink. A few eggs were served us almost raw, the Spanish phrase for a boiled egg, *pasado por agua*, proving a very accurate description. Fernsworth, who was an epicure, protested and the waiter called the *patrón* who explained, with many apologies, that the eggs had been cooked on the dying embers of a fire which had now gone out and there was no more fuel in the house. From then on, Fernsworth dropped being an epicure for the duration of the trip, with great good sense.

By some strange chance, there was plenty of bread, probably our own bread from Valencia, and we were able to buy several loaves.

As the afternoon wore on and the sun was setting gloriously, we began to meet groups of refugees, on foot with donkeys and carts, plodding along with expressionless faces and superb dignity, all dusty and worn. One group, with a man leading a donkey with a woman and little children perched on top, looked like a Holy Family flight into Egypt and the photographers exclaimed that we must stop and we did so several times. To take a picture is only a matter of moments whereas a journalist needs much more time to have a conversation, especially with simple peasants speaking in heavy Andalusian accents. We wrangled a good deal about how long we were to stop each time.

Fernsworth was so moved by so much uncomplaining distress, for the people behaved as if they had been struck down by some inexplicable thunderbolt, that he walked down the road, with half a loaf of bread in one hand which he bestowed on one family. I remember the scene vividly, Fernsworth, his small beret perched rather childishly on his grey hair, his neat, dark suit and still polished shoes, the last rays of the sun gleaming on his glasses, smooth and plump, his hand outstretched with the bread in it. And the family, cowering, too stupefied to come up to take it, hardly believing it was really for them and was not the strange foreigner's idea of a joke. Selke protested that it was our bread he was giving away and that we should need it.

It grew dark and we began to wind through weird country, all bare hills and hollows like an enlarged photograph of the moon. We saw camp fires just off the road, stopped and walked over to them. At once we were surrounded by women and children whining and begging. It was too dark to see what they looked like though one could see the silhouettes of full, gathered skirts, but I knew at once from the way they were happily settled by their camp fires, and by their professional style of playing on their poverty, that they were gypsies. Real refugees were ashamed to beg because they were proud and had been respectable people, and they were not at home sleeping out on the ground.

'*Gitanos*?' I asked.

'No, no,' they clamoured, 'not *gitanos*, *castellanos*,' but I knew they were lying.

It was somewhere between eight and nine when we reached Almería. The town was pitch dark and the streets so absolutely deserted that we could find no one to direct us to the hotel. Everything was bolted and barred with wooden shutters up and it looked as if the place was uninhabited. At last, we found what had been the best hotel, also locked and dark. We banged on the door for some time and, at length, a porter cautiously opened it a crack and, after some parley, unwillingly admitted us.

The hall was dimly lighted. I saw hardly any guests in the hotel all the time we were there but they made difficulties about rooms as if they were full up. I stepped up to the desk and started to talk to the reception clerk. Gerda made fun of me, mimicking my English accented Spanish, and I let fly and slapped her on the cheek. She had put her face close to mine and was peering up at me in a cheeky, jeering way that aggravated me beyond endurance.

'You were glad enough to make use of my Spanish in Lorca and Altea,' I cried, and it is very ungrateful of you to make fun of it now.'

'What a vixen! What a spitfire!' she said.

'If you could hear yourself speak English with my ears,' I said, 'you might laugh at that, but I have never mocked your English.'

She, Capa and Selke, like many central Europeans, had a strong guttural accent in every language they spoke. I must have appeared very unreasonable and hot-tempered. I am not like this as a rule but we were all tired and nervous. The war and the long trip had us all on edge.

It seemed there was only one single room available and I

wanted to have it, but then the only logical arrangement would have been for Selke to sleep with the driver.

'I won't sleep with him,' he said, his lip curling in distaste. 'He doesn't wash and he smells of garlic.'

'You're a snob,' I said, which was about the deadliest accusation one could level at anyone in Republican Spain.

'I'm not,' he said indignantly. 'But he snores so loud it keeps me awake; I had to share a room with him once before.'

It was arranged that Selke should sleep with Capa and I had to share with Gerda.

The hotel refused to give us any supper, saying it was too late, but after some argument someone brought a couple of bottles of wine up to Capa's room, which was the biggest, and there we had a picnic. We spread out what meagre supplies we had with us and Capa and Gerda revealed that they had brought from Paris several large, hard sausages and an entire *Bel Paese* cheese. I saw the map of Italy on the box and thought them very unpatriotic, as we in Spain were all for boycotting fascist goods. They offered us some of their food that night but looked rather put out when we tucked into it hungrily. We were much hungrier than they since they had just arrived from France and we had been on short commons in Valencia for weeks.

When we went to bed, I told Gerda she was very *mal élevé* and she apologised, but in a mocking, insincere way.

We were woken up in the morning by the room shaking as if there were an earthquake. It was an air bombardment. I jumped out of bed and got dressed as fast as I could as the whole building was shaking like a jelly, as if it would collapse without being hit, like the walls of Jericho, and I wanted to get out into the street. Gerda did not seem frightened and got up later. This hotel was similar to the one in Murcia but much bigger and not at all solidly constructed. There was a huge patio with a glass roof and a lot of galleries running round it and a perfect rabbit warren of passages and rooms off the galleries in which it was easy to lose one's way. Two broad marble staircases united in the hall.

It reminded me somewhat of prisons in American movies; I suppose it was the galleries from which one could see all that was going on in the hall and the iron railings along them. Over the galleries, at intervals, hung cages of canary birds and, when the warning sirens blew, all the canaries started to sing frantically.

I imagined all the glass shattering as I ran downstairs. As I reached the dining room there was a heavy 'boom' outside the shuttered windows and then it was all over.

I sat down, rather out of breath, to wait for a steadying cup of coffee. There was absolutely no sign of breakfast although it was nine o'clock, no waiters, no tables laid, nothing. Griffin shortly joined me.

'It was only one plane,' he said, 'I saw it out of the window. Fernsworth was doing his Muller's exercises at the time.'

'Did he stop doing them or go on?' I asked.

'I didn't stay to see, but he went on, I expect. He is a very persevering sort of chap. I've been out in the street. They say a few bombs were dropped on the harbour, aimed at the *Jaime Primero*, no damage done.'

We went to ask the reception clerk about breakfast and were told they did not serve any, only two meals a day, at one and seven, and we had better be there on time or we would not get those.

In a corner of the dining room were gathered half a dozen obviously English young men, who were having some sort of meal. They were the Joint Committee bus drivers. Most of them were much more genial than the one Canadian we had met the day before.

'Better come and join us,' shouted one red-faced youth, cheerfully. 'We brought this stuff down for the starving inhabitants. Well, we seem to come under that heading, so we broached cargo.'

One of the boys fetched a couple of chairs for us in addition to the six or eight already clustered round the window table. Another was directed to go outside to get some more tins of condensed milk, and yet another went up to his room to fetch a tin opener. They had tea and sugar and a few stale biscuits. We gathered round and presently Fernsworth came down and joined us and they made a fresh pot of tea. The journalists then got some sort of story from them but I did not really listen as no translation was needed. The others must have gone out to a café, for they did not appear. I was very glad of such a jolly English welcome in such an inhospitable hotel.

That morning it was decided that we should all go our separate ways and Griffin and I went out together. For some reason or other, we went first to the English vice-consul, who must have been a shipping agent in private life, and who lived up two flights of stairs in a shabby house near the port. He seemed surprised and not overjoyed to see us. He came to the door himself with his mouth full and wiping the remains of what appeared to have been a succulent bacon breakfast off his moustache.

We asked him if it was true that British warships were taking supplies into Málaga now that it had fallen to Franco and he said it was. We then asked if any of them were coming up here with food and he said not. As for the refugees, he said he could not think why the silly people had not stayed where they were or what possessed them to trek up here.

After we got downstairs, Griffin burst out about the attitude of the British officials; said he would never go near one of them again.

'Why, when I went up to Madrid,' he said, 'I naturally expected to stay at the British Embassy. I belong to the Empire, am as much entitled to their protection as anyone. They were so high-hat, and acted as if a Canadian was inferior to a Britisher and made such a favour of it that I took myself off. I wasn't going to stand for that. I've a good mind to make a complaint about it when I get back; it's disgusting.'

'Of course you should have stayed there,' I said. 'You're a bona fide newspaper man. I didn't care to go there because they think I'm a red anyway.'

We then went to the headquarters of a refugee committee and there met the doctor in charge of municipal health services, who showed us round. He was young and intelligent. He told us that most of the refugees were very poor and humble people, very primitive, either from the slums of Málaga or the villages and that consequently it was difficult to get them to observe the rules of hygiene when congregated in large numbers, but that they had been able to avoid epidemics so far.

He took us to an old convent where a number of refugees were camped. Washing was hanging out in the cloisters and in the courtyard some were frying vegetables over open fires. They were very different to the Madrid refugees, much more dirty and ragged. A dispute was going on because the authorities were trying to split up families, keeping the men for the army or work on the fortifications and evacuating the women, children and old people. The men did not want to stay and the doctor delivered an ultimatum that the women and children were to be ready to leave that afternoon, in Joint Committee buses, and that only they would be accepted.

He told us that we were really too late, for the bulk of the refugees had already been dispersed elsewhere. Almería was too small a town to keep so many thousands and they had been sent on as fast as possible, especially as they wanted to separate the genuine refugees from the fleeing militiamen. The latter they were trying to round up and re-form and send back to the front, but large bands of them were still wandering about the town, leaderless, for their officers had deserted.

Those we had seen on foot the night before were, he said, only a few obstinate ones who insisted on keeping together not merely families but animals as well. He laughed and shrugged his shoulders with the modern man's contempt for such unreasonable creatures as peasants.

'They will not give up their goats and donkeys,' he said, 'and, of course, we cannot take beasts in buses and they don't understand that. When they get to Alicante or Valencia they won't know what to do with the beasts either but it's no use talking to them; they must find out for themselves. Come with me to the hospital,' he said, 'there you will see those who remain because they were sick. Most of them have sore feet. Their canvas shoes wore out, you know, from walking so far. But we only keep the bad cases. We have now received a number of these individual dressings,' and he took out of his pocket a neat little packet. 'They contain iodine, a bandage, sticking plaster etc, and we give them these and they can treat themselves.'

We followed him upstairs into a light and airy women's ward. The hospital was small and he said they were opening another in an empty building. We asked if they had many air raid casualties and he said not among the refugees, but a few days earlier an orphan's asylum had been hit.

He went to look at a little girl, about nine, a pretty child, her eyes wide open. We were told not to talk to her as she was too ill, suffering from shock and exhaustion. Her mother had come to see her and, as she was not allowed to talk to the child either and was a garrulous woman, she turned her attention to us. She may have been forty but looked fifty, with frizzy, grizzled hair, a face wrinkled and burned mahogany by the sun, and a cotton dress so faded one could not guess at the original colour. She looked tough and had plenty of life in her.

'Where did you come from,' I asked.

'Cádiz.'

'What, walking all the way?' I was incredulous.

'*Sí, sí, andando, andando.*'

'When did you start?'

I was curious to know the length of this Odyssey and she was far too simple to invent in order to astonish. In fact I could see that she was not herself astonished at the feat she had performed.

'We start last August – the fascists keep coming after us – we keep moving – sometimes we stay a few days some place – then we hear the fascists are coming – we move on again. We get to Málaga – we stay there. Then the fascists are coming after us again – we go on with many other people. We get to Motril – many bombs and bullets coming from the sky, from the sea, from everywhere – my cousin she gets hit in the stomach and falls down – my brother-in-law he disappears – we get to Adra, a lorry picks us up and brings us here.'

'What did you eat?'

'The last part of the way we chewed sugar cane which grows by the roadside – from Málaga it took five days, a week, I don't remember.'

'How many of you?'

'Myself and my husband and six children and we only lost one – only the donkey died.'

She sighed and the loss of the donkey seemed to weigh her down more than that of the cousin and brother-in-law.

We turned to talk to a pale, superior little woman, very lame, for she was evidently unaccustomed to walking. She told us she was a widow and gave the name of the suburb in Málaga from which she came. She had left the town on one side as the Italians were marching in on the other. She was an active socialist with a son in the militia.

We went out on the balcony and a nurse came out with a chubby little girl, about two years old, in her arms.

'A militiaman found her sitting in the road all alone, a few miles out of town,' said the nurse. 'She is too young to talk so we don't know her name or how old she is, eighteen months to two years, I guess. We've adopted her and we call her Libertad.'

'She's a plump, bonny child,' said the doctor, pinching her rosy cheek, 'and she was clean and well cared for when they found her playing by herself in the dirt – parents probably dead, poor souls.'

The nurse said to the child, '*Salud, salud, eh?*' and the child laughed and raised its tiny fist.

'That is all she knows,' said the nurse, 'to make the Popular Front salute.'

She carried the child away with many kisses and fond clucking sounds.

We went outside and saw a queue of refugees waiting for food outside a public building. They were each receiving a piece of bread on which was a horribly unappetising brown sausage, which looked like excrement. We talked to a tattered virago with several children.

'Well,' she said, as if it were a matter of indifference. 'I lost a couple of them. Of course, I was carrying the baby and these two boys were big enough to keep up with us, but two toddlers got left behind. It couldn't be helped, it was God's will, and I have three left.'

We could get no clear account from anyone of the ghastly panic at Motril. Some thought the planes flew low and machine-gunned them, others that they were bombed. At that point many lost their relatives but, as the virago pointed out philosophically, they might still be living. Many people, to escape the firing, left the road and took to the mountains where they might still be hiding, getting their food from remote hamlets and farms. The retreat of some had been cut off by the rapid advance of the Italians, and by the destruction of bridges.

We were fairly tired by this time, from walking and standing about, so we went to a café. The Joint Committee had flooded the entire neighbourhood with condensed milk and it was about all they had at the café, though there was some sort of coffee substitute. Most of the shops were shut and barricaded. The atmosphere in the town was very bad, sullen and hostile. I have seldom seen a place where the morale was so low and I felt the Italians could have walked in easily if they had known.

The morning papers had come out and we bought some. As the paper shortage was acute they consisted of a single sheet of gaily coloured paper, bright pink or blue, of the kind generally used for the free leaflets announcing coming cinema attractions.

Half the sheet was taken up with advertisements for lost children, inserted by distracted refugee parents; they were very pathetic and I read some out to Griffin:

'Will anyone who has seen a little girl with blue eyes, aged three, answering to the name of Amelia Hernández, please communicate with Juan Hernández, Central Committee for Refugees. She was picked up by a militiaman on horseback, at Torre de Molinos, going out of Málaga. She was dressed in a blue coat, a white pinafore and socks and buttoned brown shoes. Will anyone who knows her whereabouts please inform her sorrowing parents.'

There were many others in the same vein but I was haunted by little blue-eyed Amelia, whose description still appeared in papers weeks later, in Valencia and even in Barcelona, for her sorrowing parents never seemed to give up hope of finding her.

There was no military communiqué in the paper; the rest of the 'news' consisting of an appeal to patriotic fishermen to go out fishing regardless of the danger from enemy planes or boats – an appeal which was apparently disregarded for I never saw a fish in Almería.

Fernsworth joined us. He was the only person who had really attempted to find pertinent information. He had quickly made contact with important people in the town and had tried to get an interview with the colonel who had been in command of the defence of Málaga but had discovered that the gentleman, who had been in hiding, had fled the town that day as he was afraid the militiamen he had let down would take his life. He was court-martialled later.

Fernsworth also discovered that the anarchists, angry and disappointed at the loss of Málaga, had rushed into town with the intention of bumping off the fascist prisoners held there and particularly a bishop who happened to be there. The mayor, determined to prevent a massacre, was sleeping down in the jail himself to save the prisoners – which he succeeded in doing.

'That's typical illogical anarchist thinking,' I said. 'Betrayed by one set of people, their only idea, instead of putting up a fight in the proper place, at the front, is to run back here to kill another lot of people, who were not responsible, in revenge.'

We went into the hotel lobby where we had a chat with the manager, a livery-looking little man. He was very fed up because business was bad and said the shops were shut because of looting. He did not like to have many guests at the hotel because he could not feed them. There were armed sentries at the street door and also now at the door of the dining room, near which a number of people were already loitering with intent. On the stroke of one the door was opened and they all pushed their way in, like animals about to be fed.

Our meals were always the same, a thin soup (omitted at night) and a slice of omelette made heavy with potatoes and cooked in very evil-smelling oil. We each received a small piece of bread which got progressively staler and harder so that I imagined it was always the same which had been sent from Valencia. Spanish hotels, unlike French ones, always make *pensión* terms and these must have been very advantageous to the management when they had the excuse that no food was available. It is most unusual in Spain for people to eat before two in the afternoon or nine at night but during the war they kept making the meals earlier and earlier.

As we had not seen each other for some hours we were fairly amicable at lunch and all went out together afterwards for a walk. Capa and Gerda were taken up by the police for venturing too near the barracks with their cameras and had to go off to get some more permits. The rest of us went down to the port. The shed over the dock had several holes in the roof and the quay was scattered with rice as some sacks had been split in a bombardment. On the dock sat a crowd of refugees with their bundles. They were waiting to embark for Tarragona and had been sitting there for several days. Two days later, I was relieved to see they had actually gone.

We walked along the sea-front on what had once been a boulevard. It all looked as if a swarm of locusts had passed, or as if we had arrived in the aftermath of some grim bank holiday. The grass was trampled, and blackened by innumerable camp fires. The palms had been stripped of bark to supply fuel. Papers and rags were flying about in the dust. Further up the hill were some cave dwellers which greatly excited the photographers, who had caught up with us again, but I was of the opinion that the people had always been living there as they seemed settled and fairly comfortable.

We walked back along the river bed but were driven up to the road again by the stench. It was a stench of combined drains and decaying corpses. Dead donkeys, mules and horses were lying about swollen and covered with swarms of flies, like the worst of Dalí's surrealist nightmares, and among the dead stood or lay the dying. There was one white horse. It was like the skeleton of a horse with a hide stretched over it. It got waveringly to its feet and started in a melancholy fashion over the bodies of the others. Fernsworth plucked a bunch of something green and placed it under its nose but it seemed too far gone to eat. Two days later, when we passed there again, it was dead and hardly any animal was stirring in the river bed.

We Anglo-Saxons were rather indignant that no Spaniard could spare a few bullets for these beasts, which the refugees had abandoned when they could go no further, and I intended to mention it to the town doctor, but never had an opportunity to do so. We could not be out after dark as the town was under a curfew, there were no lights and the hotel was locked at seven, so we had to get back.

Selke called a conference and announced that, as the photographers had been disappointed of material in the way of refugees, he suggested that we took a trip to the front the next day. Passes to go had been obtained for all of us. The driver did not want to go and said he had promised not to run himself or the car into danger, but he finally agreed and so did we. Fernsworth said that of course it was a waste of time as the military never gave one any information. Griffin said that, for his part, he regarded the whole trip as merely an opportunity to see the country.

We started very early in the morning. Gerda had wrenched some buttons off her skirt and I lent her a needle and cotton. She exclaimed at my foresight in bringing such a thing and at the same time called me an old maid. She was very modest about dressing and undressing and seemed to be always completely clad or in her rust coloured pyjamas. I barely got a glimpse of any part of her. I was rather unaccustomed to this manoeuvring or 'moral gymnastic' way of dressing as Kitty, like many Americans, was completely without self-consciousness about appearing naked in front of her own sex.

As we left town along the completely empty coast road we saw a few more dead animals, articles of clothing, mattresses and even parts of iron bedsteads. Refugees who had set out with all their worldly goods were abandoning them bit by bit.

At first the road ran at some distance from the sea, which was just visible beyond a mile or so of flat fields. There were the trampled and wasted remains of the sugar cane the woman had spoken of, and the outlines of a couple of white, red-roofed, summer villas against the blue of the sea. Some of the land looked like marshes.

On our right, we passed a turning signposted Granada – romantic, unattainable place! I had never been to the city of the Moors and the gypsies, the heart of Andalusia, and now it was impossible. It was not far in kilometres but the war lay between, an impassable barrier. I wondered what it was like and remembered the death there of the poet Lorca at the hands of the Civil Guards, those sinister cloaked figures he had described so well; and the death of the girl Lina Ódena, on this same front, who saw the Moors coming in September 1936 and shot herself rather than fall into their hands alive. She was a small, over-worked seamstress, in her teens, with a sad, intense face.

We stopped at a village which consisted only of a row of white, one-storeyed houses on either side of the dusty street. I think this was Adra, and we must have stopped there either because there was something wrong with the car or to enquire the way. We were ravenous as we had not breakfasted that morning and Fernsworth led the way to what had been a *fonda*. It must have been a wretched place at the best of times, only one dark room with a few wooden stools and a cloud of flies. Fernsworth gave them some eggs and tea he had brought, to cook for us, as there was nothing to be had there. The owner said the refugees and gypsies had ransacked the whole village and stripped it of everything and had even carried off his crockery, spoons, pots and pans.

I went back to the car to fetch a bit of bread and found the other three enjoying a hearty meal of sausage and cheese which they did not offer us but put away in disconcerted haste as I approached. As we had to wait for the water to boil, they were finished first and Selke was impatient to be gone. I went behind the houses and found some women holding a sort of market with a few lettuces and things spread on the ground and I was glad to be able to buy some raisins.

When I got back, I found that all were ready to start and Selke screamed at me for delaying them, like a nagging woman scold-ing a servant. We went on. The others talked in German and were apparently abusing us roundly, for Fernsworth suddenly said, 'I can understand every word you're saying.' They lost the power of speech completely, absolutely flabbergasted, for they had not thought previously that any of us could understand their conversation. After Fernsworth had dropped this bombshell the atmosphere in the car, crowded as we were at close quarters, remained awkward to say the least.

We were now driving round steep cliffs and came to a tunnel in which munitions were stored and militiamen were sleeping. We crossed frequent ravines on shaky plank bridges as the retreating anarchists had blown up all the bridges, leaving some refugees stranded and making it impossible for the relieving troops to get at the enemy until they had been repaired.

At last we were challenged by a sentry, got leave to pass on and soon came to the staff headquarters at Castel de Ferro. This was a beautiful village, a row of houses under a cliff, the road and then a shingle beach. Some lorries were drawn up in the street. A battalion of the International Brigade was there. It contained Austrians and Hungarians and Capa and Gerda quickly found some acquaintances and were surrounded by a chattering crowd. A pretty girl like Gerda caused the greatest excitement and she gave out Lucky Strike cigarettes of which she had brought a quantity from Paris. The tobacco situation was bad in Almería, hardly any of the worst Spanish cigarettes could be had and at the front there were none, in fact the soldiers had hardly any supplies of any kind. The country around had been scraped bare by the refugees and everything had to be brought from a great distance.

We were invited into staff headquarters where Selke interpreted, though with an ill grace, as German was the official language. It was in the biggest house and they had a map and a telescope on the balcony of white-washed pillars, but little else. They said they had seen one foreign warship that day.

As Fernsworth had foreseen, they told us nothing; were merely very cheerful, said the line had been stabilised just this side of Motril and that we had even made a few gains, *coups de main*, in the mountains. I think this line remained substantially the same right to the end of the war.

Capa, looking very black and hairy, went bathing in his underwear, with some soldiers who were also swimming. We had lunch with the officers, bread and some kind of sausage and cups of condensed milk. We sat in a fantastic room which had been the parlour of the house. It was full of knick-knacks, fancy lampshades and garish dolls. In the midst of all this muslin and flowered cretonne sat the Commander, sweaty, in shirt sleeves, a stout, sandy-haired, stocky German figure in heavy leather belt and boots. I felt he was very likeable and dependable, a rock who would certainly hold the line.

After lunch, the others went on further to inspect the outposts. There was a discussion about this. We did not really want to go but as they obviously wanted to leave us behind, Fernsworth developed a contrary wish to go but, in the end, we stayed behind. They had the usual trouble persuading the chauffeur to go on into the unknown but he went eventually.

We spent the afternoon lying on the beach in the sun. Griffin talked about his wife and schoolgirl daughter back in Canada and gave me some long explanation about a new and superior form of heating that they had installed in their house. I think it was oil-burning.

'Does away with all the dirt and work of a furnace,' he continued. 'It wouldn't be fair to them or my paper to run into danger – in fact I have instructions not to.'

'So have I,' said Fernsworth, idly hurling a pebble into the sea as if he had been in Brighton. 'We shall get dreadfully sunburnt if we stay here much longer, my skin catches very easily.'

Fernsworth had particularly beautiful hair; it was grey but curled naturally. I made some remark about it.

'You know, when I was a little boy I used to wear it in curls on my shoulders,' he said.

'Like little Lord Fauntleroy?'

He ignored the interruption and went on in his slow, careful enunciation, 'Once, my parents were taking me on a boat somewhere. Some people admired my hair but mistook me for a little girl. How mortified I was. I cried with rage.'

'An only child?'

'Yes,' he replied.

Griffin, his beret pulled down over one ear, smoked his pipe and gazed out to sea. It was calm and blue and everything looked very peaceful. Fernsworth fell asleep.

Griffin and I went for a stroll and came upon some militiamen throwing pebbles at some small object they had set up. They were Spaniards who had been sent down from Valencia. One was an Andaluz. He wore gold earrings and a red neckerchief like a gypsy. We saw that the object was a small ivory crucifix with a figure carved on it.

'Where did you find it?' I asked.

'Washed up by the sea,' they said.

'I should like to keep it as a souvenir,' said Griffin.

They gave it to him and he put it in his pocket.

It began to get dark and chilly so we walked up the road in the direction the car had gone but there was no sign of it. The road was quite bare and empty and wound on over the hills into the country as if it led to no war. There were no barricades and sentries here.

Night fell. A soldier set a chair for me at the door of staff headquarters and I remained there until I was quite stiff. The others loitered about impatiently. When at last we saw the headlights, we were too glad of the sight to complain, and bundled into the car in haste to get back. The other three said they had climbed on foot among the mountains for at least an hour but had not seen much. They were very tired.

Capa was feeling ill; his dark face had a greenish pallor and he said he had a splitting headache. Gerda whispered and sympathised with him. I thought he had probably caught a chill bathing for it was early in the year and the sea was still cold. All our spirits were low and to beguile the time Fernsworth started to sing. I do not remember exactly what, but I think it was *My Little Grey Home in the West* and *There's a Long Trail A-winding*. I cannot pretend that Fernsworth's talents lay in this direction.

The others, though not of a type Hitler would have welcomed, were Germanic enough to be *musikalisch*. They made it quite evident that his cheerful noise was torture to them. They held their heads and stuffed their fingers in their ears. Capa added a groan to the loud notes but they did not quite dare to ask Fernsworth to cease so he continued his performance. We stopped at Adra and Selke went off in search of aspirins, but of course he could not find any.

On our return, Capa went straight to bed, though Fernsworth offered him a boiled egg, and it appeared we were not on speaking terms. Up in our room I tried to reason with Gerda about Fernsworth.

'I know,' she said peevishly. 'I know we have to manage his caprices. We put up with a good deal, but he is a complete egoist, really insupportable,' and she made a grimace.

'We always see the egoist in other people and not in ourselves,'

I said. 'Of course, everyone is an egoist. But Fernsworth is a good writer – you must take my word for that as you have not read his stuff – and, in many ways, an admirable person. And, what is more, owing to his standing in his profession he is a very important person, the most important one among us. He should be deferred to.'

Gerda took everything I said the wrong way.

'Capa is a great man too,' she flared up. 'He is one of the best photographers alive and you talk like a reactionary, as if Fernsworth's work were more important than ours!'

I was becoming impatient and tangled up in my speech. We talked in French and she had a much better command of the language than I, and I burst out, 'That's not so. But you must see that from the point of view of world public opinion Fernsworth's paper, which has an enormous circulation and reaches people normally unsympathetic to us, is of far greater importance than any miserable little Left rag that only tells a few of the faithful what they believe already!'

Gerda was justly incensed and swept out, in her pyjamas, to sleep in the room occupied by Capa and Selke. At that time, I knew nothing of Capa's work. He was in fact an excellent and imaginative photographer, quite renowned, for his age, and has since become more so. However, I felt very strongly that Fernsworth and Griffin (who never put himself forward) were, as old men in established positions, entitled to more deference than they received.

We had expected to leave early the next day but found that the others had arranged to see over the *Jaime Primero*. Fernsworth, Griffin and I were by now firmly welded into an opposition block. We went down and sat on the quay. 'Of course it's not worth seeing, but if they intended to waste the morning over it, they should have got us passes to go on board too, at least,' said Fernsworth, and then, after a disgruntled pause. 'It's no use, we're just in the hands of another Jewish combine.'

I laughed and kicked my heels against the wall on which we sat. We were immediately opposite the *Jaime Primero*, a rusty old black boat, which had been damaged early in the war and never ventured to sea again. The sailors, looking rather slack and untidy, were lolling about on the decks. Gerda, Selke and Capa appeared and ascended the gangplank. We went away.

We were very hungry and Fernsworth got us inside a shop, I think it was a chemist's, which had a few tinned goods in it. Of course there was nothing but Worcester Sauce, Colman's Mustard, pickles and a very rusty tin of shrimps. Fernsworth turned it round and tried to read the date, which was obliterated. We discussed whether rust would affect shrimps, finally decided that it would and put it back on the shelf.

Griffin and Fernsworth went back to the hotel and I wandered about the town by myself. I entered some mean streets and there I saw a funeral. It must have been that of a child or young girl for the coach was all white and glass, like Cinderella's magic one, and the horses were white with white ostrich plumes on their heads like debutantes. There were more white plumes on top of the hearse. It was very pretty but seemed strange, this funeral with the pantomime coach, at a time when there were so many violent deaths.

When we got back to the hotel, we expected to start for Valencia but Selke suddenly put forward a proposal that we should extend the tour still further. He said that the photographers had been disappointed in the trip so far and wanted to go to Jaén, embracing an entirely different part of the southern front, and to return by Albacete. This would have added immensely to our mileage and taken another week.

Selke began the conversation in a pleasant tone, said it would be very interesting, and held out Albacete and more interviews with the International Brigades as an inducement.

'I think one can soon see enough of International Brigades, especially when they happen to speak nothing but German,' murmured Griffin.

'But there will be English and Americans,' said Selke.

'It is out of the question,' said Fernsworth in his deliberate way. 'I have been away from Valencia quite long enough; my paper will be beginning to wonder what has happened to me.'

'I ought to get back as well,' said Griffin.

As there was no censorship nearer than Valencia it was impossible for either of them to send anything to their papers until they got back there. I, of course, was opposed to the plan, as it meant no Murcia on the return journey. I also thought I ought to get back to the office, but it was not of such great moment to me except for the sake of the others.

Fernsworth turned to the driver and asked him what he thought of the idea, in Spanish, which infuriated Selke. The driver said that he was most averse to going further, that the car was in bad shape, and if the idea was pursued, what with bad roads and so on, he could not be responsible for the consequences. He then proceeded to guarantee that the car would break down and we would be delayed still further. In fact he could not say when or how we would ever get back to Valencia.

'There, you see?' said Fernsworth. 'You heard what this good fellow said. That settles the matter.'

'He only said it to please you,' said Selke, and he began to bully the driver. The driver was not the type to be put upon. He bridled like a bantam cock and let out some choice swear words.

Gerda and Capa then intervened, pleading at first ingratiatingly, then, as we were all obdurate, angrily.

'All right,' blustered Selke. 'We'll take the car and leave you here. You can try to find another car and petrol to take you back. Just go to the transport committee and try it, that's all. You shall not spoil our trip.'

Fernsworth was boiling with wrath at being spoken to in this unceremonious fashion. He and Griffin went upstairs, announcing that they were going to pack. My heart sank at the threat to leave us stranded as I knew quite well that we should never get a car in Almería, and I believed all the Joint Committee buses had already left. I sat there, a prey to all the feelings which diplomats must have when it is announced that 'negotiations have been broken off entirely'.

Halfway up the stairs, Selke turned and beckoned me.

'As for you,' he hissed, like a screen villain, 'you have not heard the last of this! You are a traitor to the office that employs you. You have sabotaged everything.'

'What on earth do you mean?' I stammered. 'Griffin is my employer here. It doesn't matter to me in the least where we go.' This was not strictly true for I had set my heart on returning to

Murcia. 'I have only been defending my employer's interests, which is my duty. It's not my fault they won't go to Jaén.'

'I shall tell Rubio about it. I shall get you fired!' shouted Selke.

Gerda spoke to him, I think defending me, and they all disappeared.

Of course, Selke was only letting out on me the spleen he was too cowardly to vent on the journalists. I was in a subordinate position and he could insult me without fear. Nevertheless, I was considerably shaken by his threat to have me fired. He was quite capable of it. Everybody regarded him as Rubio's right hand man and a person of influence, though he was later fired with ignominy himself.

I could not bear this crushing position without support and went up to the room occupied by Griffin and Fernsworth and, very much agitated, recounted to them the scene which had just taken place. They were nobly indignant on my behalf and Griffin said he would tell the office I had behaved perfectly, and Fernsworth, with all his chivalry aroused, said he intended to lodge a formal complaint about Selke's behaviour.

'The complaining will not be all on one side,' he declared, 'that little rat!'

We went down to lunch and saw the others sitting at a separate table, much subdued. They sent the driver over to tell us that we were all starting back after all. They had thought better of their threat to desert us, for which I was very thankful.

The state of our tempers can be imagined and we were all very silent. Unfortunately, the car was going badly from the first; one of the troubles was the poor quality gasoline which did not flow properly from the tank to the engine. We stopped once or twice and then were able to go on again, but around the middle of the afternoon we broke down completely. The chauffeur was not a good mechanic; the symptoms puzzled him and he began to pull the car to pieces in a manner which was the more ominous in that it looked so haphazard.

Inevitably, we were miles from the nearest village when this occurred. None of us understood cars so we could only wait. There was a single house a little way back from the road. Fernsworth went there to talk to the people and bestowed on them the remainder of our eggs.

We all walked away from each other. Griffin and I came to rest on a prickly bank. Griffin, his beret pulled down over his lean, weather-beaten face to shade his eyes, stared ahead and talked about the brisk fall weather in Canada and how, just now, the snow would be beginning to melt. I could see he had a spell of homesickness as we sat in the midst of the arid, sun-scorched wilderness. It was a very awkward wait; no other cars passed which might have provided a lift or expert advice. We were all thinking we might have to camp for the night where we were, though none of us said so.

At last, we were able to go on and reached the next village at dusk. Selke was in favour of pushing on all night. This was partly because he wanted to be rid of his troublesome passengers as soon as possible. The responsibility he had assumed and then made such a mess of worried him. I think he may have also wanted to effect a saving on the expense account. Fernsworth vetoed this idea. He said it would be foolish to risk a breakdown in the dark and the driver agreed with him.

So we found a small *fonda*. We sat in the hall while arrangements about beds were being made. These were even more inconvenient than before. Most of the rooms contained *matrimonios*. None of us was in matrimonial mood, and only one single room. Again it was suggested that Gerda and I should sleep together. I did not object but I heard her arguing with Selke, and she repeated in French, so that I should not miss it, 'I'd rather sleep in the car than sleep with that girl.' I do not know what the others arranged but I got the single room.

We had to wait some time for dinner to be prepared and we ate it at separate tables in a small dining room where there were no other guests to relieve the embarrassment. The meal took an endless time to serve and neither party spoke loudly lest the others should overhear. The people at the inn thought we were quite crazy. I was very depressed and would have liked to get drunk, a feat which the driver accomplished, but Fernsworth and Griffin were not people for excessive conviviality.

I could not sleep; the room was hot and stuffy, with a window only a few inches square which would not open, and the bed was hard and lumpy.

The next morning, Griffin said, 'Did you think last night, in that forgotten village, that it was the first time since we came to Spain that we could sleep entirely out of danger? It was a strange relief to me.'

'It's a solemn thought,' I said, 'but it did not occur to me and, however safe, I slept very badly.'

The car needed constant fixing and broke down once more but, in the course of the morning, we reached Murcia. Once more we stopped for something to be done to the car and all went into the Victoria Hotel for a vermouth. There I announced my intention of leaving the car and travelling the rest of the way by bus.

I wanted to stay a night in Murcia but my plan was interpreted, with some justification, as showing my inability to bear the company any longer. Fernsworth said it was a crying shame that I had been driven out of the party and offered to stay with me and go back by bus too. Selke became very uneasy as he knew he would be blamed if he came home with the car and his friends but without Fernsworth. I did not want him to stay as I meant to spend my time at the hospital, where I could not take him even if I wanted to, and so much championing was a bit embarrassing when my motive was a selfish one.

I told Fernsworth that it would not be fair to desert Griffin and he agreed to that. I said that I really preferred to go by bus, which was true enough, and Griffin, dear soul, insisted on giving me some money, and we had a last drink together. I felt charitably disposed towards all the world now I was quit of the party, and smiled and waved to Gerda and Capa. If I lost my job Griffin said I could work for him, and both he and Fernsworth assured me that I was too useful to lack work.

I went out into the plaza, where the car was parked, to get my rucksack which was tied on the front between the mudguard and the bonnet. The driver helped me untie it and was very upset by this dénouement. He said that Fernsworth and Griffin were real gentlemen, that he was very sorry there had been so much trouble which was not of his making. He cast a baleful glance at Selke who was of a type always to antagonise the working class. He continued, beating his breast for emphasis, that for his part he would have been only too delighted to drive me to Valencia or the ends of the earth for that matter. He hoped that my leaving the car was no reflection on his driving. I assured him it was not, though I was thinking that the car was in such an infirm state that I might well arrive back before they did. We shook hands and parted.

I tidied myself up and went over to the hospital. Outside the door stood a lorry from which wounded were being unloaded in an apparently ruthless manner, as if they had been carcasses of meat arriving at market. I squeezed past and went inside. Men were sitting about, dirty, in bloodstained bandages, waiting to have their wounds dressed and beds found for them. There was blood on the floors and the staff was evidently overwhelmed. On some front there had just been a big battle and this was the result.

I went upstairs. In the galleries were men for whom there were no beds, lying in rows on stretchers. One man called out to me in English and I stopped to speak to him. He was an American. I should have known that the men who call out and complain are not the good soldiers and that this man did not deserve my pity, but I was taken in by him at first. No man's face looks repulsive when he is lying helpless.

I talked to him several times that day and every time I passed his stretcher he tried to detain me from going on to Jan by grabbing my hand. He told me he had been wounded in the legs. This was untrue; he was shell-shocked. As, for a long time, there was no special hospital for such cases, they were distributed among all the hospitals, much to the inconvenience of the other patients. A comrade of his told us later that he had fallen down on the first day at the front exclaiming that he had been hit. His legs seemed paralysed and he could not walk, so he was carried off the field, but on examination no wound was found, not even a scratch.

He told me that he had come from America as an instructor in gunnery and had been shanghaied off to the front, which he had never intended. He said that he meant to get back to America as soon as he could move because he had been deceived. He showed me a photo of another boy who, he said, was also dissatisfied and meant to run away. He also told me he was Milly's cousin, appeared to know all about her and gave me a message for her.

I went into the ward and told Jan all about the journey, hoping our adventures would help to take his mind off his own situation. As he was still in plaster, there was an end of my fine dream of picking him up in the car and carrying him back to Valencia, which would have been impossible as it turned out.

I told him about all the wounded lying in the passages and that he was lucky to be in bed in a ward. He said he knew there had been a big battle and that the English and American battalions had been thrown into the line for the first time and the losses had been terrible. It must have been Jarama.

He told me to go over to an elderly Irishman, who was lying in a corner, and to tell him he was well off, as he was always grumbling.

'When he first came here,' said Jan, 'he complained of the bed and the doctor said 'all right, we'll change it for you,' being sarcastic of course, and the guy believed it and kept asking every day when his new bed was coming!'

I went over to the bed. The Irishman said he had been in the Great War but this was nothing like it, no, this was much worse.

'It strikes me,' I said when I got back to Jan, 'that these new volunteers are not up to the standard of the first lot. Wherever did they scrape them up from?'

'You are darned right,' said Jan. 'A lot of them are just unemployed and not sappy idealists like we were.'

'You don't regret coming to Spain now?'

'No, of course not. I couldn't have done anything else.'

'A cause isn't spoiled by a few bad people in it.'

'No, of course not.'

As soon as I had had lunch, I went back to the ward. The pneumonia patient had died and in his bed, opposite Jan, was installed a Frenchman with a big nose and long, comical face, looking like an Apache. He should have been wearing a peaked cap and muffler as if he had spent all his life in low dives in Montmartre.

'Aha,' he grinned across at us. '*Je vais danser avec ta femme, le quatorze juillet,*'[85] and he hummed a tune and held out his arms as if he were encircling an imaginary waist and jigged them about. '*Tu n'est pas jaloux, hein? Ah, c'est parce que tu sais que ce n'est pas vrai – seulement une plaisanterie,*'[86] as Jan smiled at him and shook his head.

We wanted to make some arrangement for Jan to be transferred to Valencia and I chased all over the hospital to find the *responsable*. This was now a fat French woman with untidy, frizzed hair in a fringe, and a shrill voice. I found her at the door, checking over the names of the boys who had been out on leave in the town as they came in. She was frightfully busy and bustling. At last she had hauled all the soldiers through the door and I followed her into the office.

'*Mais oui,*' she said, when at last she understood what I was after, 'he can go to Valencia if he wants to.'

'Will they send him in an ambulance?'

'Ah no, there is no transport going that way. We never send men to Valencia. If you can arrange the transport he can go.'

This was not a very bright prospect but I hoped I could fix something and we kidded ourselves we could do it. I wanted to speak to the doctor but, of course, he was up to his eyes in work. Jan said he not only operated but all the difficult dressings he had to do himself. I got hold of the pale English nurse and she said that when he had a moment she would ask him to have a word with me. She was paler than ever and soon afterwards had a breakdown from overwork and had to take a rest.

The doctor was doing dressings and a line of men were waiting to be attended to. He came out and I hardly recognised him. He must have lost at least a stone in weight and he had lost his colour too. He shrugged his shoulders and said he had no objection to Jan going to Valencia, but as to transport we must arrange that.

I went back to the ward. It was evening again. A rosy old man with walrus whiskers and a colossal beret appeared with two or three other people and started walking round. With them was a hard-faced female in a dark coat and also a beret, I think his wife. My presence seemed to annoy her and she called out suspiciously, 'Who is that woman?'

From all sides came a chorus of, '*C'est sa femme, sa femme,*' and that silenced her, though she still looked at me with disfavour.

The old man was André Marty, communist deputy and author of *Revolt in the Black Sea*. The book was about a mutiny of the French navy at the time of the Russian revolution, and allied intervention against it, in which he had taken part as a young sailor. The old sea dog went round the ward shaking hands with the men, asking them about their wounds and addressing them as *camarade* or *Genosse* according to nationality.

When he had gone, I asked Jan if they had many such distinguished visitors. 'Thorez came one day,' he said, 'he is a very hefty fellow, a thorough navvy. He is very popular. Harry Pollitt never came,' he continued. 'It doesn't matter to me but some of the English boys were very disappointed that he didn't come round as we heard he had been in Spain, and they had boasted to their French comrades that he would be sure to come, and I think he should have done.'

As I had to catch a bus very early in the morning I said goodbye to Jan that night.

At the hotel an aviator asked me to have dinner with him which I did. He looked like an Indian but was surprised when I guessed, rightly, that he was a Mexican. There were a lot of aviators at the hotel as a new airfield had been made near Murcia which we had seen, more or less camouflaged, from the car. One of them was an American we called Texas and he hailed me. We had a talk and he asked how his wife was. He was crazy about her and said he often got permission to make long-distance telephone calls to her. I told him she was well but did not tell him she was leading quite a gay life with other admirers.

That night I was awakened by loud knocking. I had asked to be called early and was not surprised it was still dark. In my sleepy state I was sure that I was only being called for the bus so I did not get up but merely shouted, '*Sí, sí*, I heard you.' The knocking continued and at last I went to the door in my night gown still with my eyes barely open. It was the police. I produced my papers and escaped from the encounter, though I had no brain, at such an hour, for Spanish explanations.

It was then midnight and it seemed I had only been asleep a

few minutes when I was really called for the bus, which left at six. Unwashed and weary I stumbled off. In the dark, a long queue of women was already waiting for bread. They had settled down happily; it was cold and some had made small fires; they were singing as they waited. Somehow I found this a heartening sight.

I had an hour or so to wait in Alicante but got back at about seven in the evening and rushed straight to the office with dread in my heart. Liston and Milly ran out to meet me and embraced me with much jubilation as if I had been the prodigal son and they swept me off to a café.

'Did the others get back?' I asked.

'Yes, last night. We went to meet them and were so surprised and disappointed when we saw you weren't with them.'

'We asked them what they had done with you,' said Milly.

'What did they say?' I asked nervously.

'Not a word. They sort of slunk off.'

'Did Fernsworth and Griffin say anything?'

'You bet they did, and plenty. They told us all about the ghastly time you all had.'

'Did Selke complain to you or Rubio about me? He said he'd get me fired,' I said.

'He hasn't said a word to us,' said Liston. 'He seemed to have his tail between his legs. And if he has said anything to Rubio I haven't heard anything of it.'

'If he gets you fired we'll all resign, won't we Liston?'

Liston assented to this and I felt cheered by so much solidarity. In fact, Selke's threats never materialised. Fernsworth, however, carried out his intention of making a formal complaint but he did not succeed in ousting Selke, who lasted several more months. Subsequently, Gerda went on her trip to the south and Jaén with another journalist. On this occasion she retained an interpreter, over whom she had cast her spell, and a car, and the journalist had to make his own way back on lorries. So the situation was probably similar. When he got back, he did not complain, he merely said, 'The young lady wanted to go on taking photographs.'

Chapter 11
Back to Valencia

Before I left for Almería, I had done everything possible to retain my room at the Inglés. I was very much put out to find, on my return, that my belongings had been transferred to Kitty's room. She had left a wild note saying that Tom had been wounded and she had gone to see him somewhere near Alicante. She had thought it a waste to keep two rooms. I felt that this would turn out badly but tumbled into bed as I was so tired. I was, however, wakened early by an air raid warning, the first in Valencia.

When I reached the office, I told Milly about her alleged cousin who I had found lying in the passage at the hospital. She said she had never heard of him. His surname was the same as hers, which happened to be Bennet. I was desperately tired and over-wrought and fainted, so I had to go back to my room and spend the rest of the day horizontal.

In the evening, they telephoned me from the hall to say that a friend was downstairs, and when he came up it was Humphrey. He said I was looking becomingly pale, like a Byronic heroine. He told me he was going back to England to report that the war was being lost. It was the time when the Italians were driving to cut communications between Valencia and Madrid. After this visit to England he gave up journalism and joined the Brigade, where he remained until he got typhoid.

Humphrey and I had a languid dinner together. I told him about Jan.

'Could he possibly ride in my little Ford?' he asked. 'I suppose not, it's too uncomfortable and Gabriel is such a bad driver.'

We went round to the Victoria to visit some people but it was a dry evening. That hotel had put up the '*no hay café*' (no coffee) sign that had long been up at the Inglés. They closed the shutters at night because of air raids and it was very hot indoors. My head ached and, at an early hour, Humphrey walked me home in the moonlight, past the *Tot Va Be*, and down the narrow passages that made a short cut between the two hotels.

The Guadalajara drive was on and the Spaniards were again wearing long and anxious faces. The next day *The Times'* man from Madrid arrived.[87] He was an imposing figure with a white beard, who wrote in longhand. As he never left Madrid and was now going home, his arrival caused some perturbation. He and his wife later returned and spent another winter in Madrid.

He was an amazing person. He had lived many years in Madrid, I think nearly twenty. Geographically he was familiar with all the country around Madrid. He could point out on the map every ditch and wall.

He would say, 'I know that road; it is very bad, must be impassable for heavy transport. I went over it some time ago when attending the Duchess of Alba's funeral and, to my knowledge, it has not been repaired since, and it was very bad then.'

He predicted that the Italians would come to grief at Guadalajara, however fast they seemed to be advancing, because of the lie of the land. They would find themselves in a certain valley from which there was no outlet, and they would be mown down. After he had gone to England, the Italians were duly routed at Guadalajara.

* * * * *

One afternoon I was in the lobby of the hotel when someone suddenly clapped me on the back and I heard a hearty 'Hello'. I could not at first place the figure with the bronzed face, wearing a leather jacket and aviator's helmet.

'Don't you remember the boat from Lisbon, deck-quoits?'

It was the man from Buenos Aires. Jan always called him 'the Greek', but I thought he was a very British bad hat.

'You don't know my name and I don't know yours, but never mind, come upstairs and have a brandy,' he said.

We went up to a large room where there were two aviators who gave me Lucky cigarettes and American magazines.

'Well,' said the man from Buenos Aires, 'how's your husband?'

'I'm sorry to say he's badly wounded.'

'Too bad. We had a lot of fun on that lousy boat, didn't we? I was on my way to Spain then and so, I suppose, were you, though none of us spoke of it.'

I did not ask him what he was doing as he made a mystery of it; I expect he was gun-running.

'I'm just flying down to Murcia this afternoon,' he said.

When I told him Jan was there he said he would look in on him, and apparently he did so to Jan's astonishment.

This strange, shady figure told me he had been 'mixed up' in a civil war in South America but that he seldom seemed to back the winning side and was down on his luck when we met him. He has now vanished but I cannot help thinking he must still be 'operating' somewhere where there is what he would call a 'spot of bother' going on.

After he had left, I formed a wild project to get him to bring Jan to Valencia by plane. Jan was now out of plaster though still immovable in bed. I wrote to him to ask if he could sit up and ride with his leg up on the seat opposite. I tried to find some big car that was going that way. I even wondered if he could travel on a bus. Nothing came of these ideas.

In a few days, Kitty was back. Moreover, she brought Tom Wintringham with her. They drove up in an open horse cab at lunch-time, Kitty, forceful as ever, Tom in uniform, with a limp and a stick and a wistful, convalescent smile. They had been to all the hotels in town to try to find a room; of course they had been unsuccessful. Tom was tired out after the journey. He had two weeks' sick leave, so I had to move out.

Milly had a spare bed in her room at the Victoria. The hotel would fill it with any female stranger so she never knew who she would find on returning from the office. She would be glad of a permanent occupant who she already knew. I bundled a few things into my rucksack and moved that evening. I disliked the hotel; it was more expensive than the Inglés and much noisier, and they did not serve breakfast in bed.

So I had another room mate, also American, also active and dynamic, also without Spanish. So, for her too, I had to go on shopping expeditions for stockings, bathing-suits and medicines.

She got to know everyone who spoke English and at meals we were generally six or more, celebrities, nonentities, all sorts. The hotel was the *rendez-vous* of journalists, and the official place to lodge visitors invited by the Government. The waiters were superlatively rude and furious at the excessive number of chairs we gathered round one table. As we could not have it in our room, even breakfast was a social meal. We generally had it with Barry. He worked for a news agency. I translated for him and went through the first set of Febus sheets before going to the office.

Barry said I looked like Alice in Wonderland because I used to wear a ribbon tied round my hair. He discovered that one could get to the beach by tram and he used to take me for walks there on Sunday afternoons. It was rather melancholy, more mud than sand, with open sewers running out to sea at intervals of a few yards, which one had to jump. There were also dead dogs and cats and, being the Mediterranean, no tide to wash them away. All along the shore were small bungalows. A searchlight was the only sign of war.

Barry, I gathered, had been unfortunate in his domestic affairs. In his wallet he carried a photo of his children which he showed to everyone. It was rather embarrassing to go out with him because he used to stop and talk to strange Spanish babies. He was particularly attached to a weazened little baby at the breast, which a gypsy woman used to carry round the cafés. He said it looked like Queen Victoria and always gave the mother something, though begging was forbidden. He really should have been a mother, not a father.

Milly, who was dreadfully short-sighted and always afraid her eyes were getting worse, always used to give to a blind old man who played *The Internationale* on a guitar in a back street by a burned-out church.

Sometimes in the evening, at the Victoria, as we sat in the lounge, with its oil paintings of sunny Spain on the walls, Barry would say the place reminded him of an ocean liner on which we were all bound on some interminable voyage with no prospect of ever reaching port.

'This place is hateful to me,' he said, putting down his empty glass and vainly trying to attract the attention of a waiter to order another drink. The waiters were expert at avoiding one's eye and sometimes told the guests that they had had enough to drink already.

'This is not Spain, nor America, nor England,' he said, 'it is just Limbo.'

'Yes,' I said, ' 'embryos and idiots, eremites and friars'.'

Milly went off into a peal of loud laughter, other people looked round and I was sorry I had spoken as I caught sight of the Canon of Córdoba sitting in a corner. He was in lay dress but I knew him.

A waiter came up and said, 'You should ring the bell if you want anything.'

'I did ring it,' said Barry. 'I want another whisky.'

The waiter looked at the clock. 'It's too late,' he said, 'we've decided not to serve drinks after eight so that people will go in to dinner on time.'

We had some additional helpers in our office now, including some to go out with visitors as interpreters. There was Aurora, petite, pretty and smart, who had been a secretary with some delegation in Geneva. There was Fernando, tall and handsome, with a moustache, a real *señorito*. At the beginning of the war he had been in the militia in the Guadarrama mountains and was always pining for the outdoor life, which he later returned to. Rubio said of him, 'He is the sort of young man who only joined the Party because the tennis clubs are closed.'

I think it was Conrad who said that there is always one Swede. We had Kajsa von Rothman.[88] She was a handsome giantess with red-gold flowing hair. She was also correspondent for a Swedish paper and typing in Swedish involved putting in lots of accents by hand. She had worked previously with Dr Bethune and had started in the war wearing trousers and riding a motorbike. With us she wore flowing, Isidora Duncan garments. She was said to have worked for a travel agency before the war. She used to bawl into the telephone: '*Aquí Kajsa, sabes, la sueca, alta, rubia!*'[89]

Among the guests at the Victoria were the last of the Malraux squadron. One of them, a big, rosy fair Frenchman, with a broken nose, spoke a little English and was on good terms with the American air attaché. The latter was also a very handsome man with smooth hair like an advertisement for brilliantine, and penetrating eyes, who went by the nickname of 'Pinky'. His fine, broad-shouldered form, in immaculate, dark blue uniform, usually graced the lobby, drink in hand. They were sometimes visited by Texas, very blond but mean looking, who had made a parachute jump which resulted, so he said, in his stomach turning upside down so that he had to wear a corset. Texas had been flying Russian planes and was loud in their praise.

Besides Pinky, who Milly had known in Honolulu, the American military attaché was living at the hotel. He was an old Southern colonel; he had a Spanish Baedeker and was always telling us about places of interest such as the Roman remains at Sagunto. The British consul also lived there until the food became too bad after which he 'boarded' at the Embassy. He was a typical Irishman, outwardly stout, warm and genial, inwardly steely. He got on very well with the anarchists with whom he had to deal at the port.

Sullivan was evidently picked for tough situations as he had held posts previously in Chicago and Marseilles.[90] The consul before him in Marseilles had been murdered. He told us, in a way that made it very droll, how he had spent his first three months there looking over corpses, in various stages of decomposition, that were dredged out of the harbour, and trying to make up his mind which of them was his unfortunate predecessor. He said that he had himself once been knocked on the head in Marseilles.

He spoke many languages so well, so fast and with such perfect enunciation that he made one think of an actor. He also played the piano and we used to gather round in the evenings to sing *The Tarpaulin Jacket* or *The Leather Bottle*, loudly if not tunefully, until the killjoy waiters stopped us. 'It's just FAI puritanism,' grumbled Sullivan.

He really liked the CNT-FAI and said they had given him a card stating that he was a member – the only member – of the union of diplomatic workers. He commissioned me to try to find him a red and black striped tie in the market, like an old school tie. However, anarchists do not wear ties. All the British diplomats had adopted, in jest, some part of the Popular Front, but no one wanted to belong to the POUM and it was foisted onto the subordinate wireless operator finally.

Sullivan was nicknamed *Komsomol* because it sounded like consul. This was the name of a Russian youth organisation and was also the name of a Russian food ship which had been sunk on its way to Spain. At the suggestion of [name missing], a *pionero's* fund was being raised to replace this ship. It was a childish idea and, after a few months, the subscription was closed but the little *pro-Komsomol* collectors in their red shirts were a familiar sight in the cafés. Sullivan collected *pro-Komsomol* literature and he had a poem, posters and stamps with the ill-fated vessel represented on them.

At that time, I acquired an admirer; a little German émigré writer. Milly said, 'Beware of little men; they are always mean.' He was a sad man, a born victim. 'I want to go to Russia, but what's the good of an unsuccessful Left writer going to Russia?' he would say.

After years of uncomfortable existence as an émigré, I expect he found the Victoria comparatively home-like but the manager, with an instinct for what he could get away with, had lodged him in a cupboard under the stairs used for keeping brushes and brooms, with a sloping ceiling and a small window at floor level. There, with a camp bed and one of the first typewriters ever invented, he lived surrounded by dusters and carpet-sweepers.

The cupboard was on our corridor and he used to pop out of it as I went by. He used to write me sentimental little notes in execrable French and shove them under our door late at night. I never found them until the next morning.

The Victoria had been the best hotel in town. It was ironical that, on the only occasion when I could afford to stay at a first class hotel, we should be on war rations and the place turned over to a committee of waiters at whose mercy we were.

It was not long after my move that Tom Wintringham appeared to suffer a relapse. He began to run a high temperature. We found a local doctor, smooth shaven, plump, bourgeois, with a soothing bedside manner. He thought he knew a little French but I was called in to translate. The fever might have been caused by Tom's partly healed wound. It might have been caused by bronchitis which he had also. But Dr Millán knew Valencia. He looked round at the bright spring weather, at the delicious wood strawberries on street barrows, he sniffed drains and he said, 'Just the time of year for typhoid and it always catches foreigners.' Samples were taken and sent to a laboratory to be analysed.

Meanwhile, Tom's fever went up and up. A day or two passed and the result came back – typhoid. Our alarm was increased by the word '*tifo*'. At first we thought it might be typhus.

'I had a friend who caught it in the Near East during the war,' said Basil Murray. He was unconscious for six months and when he woke up the war was over, the lucky fellow.'

'He was lucky to wake up,' said Milly. 'A woman I knew got it in Russia and she was ill for months and then died.'

'Unconscious all the time?' enquired Basil, hopefully.

'Unconscious or raving,' said Milly. 'In the Soviet Union, there is an inoculation possible against it, but they wouldn't have anything like that here.'

English-Spanish dictionaries, like maps of Spain, were unobtainable by that time, but there was one at the office which we studied. We asked the doctor if it was the same disease that they had feared would be brought by refugees from Málaga, carried by lice, and we found that it was *only* typhoid, as the doctor said, but Tom was dreadfully ill.

Kitty went first to ask for advice from the delegation of the Brigade. They told her he would have to go to the fever hospital outside town, which had a ghastly reputation, and that everything must go through the usual military channels. Tom was critically ill and the usual channels were not good enough for Kitty.

She nursed him herself, night and day, snatching a little rest on a mattress on the floor. At the same time, she was taking anti-typhoid injections. She had no experience of nursing but she followed all instructions to the letter. When I could, I went in to sit with him for a few hours while Kitty tore about and tried to make arrangements to have him removed from the hotel, which was imperative. The doctor had, of course, informed the hotel because of the need to disinfect the linen and utensils and the room itself after they had left. He was on the staff of one military hospital and knew all of them but none wanted to take an infectious case. At last a private room was secured in a small convalescent hospital. Then it was difficult to find a conveyance. There were plenty of ambulances but no one wanted to disinfect one afterwards. At last, a car was found and Kitty and Tom went off.

Kitty stayed at the hospital. She bought a spirit lamp to prepare Tom's food when he could take any. She had sent a telegram to England asking the Medical Aid people to send a trained nurse. The nurse came, but not until the crisis had passed. Kitty had then nursed Tom by day and the nurse at night. No one caught typhoid from Tom who, we surmised, had got it from a salad at the other hospital. Basil, who was sensitive to other people's troubles, used to go to sit with him.

At this time, naturally, Kitty was insatiable in her demands on us. Milly and I had to buy a bedside lamp, fresh vegetables in the market, extra pillows, white overalls for Kitty to wear. She managed miraculously well considering the difficulties she faced.

Kitty saved Tom's life but, after he had fully recovered, she was expelled from Spain as an undesirable. She always put this down to the machinations of the British Communist Party, of which Tom's wife was a faithful member.

Kitty bequeathed to me the duty of writing her articles for the *Manchester Guardian*, but I think she only wrote in a very unofficial capacity. The *Guardian* had no regular correspondent in Spain, but occasionally sent one in on a visit.

During this episode, I started taking anti-typhoid shots, one a week for four weeks, which Dr Millán gave me at the Museum Clinic. He put them in my back as he did not want to incapacitate me for typing, but I always had a very bad reaction. He was short of hypodermic needles and the one he used was terribly blunt. The Museum Clinic was really a casualty station, always open for accident cases or victims of air raids.

Also during this time Stephen Spender, the poet, turned up.[91] I saw him one afternoon in the outer room at the office where he was patiently waiting to see Rubio. No one was there as it was only three o'clock. He was a very tall, thin young man, with open collar and a leather jacket. He had a rather bony, Viking face and wildly straying hair. He looked red and wind-blown and rather distrait. He showed me a letter inviting him to speak on radio UGT. There was no broadcasting station in Valencia and I broke this news to him. He went on to Madrid and also to Albacete where he had obtained the entrée before leaving England.

He came back one day and joined us for lunch at the Victoria. I was feeling awful after a typhoid shot and some people were advising wine and others were advising against it.

Spender was much upset by what he had seen in Albacete. He was not indiscreet but he had been shaken. He said that, in order to win the war, all the things for which we were fighting had to be given up. That was disillusioning. He did not like the stranglehold the Party was establishing over the Brigades. He said that in Albacete they were singing, 'Deviation, deviation, deviation from the Line, thou are lost and gone forever, Oh my darling Clementine!' He did not like the newspaper censorship which was very obvious because, after the papers had been set up, whole columns were blotted out so that they looked like Sanskrit; sometimes just the headlines remained and from those we tried to guess what the columns had been about.

I think the Republican Government was becoming uneasy about the Communists too. It was a Popular Front but the Communists were trying to steal the show and they had Russia behind them, or thought they had, while the Government was still trying to placate the democracies. In addition, there were secret police operating over whom the Government had no control.

Partly because he wanted occupation and partly out of kindness, as I was doubled up with back ache, Spender sat down and addressed hundreds of envelopes for me at the office that afternoon, slowly and painstakingly, his tall figure bent over the typewriter, his long fingers picking out the letters.

In one respect, Spender seemed to fit into the scene better than Auden had done. He made friends with all the Spanish advanced poets and intellectuals and assisted in translating their work. Poets seem to get on regardless of nationality and I remember one calling on Spender at the hotel and presenting him with some lovely old calf-skin volumes of Shakespeare because he had mentioned that he had no Shakespeare with him and wanted to look at one of the plays.

* * * * *

When the nurse arrived for Tom, she caused a sensation. She was a lovely, earnest creature called Patience.[92] She was tall, thin, angular and virginal. She had a mass of ash-blond hair done up in a bun, but usually covered by a white kerchief. Her face was pointed and eager, with a full mouth, rather large nose and very striking, very blue eyes. She used to come into the office in the afternoons to read the English papers and became popular with the journalists and British Embassy personnel. She looked like the kind of beautiful hospital nurses one dreams of and, when she came to lunch with me one day Kurt, the German writer, murmured, 'Miss Barclay, *A Farewell to Arms.*'

Patience's only rival for the honour of being the most popular woman in Valencia was Mary Mulliner, sometimes called Madame Mulliner, and by Milly '*La Mulliner.*'[93] She was quite a different type to Patience, a little stout and matronly she appealed to men who liked someone kind and motherly. She was also fair, bleached as she was going grey. She dressed as though for a bridge party in Bournemouth, in floral silks, her hair looking as though she had crimped it herself with tongs. She had a milk and roses complexion and a soft Irish voice, was very feminine and a nice little woman.

Her appeal was chiefly to the British. Kurt said she was a cow and the most '*coolant*' (gluey) woman he had ever met and fled when she approached. She was certainly a lion-hunter. At every meal she was seen *tête-à-tête* with a different celebrity, the Governor of the Bank of Spain, or a general or some diplomat. A command of schoolgirl French enabled her to chat with most people. She was very conventional and was always worrying about her reputation.

Her reputation was that of a mystery woman. She lived in a sort of bridal suite at the Victoria, with a private bath, seemed to have plenty of money, and said she wrote for provincial papers. She did not often appear at the press office. She said her husband was a tea-planter. Perhaps we should not have doubted her account of herself if she had not had such an evasive manner as if she were always inventing some tale on the spur of the moment. She did flirt but could never be convicted of having an affair with anyone. She behaved so much like a spy that, in my opinion, it was impossible that she could have been one.

'I'll tell you what it is,' one journalist suggested, 'it amuses her to *think* she is a spy. It's just harmless pretence.'

If she was a spy, I could not guess which side employed her. At the Victoria there were spies and detectives spying on them and people under house arrest, so it was rather confusing.

Mrs Mulliner had some sort of pull with the hotel manager which enabled her to get good rooms at reduced prices, and she had diplomatic pull which procured her a perpetual supply of cigarettes and food from the warships.

She was very social and the moving spirit in several festivities that took place at this time. One was a Press luncheon. This took place at the Ideal Rooms in the Calle de la Paz, which had been the best restaurant in Valencia. The luncheon was given by the American military attaché. The dear old man was very fond of Mary. It was quite grand with nosegays of violets beside the plates of each lady guest.

On another occasion, there was a little dinner at the British Embassy, to which Patience and myself were invited. I bought a pair of stockings and a new hair ribbon for the occasion. Patience could appear in uniform and Mary had plenty of dressy clothes.

The Embassy was housed in the usual sombre Spanish palace with tapestried walls and dark, heavy furniture. I was painfully on my best behaviour and did not dare to take a second helping of anything. I had quite lost the knack of getting along with public school types and felt my accent was very vulgar. I could hear Patience across the table becoming very earnest and rather shrill about Medical Aid in Spain.

'How many are there in your unit? Really? So many. I had no idea it was such a big show,' said her neighbour politely.

When we were getting into the car to be driven home and the *Chargé d'Affaires* was wishing us goodbye he said, 'Well, I hope we shall see more of you now that the ice has been broken.' I was not invited again.

Finally, Mary borrowed a summer villa and invited a party of us to dinner. She liked to assemble incongruous groups and this party contained a fair sample. Milly, Micky and I were asked, also Griffin Barry and Basil Murray and a 'very important' political commissar from the Brigade, an Italian, called Gino. He was a short, thickset man with the neck and shoulders of a bull and a fine Roman head. He had a small car into which we all crammed with much merriment.

Mary was staying at the villa and when we arrived, after some rough riding over tram-lines and cobblestones in the pitch dark, she welcomed us in like a suburban hostess. Basil was already there and had mixed cocktails. He was ineffectually engaged in opening a tin of chicken, obtained by Mary's mysterious influence.

There was a maid in black with a white apron who waited at table. She was a very old peasant but looked quite like an old family retainer. The meal went off in a lively manner after the cocktails. At the end of the dinner we drank toasts and Mary got up and she made a little speech. She asked us all to state in turn what we had come to Spain for.

It was like a series of responses in church, as we each got up and began our declarations with a routine solemn: '*Parce que je suis anti-fasciste.*'[94] We had to speak French because Gino and his driver did not understand English. I said, '*Parce que je suis anti-fasciste et mon mari est blessé de la Brigade,*'[95] at which Gino clapped and said I was the only one who had given a good reason and a true one.

I could see why Gino was a commissar: he was a born leader with a strong personality, full of animal magnetism, and with a hypnotic gaze. He was accustomed to organising people, having to occupy his charges' spare time, and after dinner he soon had us dancing in a ring what he alleged to be the Carmagnole.

We also sang the Marseillaise and '*Oh ça ira, ça ira, les aristocrats seront pendus*'[96] which we did with the greatest gusto, hopping about hand in hand.

However, Mary was never satisfied unless she had some melodrama going on, something more personal than jolly community singing. She tried to work something up. She tried to make Basil, poor dear, limp rag that he was, jealous of Gino who was aggressively virile. Gino was paying more attention to the young and juicy Micky. He tried to lure her into the garden, where there was a fountain and orange trees, but the night was too cold.

Then Mary told some preposterous story about how, next morning, she was going to drive to Paris with a Pole but nobody cared and Gino merely said, '*Oh, assez des Polonais, je m'en fous des Polonais.*'[97]

We all gathered round the fire. Suddenly she announced, 'It is midnight. The last train has gone. You will have to stay the night here.' The place was served by an electric railway on which we had planned to return.

This time she had really started something and a storm of protest arose. Basil could not have squeezed into the car but Gino refused to take any of us back. He said he could not park his car on the street or it would be stolen and the garage would be locked up by now. It appeared that we really would have to stay.

'But you must all be out of my house by seven in the morning,' Mary stated darkly.

'Why?' we all shouted.

'Because at half-past seven the Pole is coming with his car.'

We were not impressed. Mary wrung her hands. She took each of us aside and said that she was sure Gino and Basil would fight the Pole, and at all costs they must be prevented from meeting. We said that it was entirely her affair.

It got later and later, the wind howled, the fire sank and, what with the remoteness of the house and Mary's well-simulated despair at obstacles which seemed to us to be completely imaginary, the whole thing began to resemble a bad play.

Barry, very sensibly, went to be in a room with the chauffeur while the rest of us were still discussing where we should sleep. Accommodation was limited, Mary was fussing about the proprieties, and we soon reached a deadlock. She invited Milly to share her double-bed and lent her a diaphanous night-gown. There remained two rooms, one with a double-bed and one with two singles. Micky and I grabbed the two single beds. After we had retired there came a knock on the door.

It was Basil. Men never liked to share what the Spaniards call a *matrimonio*, particularly when the bed is small, and when one of them is stout enough emphatically to require a whole bed to himself, and even less when they are supposed to be jealous rivals. Basil and Gino were still up and arguing with Mary.

235

'Look here,' said Basil, 'it's impossible. You must see that. Won't you two change with us?'

We were half asleep already, but it was very cold, there were not enough blankets, so we agreed to change as we thought we would be warmer together.

The next day we got up in a filthy temper but were just beginning to brighten up at the sight of coffee when the sound of a car was heard.

'Hush,' said Mary, 'it's the Pole. Please don't show yourselves. I'll go out and reason with him.'

'To hell with the Pole,' said Milly, who had a hangover. 'The coffee will get cold.'

Basil and Gino were not looking like fighting anybody. Basil was drooping in a corner; Gino glaring in front of him looking rather green as dark men do when they are cold.

'I've had about enough of *La Mulliner's* antics,' said Milly.

Mary returned shortly and we heard the car drive away.

'I've decided not to go to Paris,' she announced momentously. 'I've persuaded the Pole to go away.'

Silence. Basil looked out of the window.

'It's a fine day,' he said. 'I think I'll go for a walk in the mountains.'

'Oh, but you can't,' said Mary. 'I forbid you to stay after the others. What would the servant say? What would the neighbours think?'

The neighbouring villas were uninhabited.

Basil persisted in his intention. He said he needed solitude and to commune with nature. The fire was smoking and making our eyes sting. We all looked sourly at each other and could not understand how we had come to sing 'the aristocrats will be hanged' with such harmony and abandon the previous night.

Gino's driver did not want to take us back; he said something about the springs of the car but we did not want to risk spending half the day on a station platform. The electric railway was one of the proudest collective enterprises of the CNT and we did not trust its efficiency.

We all piled into the car much as before. But when one is not feeling expansive and cheery, sitting on top of people with arms

236

wound round their necks is very uncomfortable particularly if they deliberately make themselves bony and unyielding. I am too tall for sitting on knees and kept knocking my head on the roof as the driver took the cobblestones with a heartless disregard for the jolting of his passengers.

When we were fairly off the premises, Gino opened his mouth for the first time that morning.

'It's an outrage,' he said, 'I have never been so treated.'

'Yes,' said Barry, 'too bad not to tell us the time. Getting stuck like that. It would be just my luck to get scooped.'

'That clown, Mary,' said Milly, wiping her glasses which had been misted by smoke.

'It's monstrous,' went on Gino, beating his breast, 'to sleep the night in a house, me, and not to sleep with a woman! Not only that but for *all* the women to sleep separate from all the men. I never heard of such a thing. Never before have I undergone such a humiliating experience, never. And before my driver, too. You can see the boy is laughing at me; you can see it by the way he is driving.'

'Yes,' gasped Milly, on whose knee I was perched and whose head struck me on the chin at a sudden bump.

'An English house-party, huh?' said Gino sarcastically, and relapsed into a moody silence, his phenomenal chest swelling still more with indignation and nearly precipitating Barry, who was but a morsel of a man, out of the window from which his head and arms were already hanging.

At lunch at the hotel, we were able to laugh about it and were joined by the Consul and Gino who, though ideological opposites, had a good time quoting Dante together.

Marion Merriman turned up because her husband, Bob, had been wounded. She appeared in the office one morning, looking very hot in a fur-trimmed coat and carrying a hat-box. She was an attractive girl, well-groomed, with brown eyes, long legs and splendid teeth, a typical nice American college girl, but with a very harassed look.

'Gee, she looks fretted,' commented Milly.

She came back to our room to wash and change and park her bags.

'I had a dreadful time with the Prefect of Police in Paris,' she said. 'I had to weep over him and swear my husband was dying before he would give me a permit to come. I came on the plane, gosh it was lovely flying over the Pyrenees in the early morning. It cost me nearly my last cent but I was in a hurry, and they are nicer to you in Paris if you travel by air.'

Bob was in Murcia. While she tidied herself, Milly and I told her about Jan.

'Maybe I could bring them both back here, somehow,' she said. 'Anyway, I'll try. How I hate wars and politics and men who will fight. You may be sure I'll do my damndest to get Bob right out of Spain and the whole business. The worst of it is he believes in the cause you know. It's going to take some doing. I've brought his palm beach suit with me and I just imagine us lounging on some '*plage*' on the Riviera, so he can get over this and forget all about the war. Maybe you and Jan could come too?' she said, turning to me.

'How I wish it could be,' I replied.

She seemed so young, from a different world, still believing in normal human happiness, which we had all forgotten.

Basil took a great fancy to Marion. He borrowed some money from her and then bought her a huge bouquet, and insisted on accompanying her as far as Alicante. While there he found the light on and a policeman in his room in the middle of the night.

When he returned he was called to the police to explain a telegram which she had sent him to announce her safe arrival. It was so full of feminine names, some messages for us, that the police thought it was in code. These incidents upset Basil.

Marion wrote to me several times. She found Bob with a shattered shoulder. It had happened after only a few days at the front when Bob was temporary commander of the Lincoln Battalion. The first commander, a tailor from Chicago, sound in politics but not in nerves, had gone mad the first night. He led a lot of men out up a moonlit slope and those who were not killed crawled back as best they could, and he had to be locked up.

The x-ray machine happened to be out of order so Bob's shoulder had not been set properly and had to be re-broken and set again. Then they ran out of surgical plaster and set it in builders' plaster which, as Marion said, 'weighs about a ton, so after he has been walking about half an hour he is tired out and sweating and has to rest.'

They went up to Madrid for a few days so that Bob could speak on the radio and this changed Marion's attitude completely.

She wrote, 'I am ashamed of all I said about getting out of the war. I am 100 per cent behind Bob in his work here. I shall stay. Later he will be able to go to Albacete to train fresh recruits. Bob is in the hospital that was the University and Jan in the Secondary School. I go to see Jan often. He still can't move and is in bed. I admire his cheerfulness and courage.'

Basil Murray was a most unhappy man. I do not remember what reason he gave for being in Spain at Mary's party, but I guessed it was personal. He was employed by a News Agency but it was a quite unsuitable job for him. Every day, in the square, there was a performing goat which stood, with all four legs together, on top of a pole. This amused him and he frequently mentioned it in his despatches; such frivolity shocked the censor. After a few months of this he was fired.

The Agency sent a replacement called Angelopoulos who signed his despatches 'Angel'.[98] If Basil had been too lethargic a correspondent, Angel was in some way too active, for he was imprisoned. None of us liked him, but we felt we ought to stand together, so we presented Rubio with a petition for his release. Rubio was a clever talker. He told us that Angel was much more comfortable in prison than we were at the Victoria as he had a whole cell to himself. However, after the fuss, he was released and expelled from Spain. Unfortunately. all this happened too late for Basil to know about it.

The loss of his job affected Basil's spirits a good deal; I do not know how well off he was but he would not consider going home. Sometimes he would talk about joining the Brigade; sometimes a pretty yacht in the harbour would catch his eye and he would suggest going sailing – as if the police would have allowed that! He was thoroughly *désorienté*, the only person I knew in Spain quite unattached to life. Lots of people said they were 'fed up' and wanted to 'end it all', but somehow, when a war is on and one's tenure of life becomes more precarious, one clings to existence more intensely.

I was not able to see much of him as I shared a room with Milly, who had no use for futile intellectuals. His room was on our corridor and he used to try to waylay us and urge us to come and talk and drink with him. I am afraid we were all very heartless and he never could get anyone to take him seriously. He was sensitive when everyone else was being tough.

He bought a monkey with sad brown eyes a bit like his own. The management protested but he said, 'What about all the other monkeys who live here?' and they gave way. It was not a nice monkey; it was too big for a pet and very ill-tempered. It had a habit of snatching at one through the open door as one passed, as if conniving with its master to drag visitors in. He named it after a girl he had been in love with.

He was chronically lonely but used to try to work up some interest in girls occasionally.

'I had Aurora to lunch,' he said one day. 'She's a pretty little thing and a nice girl too.'

'Very nice,' I said.

'No good, of course, not that I really care. She's engaged. Even these *modern* Spanish girls are no go. All Spanish girls are either whores or forbiddingly respectable. It's quite Victorian; there is nothing in between.'

'The Socialist Youth (of which Aurora was a member) are very pure and moral,' I explained. 'You see it's the first time those girls have been emancipated and allowed to go about on their own and work. So the boys feel it's up to them to treat them with the utmost respect.'

'Have some strawberries,' said Basil.

'What about typhoid? You haven't been inoculated.'

'Oh, never mind, we'll drown them in kirsch to kill the germs.'

One evening I was told he was ill and went up to see him. He was sallow with brilliant eyes. He was much excited, made a great fuss, and demanded a doctor. I thought he was putting it on as he complained so much more than Tom had ever done. He had been very sick. He said he had lunched on shrimps and beer. I did not want to disturb Dr Millán as it was ten o'clock, but Basil insisted that he could not wait until the morning so I telephoned and stayed to translate.

Several friends came up to the room, including Pinky and the French aviator. We all stood around the bed. The monkey had gone. Basil was yellow and waxen, his big eyes very luminous. He showed us a towel on which he had spat blood. The doctor looked at the bottle of whisky and the bottle of sleeping pills beside the bed. He diagnosed internal inflammation. Basil complained of pain in the diaphragm and difficulty in breathing. The doctor said it was probably a gastric ulcer and he must keep very still and eat and drink nothing.

Basil was quite clever in his head and conversation. He had no fever but a weak pulse. He said that in the afternoon he had walked about as it seemed to ease the pain, and that he was very thirsty and had drunk two bottles of Vichy water. The bottles were rolling about on the floor. The doctor told him only to suck lumps of ice.

When we got outside, I told the French aviator that Basil was always inclined to feel sorry for himself, and wanted attention, but I thought he exaggerated his symptoms and that there was not much the matter with him.

The next day, when Patience came to the hotel, I told her Basil was in bed and suggested she might go up and have a look at him. When she came back she scolded me for my indifference.

'He's a very sick man,' she said. 'If it's a gastric ulcer it's dangerous, but I don't think it's that. He's much too ill to be left to what attention the hotel can give him.'

She fetched a few things from the hospital and stayed all night with Basil. She contacted the consul, and arranged an ambulance to take him to Alicante the next day. She accompanied him and took him on board an English hospital ship which was anchored off there.

When she came back she said, 'It's pneumonia. I suspected it from the peculiar way his nostrils dilated, and the ship's doctor confirmed it. They are giving him oxygen and doing all they can.'

But Basil died at sea, floating between Alicante and Marseilles and, to the last, trying to send radio messages to various women. The consul paid his debts. Mary was away at the time of Basil's death but on her return she assumed he had died on her account and that she could have prevented it. She put on black.

Not long after this, she left on a warship and gave away a lot of her things on departure. Milly received a bottle of perfume and I was to receive a pound of butter but the waiters embezzled it.

Chapter 12
April 1937

Milly went away on a couple of trips so there was a social lull and I used to eat either with Kurt or Seldes. Seldes was the sort of boy who could not get on for five minutes without his wife or some female to listen to him, but Helen, after she left the blood transfusion service, would not remain idle. She was a laboratory worker and, hearing that a laboratory was to be set up in Murcia, she went there. When she arrived, naturally, there was no laboratory but the hospitals were over-crowded and understaffed and she was pressed into service. She knew nothing of nursing but, as an American girl, she was probably more adaptable than the average Spanish girl.

Helen was not in the same hospital as Jan. She had charge of a huge ward with forty beds. According to Seldes's account her labours were pretty ghastly; the dressings she had to do, the interminable hours she had to work in order to get through attending the patients somehow.

Seldes pretended to be hard-boiled about it and said it was a valuable experience for her. I admired her – she stuck it for months until her physical strength gave out. However, it was obvious that he was longing for some excuse to get her away, but as a good anti-fascist he could not summon her to Valencia out of selfishness, because he missed her, when she was so necessary at her post.

He went to see her for a couple of days.

'Well, how was Helen?' I asked when he came back.

'She's awfully tired,' he admitted. 'She must be. She burst into tears when she saw me and that's not like Helen. But she had been on duty then for twenty-four hours at a stretch. It was an emergency, but then it always seems to be an emergency at that hospital.'

'How is the hospital?'

'Better than the one Jan is in – which isn't saying much. Jan is in the worst organised hospital I have ever seen.'

'Why don't you tell Helen to quit? You know you want her to.'

'I? Not at all. I think it is a fine experience for her. Of course it's hard on the nerves at first; seeing raw wounds when you don't know what is tendon and what bone.'

'It's not fit. She's not awfully strong. You wouldn't like it yourself.'

'I approve. It's all right,' said Seldes obstinately. 'I have my own newspaper work.'

He launched into some of the long words that he did not know how to pronounce or what they meant. Milly used to say, 'I can't think where that boy was raised. He has positively *no* background.' She always said that I had such a lot, as if it were an aura. I was comforted by knowing that Helen was in Murcia as well as Marion. I liked them both and knew they would visit Jan and help him to while away the time.

* * * * *

'I often wonder about that old woman who looks like a madame,' said Seldes one day. 'She's sitting behind you now.'

'You mean the one with the improbable yellow hair?'

'Sure enough. She has a couple of young girls with her. Must be white slavery.'

'They live on our floor, which is the cheapest in the hotel.'

'Ever entertain in their room?'

'Yes, they have a few visitors in the evenings, but several men come at once and talk. They are Spaniards.'

'One of the girls has a black eye today.'

I craned my neck round cautiously.

'I have no idea of the connection of that girl with the old lady; perhaps a servant. But the other girl is her daughter, I'm told. I think her daughter is engaged to one of the French aviators – not the one who drinks brandy at breakfast but the quiet one. She is always very carefully chaperoned, too.'

'Well, if we were in America I'd take my oath the old lady was a madame.'

The old lady had uncombed, badly dyed, frowsy hair and a very lined, ugly face, so she did look like a broken-down woman of pleasure. The daughter had raven hair and was as beautiful, as pale, and about as lively as a Greek marble. The mother came to breakfast in a dingy kimono; the daughter swept into dinner, eyes modestly downcast, wearing a long dark blue cloak.

Later, I learned that the old lady was an aristocrat who earned a living by betraying her former friends to the police. She did it for her daughter's sake for she had been left without means, her husband either shot or left on the other side.

Eventually, the Spanish Aphrodite disappeared and we were told that she had died suddenly. Then the old lady slipped up and got into trouble. Some friends, suspecting that they were about to be arrested, gave her some jewellery to take care of for them and she stuck to it instead of handing it over to the authorities. When arrested, the friends told the police about the jewellery.

The old lady was put under house arrest and had meals in her room. I often saw her, in her kimono, weeping and lamenting into the telephone in the corridor on our floor, trying to get people she knew to exonerate her. She was very broken up by these two misfortunes, which came close together, and aged rapidly.

We seldom saw her after the daughter died except when there were air raid warnings. These terrified her very much and she was always the first one down in the hall, her sordid kimono barely covering her stout nakedness, anxiously screwing her diamonds into her ears.

Another time, I was lunching with Seldes one Sunday. I had been at the office to look over the papers. Spanish daily papers came out on Sunday but not on Monday. All morning we had been disturbed by blaring brass bands marching round the town. When I faced Seldes's pretty, pouting face across the table, I asked him if he had heard the bands. The anarchists had the best bands in town though there was a certain monotony about *The Internationale* and *Hijo del Pueblo*.

'It's an anarchist plot,' said Seldes in a whisper.

'I didn't seen anything sinister about it,' I said. 'They were collecting for the *Hospitales de Sangre*. Kids were selling postcards and sticking up posters in cafés.'

'It was a show of strength.'

'Not much of a show then, the same bands and procession came round several times like an army in an opera, and half of them were street urchins.'

'They forced the cafés to stick the posters up with threats.'

'The posters were only of a gigantic Red Cross nurse supporting a diminutive soldier in the palm of her hand. Freud would have something to say about some of these posters. But I wish that as soon as we get one that is really a work of art they would not paste it over with something else immediately. There are altogether too many.'

'You know there is a war of posters on here,' said Seldes. 'As fast as the communists stick up something like *Mando Único (Unified Command)* the anarchists come in the night and cover it up with *No envenenéis a la infancia (Don't Poison Childhood)* or something. And the CNT have the graphic arts union in their pocket.'

Seldes looked petulant.

'I like *Don't Poison Childhood*,' I said, 'and I like *Love the Birds and the Beasts* – the one that shows a child apparently stroking a large cockroach – and I like that one resembling a Braque in brown, that shows a face side-view and front-view at the same time, reading a book called *What is Anarchy?*'

'I don't pretend to be artistic,' said Seldes, 'but you seem to miss the significance of these things. Also it must be Anarchism, not Anarchy. That poster *Don't Poison Childhood* is only because they have no child organisation themselves.'

This poster showed a child in tears being offered shirts of different colours and pushing them away.

'Every time I see that poster of a hand grasping three books like a sandwich, Marx, Bakunin and Lenin, with Bakunin in the middle, I think I'm going nuts,' said Seldes. 'If you'd read any of them you'd see how illogical it is.'

'Several people have told me I'm *analfabeta*,' I said humbly. 'I'm reading some but I can only get them in Spanish and I haven't much time.'

'You needn't bother with Bakunin,' said Seldes, 'or *Seven Red Sundays* either,' which he saw I had with me, 'it's quite superficial.'

'Have you read it?'

'No, I wouldn't waste my time.'

My other companion was Kurt. We sometimes went to the beach. He was always promising to borrow a friend's car but in the end we always went to Las Arenas by tram. Kurt was rather a snob and boasted about his friend who was in the Brigade and had an official car. This friend was very conscientious and would never lend his car for jaunts of pleasure – also it would have been confiscated if he had been discovered doing this.

'I was at the Russian Embassy last night,' Kurt would say with pride. 'I must contrive to take you there one day.'

'What does one get if one goes there?'

'Marvellous coffee and cigarettes.'

'All right, I'll go.'

He never managed to arrange this either.

When Milly came back from Paris, the food situation seemed worse, or she grumbled more. 'Why, you can see even the fish here are puny and half starved.'

The waiter, with a dexterous and professional flip of two forks, was dealing us each two skinny, bony, little frizzled objects.

'I don't know what it is about revolutionary upheavals,' said Milly, 'but it is always the same. The place gets invaded by cranks, one eats nothing but fish and there is a shortage of soap. It was the same in Russia. Now they won't give us clean towels and serviettes and when they do they are grey.'

'I think things smell worse when they come back from the wash than before they go,' I said.

'In Russia they smelt of fish. I can't think what they make soap of here.'

'It's waste from olives – it came up this morning when I was translating the new official price list. It wasn't in the dictionary and I had to ask Coco.'

'Here come the social service workers,' said Milly.

'How do you know they are?'

'By the look of them. That woman with greasy hair in a net, and a pinafore dress couldn't be anything else.'

'I think she's Swiss and the others are Belgians. What are they doing here exactly?'

'Investigating conditions,' said Milly sarcastically, but added, 'they are all right. They mean well, especially the Quakers. They do a lot of good. They bring food. They look after kids. Friends are more help than comrades sometimes.'

'*Los amigos cuaqueros*,' I said, for that was what they were called in the papers.

'I want to speak to Garratt,' said Milly, and went over to him.

Garratt was a quiet, blond, clean, rosy man with glasses, looking somehow clerical, who was in command of the Joint Committee bus drivers. He was neutral, seemed to shun soldiers as compromising, appeared to take no interest in politics, would not allow his drivers to talk to journalists. He was, within the limits of prudence, a good-natured person and always very civil so I asked him if any of his buses could fetch Jan. Either because he would not meddle, as he was only supposed to help non-combatants, or because it was impracticable, he refused.

'The buses don't go that way any more. We use them exclusively for evacuating children from Madrid; and soon we shall give that up.'

'Why?'

'Because the parents won't let them go. We have the hardest work to collect any children now. I shall return to England shortly.'

'Oh, really. I am sorry to hear that.'

Garratt smiled and said, blushing, 'I feel I am a great fraud really. I am not of much use here. When I return I intend to advocate a change of policy on the part of the committee. There are plenty of vehicles here already that are out of action for lack of petrol. The main thing now is to pour food into Spain as fast as we can, especially milk, and especially to Madrid.'

I knew very little about Garratt; I knew he had been the *Manchester Guardian* correspondent in Abyssinia. I was surprised when he later produced a book, *Mussolini's Roman Empire*, in which I was touched to find a piece praising the International Brigades.[99]

The current view was expressed in this remark by one of the British diplomats, 'I do not see why we should stand in the way of these fellows who come and get killed in Spain. We shall get rid of a lot of undesirables this way.'

* * * * *

We had not seen the last of the disgruntled Bennet, the International who said he was Milly's cousin. When I was leaving the office one day, I ran into him in the street. I did not want him to go up to the office or find out where it was and, as he followed me, we walked along a back street. He made me feel very uncomfortable. He stumped along, limping heavily, leaning on a stick. I could see the limp was put on.

'You never gave my message to Milly.'

'Yes, I did.'

'She never communicated with me.'

'She said you were no relation of hers; that she had never heard of you.'

'Oh, she did. Well I know a few things that would dish her if I chose to talk. Where does she live?'

'I shan't tell you.'

'The American consul will. I'm on my way to him now. I have some interesting information to give him about the Brigade.'

'You wouldn't be such a rotter as to gab to him about the Brigade!' I cried. 'How did you get here anyway? I believe you are a deserter.'

'Nothing like that,' he said, with a grin that made him look more rat-like than ever. 'The police haven't got a thing on me. Bennet's too smart for that. I've got my discharge from Albacete all signed and sealed. Want to see it?'

He forked it out of his wallet and it looked genuine enough, but I was still doubtful.

'No Internationals are being allowed to leave Spain now, not even permanently disabled ones,' I said. 'How did you come by that paper? Not honestly?'

He could not resist showing off and, after a lot of hush-hush and making me promise not to repeat it, he admitted that he had obtained it on false pretences. 'I went to an American officer in Murcia. Yes, a fine, noble communist. I told him I had telegraphed the consul that I was being detained against my will.

I threatened to make a big scandal. The fellow was scared stiff and telephoned Albacete to send my discharge.'

'You hadn't got any message through to the consul, because you couldn't have done.'

'Of course not. But the story worked, didn't it? I got my discharge and here I am.'

'It was just a piece of dirty blackmail. Now I hope you will be satisfied and go home quietly and cause no more trouble. What do you keep following me around for? Do you want money?'

'No, I got my back pay and plenty.' He showed me a roll of notes.

'Then quit bothering me. Just because I had a soft spot for you when you were down whining in the hospital is no excuse to take advantage and pester the life out of me now.'

With difficulty, I shook him off for the time being.

There was quite a number of deserters floating about just then. I saw a couple of Indians in a café and Milly, who collected her mail from the consulate, said she encountered a large black man there, sitting behind the door, very scared.

The American consul treated deserters more kindly than ours did. Ours said, 'I was in the Great War myself. I went as a volunteer but when I got to France and didn't like it I never thought that I could run home again. I have more respect for those men who stick it and go on fighting than for these sneaking cowards. Between ourselves, I have got most of the deserters off my hands. I let them sleep on a stone floor and give them three pesetas a day to eat on and they soon get fed up with dodging the police here and desert back again.'

I laughed. 'I am told that when they get back, they float about unclassified because the administration is too busy to nail them down, and they are known as 'the ghosts of Albacete',' I said.

Bennet did manage to corner Milly and she said, 'He certainly is a nasty piece of work but he didn't get much change out of me. I sympathise with those boys who are just scared and not cut out by nature to be soldiers though they did not know it, but he is such a revengeful bastard. He wants to damage us all and will talk plenty when he gets back to the States, I'm afraid.'

'Anyone can see what a swine he is and would discount

anything he said.'

'Some fascist newspaper would gladly make use of a sorehead like that for their own purposes,' said Milly.

One night on my return to the hotel, I found Bennet, offensively drunk, lying in wait for me in the lobby. The manager looked worried, said the man would not go away and was very abusive.

'Hello,' said Bennet, seizing me by the arm. 'Dodging me, eh? I'd like you to answer me a few questions about that precious Brigade and the way it's run. Just a bunch of reds, they are, red agitators.'

'Shut up.'

'You're a communist, aren't you?'

'No. And I'm not responsible for the Brigade, either.'

'Well, what about your boyfriend?'

'You leave him out of it,' I said angrily, for he was shouting at the top of his voice and all the very mixed audience was staring at the two of us.

'Communists, all of you. You could have let me out of here sooner. I was just kidnapped.' He looked around to see what impression he was making.

'Don't be silly. Jan has no influence in the Brigade; he isn't even an officer. You are bringing your complaints to the wrong shop. You are drunk, get out of here,' and I tried to push him towards the exit.

'Drunk am I?' he said with indignant belligerence. 'Not too drunk to know what I am talking about, and trying to push a wounded man downstairs, are you? I'll go when I choose to go.'

The big French aviator with the broken nose was standing in a corner watching us.

'I don't know what that type is to you,' he said, 'but do you want me to throw him out? Because I will *avec plaisir*.'

'Better avoid a worse scene, if possible, thank you very much.'

However, Bennet was daunted by the Frenchman and stumbled off, still muttering. He must have been repatriated for we saw no more of him.

As Seldes was American, I told him about Bennet.

'It's difficult to know what to do about fellows like that,' he admitted, 'and there will always be a few. On the other hand there were boys in the beginning who came over to fly but got shunted into the infantry and never belly-ached about it.'

'I know. I met one in the hospital in Madrid.'

'But take Trotskyists, now. What can you do about them?'

I sat back resignedly, for he was off on his favourite theme.

'When I was last in Murcia, there was a rabid Trotskyist there, making political speeches all day to the boys. Now, he had really fought and been wounded so he couldn't be chucked out of the hospital or put in solitary confinement or anything.'

'Why should he be punished? Is Trotskyism catching?'

Seldes gave me a look as if I had made some disgustingly dirty remark, but I continued, 'The boys can talk back, can't they? They might convert him. He volunteered and fought. You'll not be telling me he risked his life just for the chance of airing his opinions.'

'Fascists have joined up just to sabotage and create disorder in the ranks.'

'Spaniards might join up because otherwise they would be suspected of being fascists. Then they naturally sabotage things and set a bad example to their comrades – by running away from the front or passing over to the enemy. I suppose all cowards might be shot out of hand, some old volunteers believe in that.'

'Sure,' said Seldes, evidently most uncomfortable at this ruthless suggestion.

While Seldes and others were sniffing out anarchist or Trotskyist plots in all directions, none of us suspected Liston, head of the English section of the Information Office. He was that most dangerous type of all: an ex-communist. I do not know whether he had been expelled or had left the party. Apparently his old associates did not know, for he had come to Spain armed with what were, for a Leftist, unimpeachable letters of credit. He had lived in Europe for some years. The American Party was responsible for him on account of his nationality. I have always thought this insistence on nationality as a criterion of party membership rather stupid; the place of residence would have been better. Leading American communists could not have kept much of a watch over him, and the Spaniards took him on trust.

Liston was beginning to be a bit restless in his post. He was losing interest and discharging his duties more and more perfunctorily. He complained increasingly of his rheumatism. He said his health would not stand the damp climate in Valencia. He went up to Madrid, and talked of starting a bureau there. I hoped he would not as I did not want to leave the coast. It transpired that the heroic city did not suit him either and he went off to Barcelona, he said only for a visit, though Constancia pointed out that it was even damper and colder there. Spiritually, Liston was more at home in Catalunya, the stronghold of the POUM.

Rubio thought a lot of him and all of us confidently expected him back. We sent him copies of all our stuff and wrote often, asking his advice. I asked him to send us articles on industries in Catalunya as he had the opportunity to get first hand information, and the co-operation between the Catalan bureau of propaganda and ours was not of the best owing to age-old jealousies between the Generalitat and the Central Government which we represented. I was now officially described as a *funcionaria* and the consul said that my position as a civil servant to a foreign power was irregular but he was unable to define it as criminal.

Liston never answered any letters and at last we realised he had deserted his post.

'It's just like him,' said Milly, 'to leave a job as soon as he has got it started. He has been a failure all his life.'

The Spaniards were hurt and disappointed; they had always thought Anglo-Saxons so reliable. It seeped through that Liston was consorting with the POUM a great deal in Barcelona. He left shortly before the May rising in that town, in haste, we heard, with the police on his track. It was much later that we heard from America that he had been conducting virulent written and spoken propaganda against the Spanish Republic and the war, and that he used his position 'employed in a responsible post by the Government' to lend authority to his statements.

Fernsworth may have got wind that something was up because he went to Barcelona just before the May rising and left me to 'cover' for him. Before he went, he invited me to a dairy for ice-cream and gave me a sort of 'interview' to see if I would be a suitable person. I kept wondering what the ice-cream could possibly be made of – probably *horchata* which is a kind of nut milk. I do not think he would have left such an amateur as myself in charge if he had realised that he would be unable to get back for weeks, that the telephone would be cut between the two towns, and that there would be a Government crisis and Cabinet re-shuffle.

It was after this Cabinet re-shuffle that Negrín became Prime Minister. He was then an unknown figure and at first no photographs could be found of him. The Anarchist Minister of Justice, Oliver, was replaced by the Basque Irujo. The Basques were always regarded as right of centre. The Basque Delegation was the only place in Republican territory where Mass was legally celebrated and outsiders could attend there if they wished. There were several Catholic journalists, one of whom, by some Catholic sixth sense, had discovered a priest working as a waiter in a café.

We knew nothing in Valencia about what was called 'the May Putsch'. We were told that there had been a bit of trouble in Barcelona and that it was all the fault of the POUM which had now been suppressed and now everything would be all right.

The only instructions I ever received from Fernsworth were to keep track of 'Potato Jones' as all England was following his movements with interest. I was told he had passed Gibraltar and I was to go to Alicante to get an interview with him. I did not succeed in this mission.

Potato Jones was captain of one of the ships that ran the blockade to Bilbao. All the ships' names began with Stan – Stanlake, Stanland, Stangrove and so on – making it hard to find out which was which as the Spanish reports were inclined to garble names anyway. There were also three Captain Jones plying to Spain; Potato Jones, so called from the nature of his cargo, Corn-cob Jones, who smoked such a pipe, and there was Ham-and-egg Jones. The CNT paper, *Fragua Social*, published a eulogy in verse on Potato Jones, which in rough translation ended:

Oh Captain Jones, Captain Jones Potato
May you be wafted by fair winds into the port of Bilbao,
Seated on your potato sacks as on a throne.

While Fernsworth was away, a British destroyer struck a mine. At first it was said that it had been torpedoed. About seven seamen lost their lives. I had to ask about this at the Embassy and was told that the wreck would be towed to Gibraltar for an Admiralty enquiry. The seamen were buried at Almería and the British authorities were embarrassed by the presence at the funeral of representatives of the Bakers' Union and various Popular Front organisations. The Antifascist Women strewed rose leaves.

* * * * *

Jan and I were still carrying on a correspondence as to how he was to be brought to Valencia. I wrote in French to the doctor in Murcia and he replied that he had no objection to Jan being moved but no ambulance went that way, though he might be taken to Albacete. I was afraid that if he got there he would be detained in a place where I knew I could not go. He was still hopelessly horizontal and in imagination I kept trying to convey him in or out of trains or buses and balking at the attempt.

I made enquiries of Dr Millán as to which was the best hospital in Valencia. He said the best doctors from Madrid were at the Provincial, especially a Dr Trigo. This name stuck in my memory because it is Spanish for wheat and I was translating a lot of decrees about wheat at that time.

There was a telephone on the wall in our office and one evening, just before I left work, it rang. It was Marion who had got permission to ring from the hospital in Murcia.

'I think Jan may be coming tomorrow. Ring me this time tomorrow and I'll tell you for certain.'

I also had to get permission to make a long-distance call the next day. After I got through, I could get no sense out of the matron, who kept repeating, '*C'est la service sanitaire, salut camarade,*' and would not listen, and it all took so long that I

255

thought the call would be cut off, but at last Marion was on the line. 'It's all right. He's coming on the train tonight. There are other comrades with him. I'll see him off.'

'See he has everything he needs, and thanks a lot.'

The railways were in such a state in a divided and disorganised country that it was quite impossible to guess how long the journey would take or when he would arrive. I could not camp on the station platform though I should have liked to. When I got back to the Victoria in the evening of the following day I found a pencilled note from Jan, apparently delivered by hand, in my pigeon-hole. It said: 'I am at the Hospital Pasionaria. Can you come and see me?'

I went up to the lounge to try to telephone but the booth was occupied. I sat down to wait. As soon as it was free the phone rang and a waiter answered it. He came out, looked vaguely round, and seemed about to go away when he saw me.

'You're wanted on the phone.' I hurried to the booth.

'I'm Patience. You know, the English nurse. Your husband's come in here, the same hospital where Wintringham is . . . He asked me to call you and tell you.'

'I can't come tonight because of the blackout and it's so late, but I'll come first thing in the morning. Will you do anything you can for him, give him my love and tell him I'll come early. What luck that he's at the Pasionaria.'

'I'll give him your message. I'll look after him. Kitty was here and asked me to call you.'

'Please thank her.'

At last he had arrived.

Chapter 13
Calle Sagunto & Calle de las Comedias

The next day was a Sunday. I was up early and went to the flower market on my way to the hospital. I had never visited Tom Wintringham at the Pasionaria and had to telephone Kitty at the Inglés to find out which tram to take. It was a number six, to the other side of the river, to the outskirts of the town towards the port, Calle Sagunto, almost at the terminus. The Sala Internacional was a smallish ward upstairs, with floors and lower walls tiled in green and white. The building was a former convent school and at the end of the ward were blackboards with caricature faces scribbled on them. Outside hung a very bad, smiling photograph of La Pasionaria.

The hospital was not full and most of the men were convalescent and went out in the town in the daytime. The beds were real ones, not folding cots, and Jan said he had slept well for the first time since he was wounded. This may have been because Valencia was cooler and there were fewer flies. The shutters were half closed and it was semi-dark as it was a Spanish hospital and they knew the flies would be deterred by a darkened room.

Though the ward was called the Sala Internacional there were very few foreigners in it. A very small, thin Spanish girl was in charge, dreadfully embarrassed by the rude shouts of some of the rougher men. She told me she was a dressmaker by profession, but had wanted to do something to help the cause.

Jan said the doctors were hopeless and there was a semi-trained assistant, a man in a dingy white robe, called a *practicante,* who was supposed to do dressings but who, until that morning, had refused to take off the tight and elaborately-padded bandages which had been put on Jan's leg and foot to protect them during the journey.

He had had a dreadful journey. Marion had been mistaken about the comrades travelling with him. They had only gone as far as the junction where he had to change trains, and most of the journey he had accomplished alone and helpless on a stretcher. I was amazed that he had had the determination to get to his destination at all. He had been left lying for hours in Valencia station before he could persuade someone to telephone for an ambulance.

Though he reached the Pasionaria by chance, it was the best place for him. His operation was over, and to be in the same hospital as Tom, with Patience and Kitty always in and out, meant a lot of little extra comforts for him.

The Spanish nurses were too modest to wash him but Patience did, and rubbed him with alcohol so he would not get sore from lying in bed.

Kate & Jan at the hospital in Valencia

He lifted the blanket and showed me his leg sticking out from beneath his shirt. It was as stiff as a board; he could not move it at all. It was wasted so that the thigh looked even thinner than the calf. It was pallid, like one's fingers when they go dead from staying too long in cold water, and the foot was slightly blue. There was a huge ball of water on the knee. It did not look as if he would ever recover the use of it and I was still afraid, as there did not seem to be any circulation, that he would lose the foot.

The hospital doctor had been horrified by its appearance. Dr Millán came in to have a look at it and said we must get someone to start massage.

In the afternoon, I returned with things I had bought for Jan and some cakes and Kitty made tea and we had quite a gay little party at his bedside. Tom, of course, being infectious, had a private room, but it was just down the gallery on the same floor. Discipline was not strict, the place was informal and the Spaniards had their families to see them. Kitty and Patience used to go to the pantry to fetch what they needed.

There were a couple of Germans at the Provincial Hospital who used to visit Jan and from their accounts it was a good thing he did not go there. It was a big crowded place, the food was very bad and there were several typhoid cases there. Jan had only had one injection against typhoid, before he left England, and had never followed it up. As he was so weak, Dr Millán did not think it advisable for him to have injections then, so I would not let him eat strawberries unless they were boiled. Patience boiled them but he did not like them so much cooked.

When I got back to the hotel, I asked around to see if anyone knew of a masseur. The American military attaché knew a man who had been treating him for stiffness resulting from an automobile accident. This man, however, wanted ten pesetas an hour if he visited a patient. Dr Millán found us another man who worked at the Provincial. This man came to see Jan and we agreed upon a price, which was five pesetas a time. Jan's pay was seven pesetas a day.

The masseur came every day from then on. It hurt Jan very much but it soon began to show good results and the masseur said that the water on the knee did not matter, he would soon disperse that.

Just after Jan arrived, we had a spell of bad weather and he must have caught cold on the journey, for he developed a nasty cough. Patience said that people lying in bed were especially liable to chest complaints and I remembered Basil and was afraid of pneumonia. I bought more pillows so he could be propped up high and went with Patience to the hospital pharmacy to get a cough mixture made up. The pharmacy was a little cold dungeon on the ground floor with a haphazard mass of coloured bottles and drugs on dusty, cobwebby shelves. It look more like an alchemist's den.

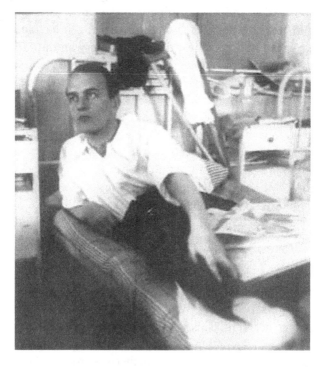

Jan in hospital in Valencia

After Jan arrived in Valencia, I felt I could no longer bear to share a room and have no place to myself where I could be quiet. I liked Milly but she was so energetic and social as to be very tiring and I was with her all day at the office. As I knew there was no hope of finding anything in a hotel, I asked around among my Spanish colleagues and something was soon found for me. It was a flat which belonged to a wealthy family who had fled from Spain leaving three servants without wages, so they were going to run it as a *pensión* and several people were wanted to share it.

It was on the top floor and my room, overlooking a courtyard, became very hot in summer, but there was a lift which made it possible for Jan to come there when he was well enough. When I first went there, there was only one other boarder, José. He was, I think, a rather luke-warm antifascist, but had been caught up on our side. He wore uniform but always looked a civilian and carried a briefcase. He was an engineer, nominally, in the army, employed on coast defences. José was a thin, dark, sickly-looking man with glasses.

The flat was near the office, in the Calle de las Comedias, a name which was later changed to Calle Maxim Gorky – not that it was ever called that. At that time I could have picked any room I liked but I was so afraid that I would be obliged to share again that I chose a small single room. The whole place was luxuriously furnished and there were two Persian cats and a canary. There was a large and splendid tiled bathroom but never any hot water.

At first José and I lived on our own there and we had Visitación, the fat old cook, and two maids to look after us. They took care of everything most conscientiously, just as if the owners might return any day.

The first evening after dinner José produced a photo of an ugly little girl of five with her eyes screwed up against the sun and said it was his daughter.

'*Muy mona* – very pretty,' I said, 'and where is the dear child now?'

'She has been sent abroad to Russia.' He shook his head sadly.

'I had no idea you were married.'

'Divorced,' he said, more gloomily still. Then, after a pause, 'You know Tatiana?' This was a Polish woman who I knew by sight. She was very unprepossessing, pallid and greasy with hair that Jan would have described as '*mausgrau*'.

'Indeed, yes.'

'She was my wife. She left me and went off with another man. Believe me it is a great mistake to marry someone who is not of your own nationality. It never works. You never have the same ideas about anything.'

'I quite agree with you. I've done it. I had a divorce too – I know one feels lost at first, but you are young and you will get over it.'

'I want the child,' said José, with an obstinate twitch of his small mouth, 'and I will get her in the end. It's very hard to be separated from your own child.'

'I see she is fair like her mother.'

'Yes,' said José with pride.

Spaniards seem to have a superstitious admiration for blondes, apparently even plain blondes.

'It's very difficult with the war and everything. I should like to get right away. But that is impossible and here we are both stuck in the same town. We are even mixed up in the same political work, and people take sides you know. And the other man is here too. Oh dear.' He put his head in his hands. Teresa, the maid, came into the vast and pompous dining room and began discreetly clearing plates.

'Would you care to come to the cinema?' He ventured tentatively.

'I'm sorry, I'm dead beat. I'm going to bed. When are your friends joining you? It will be more cheerful for you when they come.'

'In a day or two.' And he went off to the cinema by himself.

I did not think then that I had got much of a bargain in exchanging Milly for José, the deserted husband. However, the other members of the household in the Calle de las Comedias, which we called the *República*, were quite different and we were very jolly there.

There was Miguel, the maids' favourite. They mothered him and sewed buttons on his shirts. He was the baby of the party, aged about eighteen, a rosy, nice-looking boy, with an oval face like an early Picasso. He was a medical student completing his studies in a rapid, three months, course. His parents had been left on the other side. Before I left, he went back to the army as a doctor but, luckily, he was slightly wounded and returned to Valencia. The bullet had ricocheted off the revolver he was wearing. He was studying a large book with illustrations of the effects of poison gases in the 1914 war. He brought serum from the hospital and inoculated the rest of the *República* against typhoid, but the maids refused to be done.

There was Francisco. He was strikingly handsome, with big dark eyes, shining teeth and short cropped hair. He had a fine athletic figure and was a good swimmer, but he had a club foot so was not eligible for the army. He worked in the propaganda department, making posters and so on, which was in a different building to our office. He came from Alicante and was lively and voluble. He had a large appetite with the sweet tooth of a child and was always hungry. He loved to take a tin of condensed milk and spread it on his bread and once demolished, almost single-handed, a whole packing case of raisins which some friends had sent him from Alicante.

Francisco was the only one who took any interest in girls and sometimes he used to invite two who worked in his department. He really liked Luz but invited Miggie as a sort of chaperone. Luz was sixteen, Miggie only thirteen. Luz was very pretty but rather serious and austere. She was the treasurer of the Anti-fascist Women and came round to collect contributions and round us up for meetings. There were so few Spanish women who were politically conscious that foreigners had to join this organisation.

Miggie was Margarita Robles, Coco's little sister. She looked older than thirteen, her figure was budding and she was bursting out of her clothes. Everyone was very proud of Miggie for being so clever and grown up. She was very brown, with downy arms and legs, and fuzzy hair that hung down to her shoulders. She had rather broad features and a dazzling smile. She was of Andalusian blood but looked like a Hawaiian. In the last stages of the war she was sent to the United States as Spanish delegate at some young women's conference. She was the youngest delegate there. There was no one else who could be sent, for Miggie not only spoke English, she had been born in the States and was an American citizen.

The other two men at the flat were older and both came from the other side of Spain. Pablo was a little plump man with a gold tooth who looked like a priest. He had a funny flat-footed way of walking. The other man was Quiroga. Both of them worked in the censorship office.

Quiroga was short, pale, frog-faced, appeared to shave rather seldom and wore very strong glasses. He was an intellectual, perhaps a professor. His wife was in Salamanca but none of them talked about relatives in rebel Spain or knew what had become of them. We all lived in the present. Quiroga was witty and rather bitter. He read English and liked Aldous Huxley, D.H. Lawrence and Katherine Mansfield. He had translated from Proust and was translating Marx. He had diabetes and there was hardly anything he could eat.

The women who were running the *República* were Visitación, the cook, who used to make pilgrimages to her native village to forage for us and return with a bit of goat or something, and Teresa and Dolores who were young sisters. Dolores was married and had a little girl. Her husband was in the army. There was another very dull peasant girl with thick legs, like a Maillol sculpture.

It was lucky there were so many of them as they got up at dawn and took it in turns to stand in queues, for bread, salt cod, soap. One would come back and lay the round flat loaves on the table just as we were sitting down to the two o'clock meal.

The boys used to tease the maids for their Valencian dialect and because they took the CNT newspaper *Fragua Social*, whereas we took the communist newspaper *Frente Rojo*.

We made many jokes about the furnishings of the flat. 'The triumph of bad taste' someone described it as. Until we went there it did not contain a single book, nor was there a bookshelf or a writing desk. There was a pianola and a lot of china, glass and *bric-à-brac* which the maids dusted and polished. There was a bowl in which was an oval of looking-glass on which were water-lilies and leaves of painted tin. There were tapestry hangings, a white and gold Chinese tea service and the most perverse lamp-stands and shades. One was a marble column with a draped nymph on top, holding the bulb like the Statue of Liberty.

There were enlarged family photographs of the absent owners. They were broad, stolid, bovine-looking people, perfectly bourgeois and self-satisfied. There was a fat husband with a watch chain across his paunch, a broad-bosomed wife with no neck, a smirk and a double chin, and a little boy in short socks, a sailor suit and straw boater, with a face too round to permit of any expression at all.

I do not know where all the maids slept. The kitchen was at the end of the corridor furthest from the front door, after all the other rooms, and there must have been a couple of rooms for them beyond. Dolores was not a regular member of the staff but she and her little girl had joined her sister Teresa because of the war. They were very good to us and did all the washing and ironing also. There were not many modern conveniences in the flat but there was an ice-box in which I cooled white wine on occasion.

I told Visitación that Jan fancied a chicken. She tried but could not find one so she got a little pigeon and cooked it in a casserole. She also made flan, which she said was very strengthening for sick people. She packed it all up in a basket, covered with a clean serviette, and I carried it to the hospital.

As we were on the top floor, with a glass-roofed patio, the maids panicked in air raids so whenever we heard noises, even when we knew they were bombs, we always told them it was only our anti-aircraft guns, to reassure them. They would run downstairs somewhere and Teresa, who was *muy nerviosa*, had appendix attacks after air raids and had to put ice on it. On the other hand, Visitación would bustle into the dark room saying, 'You can't die on an empty stomach, that would never do,' and light a candle and concoct a green tortilla with spinach.

The rest of us would go up to the flat roof to watch, José taking a professional interest in how the defences were working. There were rabbits and hens kept up there and we would blunder into the hutches and set the poultry cackling, or nearly decapitate ourselves on the wire clothes-lines which were hung very low as the maids were all short. The red sparks of chaser bullets were pretty as fireworks, and I once saw a plane caught between two searchlight beams, like a glittering dragon.

José, though without his wife and child, seemed to have a lot of other relatives. He had a brother in the army who would sometimes turn up, a rather noisy, riotous fellow. Quiroga liked to work until late translating, with his typewriter on a card table in the parlour, fortified with tea as he was not allowed coffee, and the irruption of this brother disturbed him.

Before I left, another of José's brothers arrived with his wife. He was a doctor and had evacuated a hospital from Bilbao to Santander and then from Santander across France. They had several children parked in a colony in Alicante where José's sister was a teacher. The wife was always rinsing pink underwear in the dining room. The doctor had already got a job in a hospital and the wife spent her days looking for a flat so she could be reunited with her children. All José's relatives were very bourgeois and very fond of one another.

Extra people created great food difficulties. As we gathered round the dining table in increasing numbers, Quiroga would say, 'It is the perpetual miracle of the loaves and the fishes here,' and Teresa would laugh and nearly drop the dish. Quiroga had the worst of it on account of his diet. Once she brought in for him some very strange-looking shellfish, all tails and scales like scorpions.

'Are these a Valencian specialty? What are they called, Teresa?'

'I don't know I'm sure, *señor*,' she replied, shrugging her shoulders and laughing, 'I never saw them before. We buy anything we find in the market.'

'Don't tell me you found these in the market. You found them under a stone!'

As the maids kept a few rabbits on the roof we sometimes had *arroz* with rabbit and then Quiroga would look round to see if one of the Persian cats was missing. This jest invariably shocked the maids who would sooner have starved themselves than sacrifice one of these creatures. Once, in desperation, one of the cats stole a rabbit and Visitación angrily snatched the remains away from it and served it up to us just the same.

The cats were reduced to mere bags of bones though, like the rest of us, they did not complain. As they had long blue-grey fur, one did not realise how thin they were unless one picked them up. They were very affectionate and, for some reason, had English names; one was Tommy and the other Bobby.

José had brought a gramophone from Madrid and we all bought records for it, according to our tastes, from what was available in the shop. José brought some back with him when he went to Barcelona on business as the stock there was better. The maids, as part of the República, also produced a few discs, the Santa Espina and some Flamencos.

Teresa stood listening, her hands folded over her stomach, under her apron, her plump arms bare.

'I have been to Barcelona,' she said. 'Do you remember how on certain fiestas they used to dance Sardanas in the streets all day and all night – *bailando, bailando en las calles* – you have seen that, *señora?*'

'Yes. A circle, and then another circle inside that one, and then another, more people joining in, old people and young and children.'

'No more,' she said, shaking her head, as the sad stirring music with its strange pipes reached a climax.

* * * * *

Jan's leg improved very slowly and so did his general health. Every advance was celebrated with some little treat; from the time he could sit up and turn round in bed so that he could see the distant sea out of the window until the time when at last I got him down to the beach; from the time when he could be carried down to the wretched little bar across the street until the time I got him to a real café; from the time when he first hopped on crutches across the ward until I got him to a meal at the flat.

Jan had been reading so much he was tired of it, but he liked the English newspapers that I took him from the office. I told him all about the people I met and what it was like outside to relieve the tedium. We sometimes used to talk about the old days in Spain, how we used to like pictures and churches, folk dances and music and peasant costumes, but it was like looking back on some theatrical spectacle seen years before.

I told him about the air raid shelters which were being built. They were decorative, white concrete, with *REFUGIO* written on them in shiny modernistic letters. They looked like cinemas. One even looked like Lenin's tomb. At the doors were pots of flowers tended by the guards.

I told him about the cathedral, which was on the Calle Campaneros close to the office. It was used for storing munitions and lorries drove in and out. It had a beautiful carved Renaissance porch and there was a printed appeal pasted on the door. It showed a reproduction of the carved capitol of a pillar and beneath was written, 'Workers, respect the labours of your brothers of yesterday.'

Jan was a painter in normal life so I bought him a drawing book and some coloured crayons in a box made in the likeness of Popeye the Sailor. He used to sketch the other men in the ward and did a good likeness of the pig-like Frenchman known as *el borracho* (the drunkard). When he got his pay, he would disappear for a day or two and then be carried back to the ward again.

One morning, I found Jan busy on a poster of a woman with streaming hair, waving a red flag.

'These communists always manage to make one useful. It's for a decoration for the 1st of May. I sent out for the paint and it's the wrong colour; crimson instead of scarlet. And I can't seem to get the proletarian look on the girl.'

'You should see the posters of *Mujeres Libres*,' I said, 'if you want to get an idea of a militant, politically conscious char-woman.'

I knew there existed a fine, large book of all Goya's etchings which had been produced for his centenary. A friend brought a copy from Madrid. It was a bit difficult for Jan to balance it on his chest but I turned the pages and helped to support it so that we could enjoy the bullfighting series and the *Disparates* and the *Desastres de la guerra*.

Patience was doing duty in the fever hospital where there were two or three Internationals at this time. One was Dutch and could not make himself understood at all, the other two were unconscious, suspected typhoid cases. Another patient there was a British sea-captain, merchant service, who was later discharged because the doctors concluded he was suffering from a combination of malaria and delirium tremens.

Her crusading fervour was at its height and she had plenty of scope for it. The hospital was an ancient, insanitary building, rife with all the germs of ages, an antique lazaretto of a place. When Patience first got there, she found that the sick men had never been undressed but were lying in dirty sheets in their filthy uniforms. The hospital had no change of linen and no soap. She said that every day she expected to find them all dead but only one died.

All infectious diseases were mixed together and all were allowed to receive their families, including children. Patience got us to write slogans in Spanish and set Jan to making posters representing diabolical germs clinging to visitors' skirts or the dust on the ends of brooms.

Before she had got far with reforming the municipal fever hospital, Patience was called away to attend several English nurses and doctors who had been taken ill. It was astonishing that medical units had come out without being inoculated. Penny, the English nurse from Murcia, had typhoid, and another had Malta fever.

I went in and out of the Pasionaria freely, usually in the hot, sunny afternoons. The building had a tall, white façade with hardly any windows or decoration on the street. In the doorway lounged two Spanish sentries who sat on yellow brocade chairs, now threadbare and greasy. There was a flagged patio, and upstairs a gallery where there were two gorgeous but tattered crimson and gilt sofas and several armchairs, like thrones, occupied by patients able to crawl out into the sun.

On the stairs I often saw a young Spanish boy who was consumptive. His clothes hung loosely on him and his face was wan and hollow. He crept silently about, leaning on a stick and clinging to the banister, gasping at every step. He seemed to like to move about as long as he had an ounce of strength left. Nobody took any notice of him. At length I saw him no more and supposed he must have died.

When I arrived, a big Polish miner with protruding ears, who was very inarticulate but full of good will, would come up smiling and gesticulating, and would say, 'gut, gut' when Jan began to walk a few steps. Jan had to give up quickly as the blood running down into his foot made it swell and it was very painful, but he was brave and persevering. Dr Millán said he should have an elastic bandage to obviate the danger of varicose veins; there was no such thing in the hospital but I was able to buy one outside. Jan was provided with a pair of crutches, padded with blue velvet, which were meant for a shorter man. Patience said there were such things as crutches with springs that were much easier to use than these, which chafed under the arm.

Until Jan could bend his knee, he could not get up. Sometimes my visits coincided with those of the masseur. He was keen to show me that we were getting our money's worth and bent Jan's knee with his powerful hands until Jan broke into a sweat and begged him to stop and Patience came running with a drop of brandy.

'In England, we would give him a local anaesthetic and bend that knee to a right-angle in one go,' she said, 'instead of doing it bit by bit like this. It will work just as well in the end but it's a lot more painful.'

Sometimes I had to get water for the flowers from the bathroom. It was filthy, the drains all stopped up with rubbish and old bandages. One of the men was usually shaving in there.

Sometimes I visited Tom Wintringham. He was making a rapid recovery and we placed bets on who would be up first and able to visit the other, he or Jan. Tom won the race and left the hospital before Jan was out of bed. Tom had a lot of cigarettes and dainties sent him; I remember one parcel from Fortnum and Mason's. He would send things to Jan and Kitty would make tea.

One of the patients in the ward always came to sit near us while we talked. He would listen and then say at last, 'Isn't it strange? So much talk, gabble, gabble, and I can't understand a word.' Or he would turn over one of our English books and remark on the strangeness of that.

An old anarchist lay in the next bed and used to read aloud from a magazine, his stubby finger following each line. He did it very slowly and, I think, could not understand without this procedure. He looked like a bear with a book. He had a black beard and a red kerchief round his neck. The others used to tease him and call him *Bigotes* – Whiskers. When he got up, the inside of his bed was quite black, though the outside cover was clean. His boots smelt terrible.

There was one boy who played the guitar and another with a paralysed arm. The latter belonged to the Socialist Youth and had been three times wounded. He was always cheerful.

'I joined up last year, when I was seventeen,' he laughed, 'and I've been in a lot of battles and I was lucky, but at last they got me.' He shook his useless arm. 'Never mind, I'm learning to write with a typewriter.'

The Spaniards had friends in to see them. One man had his wife and baby and the nurses made a great fuss of the baby, tossing it up and down. One old peasant in a black smock used to visit his son nearly every day. He never spoke. He just sat for an hour, with his cap in his hand, and looked at his son and then went away again. Jan told me that the prognosis for this boy was bad. It was a hospital, not for treatment, but for convalescent or hopeless cases.

Chapter 14
Visits and Visitors

I went on few trips as I was more useful in the office but I did go to the Teruel front. This was our nearest. There was a sign in the square with a map of Spain and the words, 'It is only 156 kilometres to the front.' The figures 1 and 5 fell off and it looked as if the enemy had advanced alarmingly but, for some time, this went unnoticed.

This front was quiescent for most of the war and Teruel was taken much later. The lines were close and I saw the towers of Teruel plainly silhouetted against the sunset sky before I ducked because, despite the failing light, a sniper had seen us. It looked like an Italian hill town. The next day we had lunch with the officers in a farm which had just been re-taken from the enemy, who had left behind two flagons of sweet Málaga wine.

Rubio was exultant when Belchite was taken, and sent a party of journalists, including Milly. It had been fought very hard for and the weather was hot. Milly said it was ghastly, the stench of corpses and a sanitary squad in gas masks trying to get them buried. Shortly afterwards, Humphrey and another Englishman came through there. They said the town was defended house by house. Eventually, the men were fighting their way in by making a hole in the wall from one house to the next. Then they stepped through into a hospital ward and were taken aback by the scene. There was a smell of gangrene; there was absolute stillness. Here and there nuns were sitting beside the beds telling their beads.

I went up to a hospital in Cuenca which had mainly English medical staff, though there were a few Canadians and Americans. An American nurse was trying to get running water installed in every ward and something on the windows to exclude flies.

It was a beautiful place in the mountains, a spa, and the building had been a hotel. There was a bathing pool of fizzy, slightly warm water. The food was good, bread and mutton and wine. I was depressed by the way people clung to their national habits regardless of politics or circumstances. The truck driver who took me round was a cockney and pining for Camden Town and kippers. He looked all wrong in a pair of well-cut riding breeches. The medical staff had little parties in someone's bedroom in the evenings, with tea and plum cake sent from home, that reminded me of boarding school, midnight feasts and tuck-boxes. One night there was a concert and entertainment provided by the staff and patients.

Part of my assignment there was to write about a co-operative farm so I took this excuse to talk to the 'natives' and escaped one evening to the porter's lodge. The mayor of the town lived there and I sat with him and his family, two little children and another baby on the way. We all drank wine and one after the other the children fell asleep and were carried up to bed.

The owner of the estate was an absentee and the land had been divided up among the peasants and they were very happy and proud about it. The mayor showed me over the farm and explained how the proceeds were divided up. What I chiefly remember is climbing into a whitewashed loft which was full of wheat and, nestling in the wheat as an ideal packing, were large melons.

When I left Cuenca, I was given a lift in an ambulance. It was on its way to Albacete and as we progressed my companions became more and more buttoned up. When we reached the crossroads, they said they would have to leave me there but they did wait until an empty truck came along, on its way back to Valencia, which took me up. It was an open truck and very cold; we did not arrive until late at night. The driver lent me a *capote manta*, a bit like a Mexican *serape* with a hood, which was very warm.

If I had been surprised at the English clinging to their habits, I was also surprised at the way other people did. There was a street vendor who sold cigarettes because he had always done so. There were two kinds: one was absolutely non-inflammable but it might console one just to have it hanging in one's mouth like a baby's dummy. The other kind was made of some paper which immediately flared up and burned down to one's lips.

The Spaniards in the office sent out to the café for glasses of coffee in the afternoons. There was no coffee or milk or sugar.

There was a coffee substitute called *malta* which was terrible unless 'cut' with something, as they said, speaking of it as people used to speak of bootleg gin. Drinks were sweetened with honey, that honey made from orange-blossom that is so expensive in London. There were two kinds of synthetic milk, *leche vegetal* (probably made from nuts) and *leche en polvo* (which I believe was chalk). This last just sank to the bottom of the glass.

There was home-made vermouth in a corked, unlabelled bottle like a medicine bottle. This tasted like vinegar and water.

Some people were so accustomed to night life that they would never give it up. Barry was one of these. He would sit in the Wodka café until it closed at about half-past ten and had then discovered several other possibilities. In one sand-bagged building in the Plaza Castelar was the office of the Febus News Agency which was open all night, so he would look in there. Above it was an illegal café which I only ever visited at midnight and could never find again. Once we tried to get into a brothel by mistake as we saw lights under the door and heard sounds of merriment; we were on the wrong floor.

The café was large and bleak with *Izquierda Republicana* posters on the walls. Sometimes a radio played. There was only one waiter and it was almost impossible to get served. Most of the time the proprietor was making ineffectual efforts to persuade his clients to go home so that he could close. In the end a few groups would be left drinking *gaseosa* (sweet fizzy pop) while the patron's wife raised a dust with a broom, the waiter washed up and the children cried to be put to bed.

The summer of 1937 was the time when we were so inundated with visitors that Valencia might have been a tourist resort. A lot of them were important people but some came for frivolous reasons because it was the fashion. First Kajsa took them to the police to have their passports stamped. The police, as everything had been moved to unexpected places, were installed in the Medical School which had a skeleton in a glass case in the hall. This intimidated some people and, I think, Kajsa later contrived to fix up the passports in batches herself.

I did not usually go out as an interpreter except when we had so many visitors there was no one else available. My Spanish was not good enough to do the sort of diplomatic translating that is required of an official interpreter.

The itinerary usually included a trip to the front, University City, Madrid. Quiroga sometimes had to go to the Censor's office in Madrid and he said he wondered how the tourists were fed unless they brought supplies with them.[100]

'Last time I was up there,' he said, 'we had stewed cat one day and dog's head the next. It was a big dog and we pretended it was a calf's head.'

Madrid was shelled every day but it was not dangerous to the residents as they knew the time of day to expect it and where the gun emplacements were, so they walked on the safer side of the street.

Sometimes, Constancia sent people to the Teruel front which was nearer and safer. Among these was the American Socialist leader, Norman Thomas.[101] He was a big pale man who had been, I think, a non-conformist minister. Such a combination of views would have been unthinkable in a Spaniard, as Spanish liberals were automatically anti-clerical. The Thomases were also total abstainers though we had little to offer other than alcoholic beverages.

The day Norman Thomas went to Teruel, I was deputed to keep Mrs Thomas amused and accompanied her to a colony for refugee children at Perelló. We drove some of the way on a raised causeway through the flooded rice fields where peasants in punts and large straw hats were paddling about, making a very far Eastern scene. The houses had steep gables and thatched roofs.

The colony was for the children of men employed in the public services in Madrid, tram-drivers, dustmen, firemen and some of the printers' and book-binders' union. They were housed splendidly in a requisitioned villa. The teachers were very young, one with her hair down in a plait. However, they were hungry.

'We dare not take them for walks on the beach,' said one teacher. 'It gives them too much appetite. And we have only beans to give them; not good for little children.'

The children sang for Mrs Thomas. They were making little boxes, cardboard covered with coloured paper, which they said were for *bonbones*, which seemed rather sad as they could never

275

get any sweets to fill them.

If one acted as a courier, one usually got some perks and Mrs Thomas gave me her wilting bouquet and a packet of soap-flakes.

I made the mistake of offering a drink to another visitor who was a rabid teetotaller. This was Willy Gallagher, our only communist MP.[102] He had a very red little nose but this must have been caused by dyspepsia. I saw him sitting alone in the lobby of the Victoria looking miserable, with everyone around him drinking. I was told afterwards that he had seen so much drunkenness in the slums of Glasgow that he was violently against liquor and lived on bread and jam and tea.

Some visitors did not need interpreters, only cars and drivers. One such was Hemingway,[103] who always came with a large entourage and always wanted to go to Madrid at once. He was a huge, red man, in hairy speckled tweeds, with a crushing handshake. He looked like a successful businessman which, I suppose, was the impression he wished to make. The first time I saw him, he came with Sidney Franklin, a former bullfighter,[104] and two Dutch cameramen, to make the film *Spanish Earth*. One always had the feeling that there were several shadowy, unidentifiable, obsequious figures in the background while Hemingway, the great man, was in the foreground.

The second time I saw him, his main companion was Martha Gellhorn.[105] While he was with Rubio, she waited in the ante-room where a long table of heavy oak, like a refectory table, was spread with newspapers. She was handsome in a rather predatory way, with a beaky nose and brilliant eyes. She had an elegant coiffure, a linen dress and a perfectly even sun tan. She wore her skirt rather short, and sat on the table swinging her long, slim legs in a provocative manner. The Spaniards disapproved of this. They believed that sexuality should be directed only at one person at a time, preferably in private.

There was often an awkward gap between the manners of our visitors and those of their hosts. Some of our visitors were exceedingly proletarian, crude and unpolished; the hosts were all urbane and civilised to Geneva League of Nations' standards. Many of the Spaniards and most of those in the Government must have seemed disappointingly moderate liberals to our guests.

The man who was cleverest at smoothing things out with everybody was Otto Katz.[106] At the time, he was head of the Spanish Press Agency in Paris and went by the name of *Simone*. No longer young, he was a very charming man, an artful propagandist amazingly good at ingratiating himself with the most diverse types and making use of them for propaganda purposes without their realising it.

Among our visitors was a party of three British women MP's determined to investigate facts and no nonsense about it. One, the Duchess of Atholl, was stout and wore a coat and skirt of some rough durable material like the upholstery of a railway carriage.[107] The others were Eleanor Rathbone and Ellen Wilkinson. Eleanor Rathbone was earnest and austere, interested in prison reform.[108] Ellen Wilkinson was small, wore high heels, had red hair and was the only one who used face powder.[109] None of them was young but Otto said, 'After all – they are *women*,' and set out to flatter and conquer them – or at least to persuade them to a favourable point of view. I spent one evening with them, in their room at the hotel, eating chocolates, and everyone quite unbent thanks to Otto.

Another visitor was Lillian Hellman.[110] She rushed about and was terribly impatient because we were unpunctual and unbusinesslike. She made no allowances for the hasty and provisional nature of everything or the war. I did my best to provide her with the information she required. We had built up the files as best we could from the time that we managed to get a carpenter in to make a few shelves for them, and we knew from experience the questions visitors always asked. The headings were: Religion, Education, Industry, Agriculture, membership of political parties and trade unions.

There was complete freedom of worship for protestants (of whom there are very few in Spain). The British and Foreign Bible Society was doing good business. 'The Bible, a *must* for your library' was their advertisement. As for the Catholics, a few, such as the Canon of Córdoba, had declared for the Republic, and there were always the Basques.

The Ministers of Education and Agriculture were communists.

They were well organised and produced pamphlets in plenty. Reading was all the rage. There cannot have been any paper shortage; every town was full of outdoor bookstalls. The books were political, technical, Spanish classics, the poems of Lorca and other modern writers. Everyone who could read was enjoined to teach others and a primer was produced which was supposed to teach reading and writing simultaneously. At the end of this illustrated book was an epilogue: 'Soldier of the Republic, now you have learned to read and write. With your rifle in one hand and your primer in the other you seem to be mounting guard over your right to education'.

Some of the old nursery rhymes and stories, such as *Little Red Riding Hood* were re-written with an anti-fascist turn.

One day on a bus journey, I met an old anarchist who was reading a tract which said that all human ills could be cured by a diet of oranges. This was a very useful theory for the time and place since oranges were our staple diet.

The Minister of Public Works was a professor, a most gentlemanly and cultured person, but totally unpractical. He could not do anything about roads and railways at such a time except authorise first-aid patchwork.

The political parties and trade unions were very difficult to assess, particularly the CNT-FAI. The anarchists were certainly more numerous than any other political body in Spain, and the most truly working class, but they lacked educated leaders, especially after the dissolution of the POUM which had worked with them. They denied that they were a political party – they were a federation – and did not believe in government. At first they had been genial and welcoming to all comers but after the May rising in Barcelona they took fright and would not give out information. It may also have been true that their records were so disorderly, or non-existent, that they did not know their own strength. They told me that they thought the CNT membership was 'about three million'. I came across a book which was an account of the landing on Ibiza. Anarchists set sail from Valencia early in the war, 'took' Ibiza but were obliged to leave again very rapidly. This was the description of the troops: 'They were men with hands horny from toil, sweaty shirts . . . How many were they? We despise statistics. Numbers freeze the blood and paralyse the brain. They were many, a multitude.'

This quotation pleased Milly so much that she wanted to put it up on the wall of the office but she was not allowed to do anything so frivolous.

I went to interpret for Louis Fischer[111] and a trade union leader, which was Otto's idea, but I found it such a strain listening to the words of an unfamiliar vocabulary and accent that I paid little attention to the facts. The talk took place at a banquet. It was a banquet in style, though there was not much to eat. It was held in a palace, on the first floor, at a long table, under very dim lights which seemed to make it harder to hear. Negrín was present and some officers in uniform.

I accompanied an American alienist on an interview with a Madrid specialist in the same field. The Madrid doctor was soothing about the lunatics. He said they did not mind bombardments because they were so absorbed in their own illusions. He said there were not many shell shock cases in the army except in the International Brigades – he excused the latter on the grounds that they never had leave to see their families.

I went twice as interpreter to prisons. Constancia and Aurora could neither of them bear to talk to Spaniards from the other side. I went once to a military prison. It contained some Falangists and Civil Guards, a few Moors, two very sulky German aviators and several hundred Italians.

At the gate was a scrubby little Moor, his hair hanging in wispy ringlets, his head through a hole in a very dirty blanket. He grinned.

'He's a trusty,' said the officer in charge. 'He's very glad to be here. He's scared of aeroplanes.'

The Moor, who had a rather primitive face, fingered an amulet he wore round his neck and made several jerky salutes, varying the clenched fist with the upraised arm in a dubious way, as if one or the other should ward off the evil eye.

'Funny thing is he comes from French Morocco,' said the officer, 'some press gang or other roped him in. It's not often we get live Moors. They are so dreaded and hated by the people, sort of bogey-men you know. You must have seen Saracens' heads in churches. St Iago is depicted slaying Moors. The people are a mass of superstitions.'

'How about the Civil Guards?'

'Ah, that is a different story. They know what is coming to them and generally fight until they are all dead. And if they surrender and declare for us we can't trust them. In Málaga, they put on their old uniforms and welcomed the fascists in.'

'What will happen to them?'

The officer was evasive and said they would be tried. I concluded they would be shot. Civil Guards are particularly loyal to a reactionary régime. They are not young men but all old soldiers who were never loyal to the Republic, which only dates from 1931. They look like reaction personified in their eighteenth century costumes, their long cloaks and tricorne hats. The Civil Guards were old and battered, their faces dried and seamed, here and there a tooth missing. They carried themselves with hostile pride. They had been besieged in a sanctuary, Santa María de la Cabeza, since the early days of the war and had no news of what was going on.

'Were you surprised to find it so cosmopolitan here in the prison?' we asked. They shrugged their shoulders. 'Those –' They looked scornfully at the cheerful, chattering Italians, 'it is almost unbelievable.'

'Aeroplanes drop fascist emblems for you.' We showed them one.

'Those things. We wouldn't demean ourselves to wear them. They are toys for boys.'

I tried to look at them impartially but even if one knew nothing of their ruthlessness it was plain in their faces.

In Belchite, the Civil Guards held out to the last, defending the church from the tower for several days after the rest of the town had fallen. The streets of Belchite were littered with capes and tricornes. One journalist brought back a black tricorne as a souvenir but a waiter at his hotel tore the hat into fragments and jumped on the pieces, wreaking an age-old hatred on this symbol of oppression.

I visited the women's prison with a party of women journalists. It was some distance out of town by tram. There was a long drive, shaded by trees, running through a garden up to the building. It was an open prison, without locks or bars, but the prisoners would know that they were safer inside than out. The building had been a Jesuit monastery. The inmates were all Spanish but very mixed socially. However, they all had their own cells. Some of them appeared to be prostitutes who had been taken up for spying, others were high-born ladies. The latter were held as valuable exchange prisoners. Their relatives on the other side arranged to exchange them for aviators who had been obliged to bale out over enemy territory and who were very scarce and precious to us.

There was Franco's niece with her baby in a cot covered with netting to keep off flies. Aurora covered her embarrassment by cooing at the baby. There was Millán Astray's sister and a very ugly old lady in black who was some relation of the Duke of Alba but proved a rather bad investment as he did not seem anxious to ransom her. There were three lovely girls, titled sisters. Later, when I told Humphrey and another Englishman about them, he said, 'I remember those *débutantes*. We captured them after Guadalajara. They were hiding in the straw in a barn dressed up as Red Cross nurses. We were a great surprise to them. Not their class quite, but not too far off; they had expected Tartar hordes.'

These girls spoke good English as they had had an English governess. They looked quite elegant. Someone from the British Embassy visited them every week and brought them reading matter. They had the *Sketch* and the *Tatler* and a novel by Anthony Trollope. On the wall was pinned a coloured print of butterflies. They were cheeky. I was wearing a hair band of twisted raffia, red and straw colour. 'You are wearing our colours,' they said, meaning red and gold. We were offered a plate of prison stew to taste and I told them it was as good as we got at the hotel, but they did not believe me. They said they were very bored but were annoyed with the prison governor, a lawyer, because he made them work.

'We either have to make shirts at the machines or clean the house, scrub floors, but we clean because it is over quicker.'

They looked with suspicion at Aurora because she was evidently a lady. When I left, they offered to shake hands with me. It was not long before they were exchanged.

* * * * *

There were a few visitors who slipped in and out without any visits to the Press Department, who went where they wished and had cars and petrol. These were communists in good standing. When I reached Spain, my political ignorance was such that I had barely heard of Marx and Lenin. I had never heard of Tom Wintringham, who was then an important figure in the British party, until Humphrey introduced him in Barcelona. I had never heard of André Marty, the Commander of the International Brigades, until Jan told me about him. While Jan was in the Pasionaria, his book on mutinies came out in England and Jan received a copy.

Other important visitors were unknown to me also. They were pointed out to me at meals in the hotel. One was Egon Kisch.[112] I was told he had performed some heroic feat in Sydney which involved swimming from a ship to the shore with a broken leg, I forget why.

Another was Ilya Ehrenburg, who was having breakfast with his secretary on what we called the blue verandah because its glass was painted blue to conform with blackout regulations.[113] The secretary was rather thick-set and coarse but Milly, who had been in Moscow, said she would have been considered a *belle* there. I was only familiar with the White Russians, elegant and glamourous, from my days in Paris working as a mannequin. Ehrenburg looked like an old grey rat.

Other visitors may have come and gone without my ever meeting them. One, who I only met casually once, was Dos Passos, yellow, small and bespectacled. I think he was with Barry who introduced me and we chatted briefly on the street corner. Dos Passos must have been sadly disillusioned in Spain for he arrived at a time when a friend met with a tragedy.[114]

Coco Robles' father had been a professor in an American university and Dos Passos was a friend of the family. He came to Spain expecting to renew this friendship and, no doubt, to take an interest in the republican cause. Coco's father was working very closely with the Russians as an interpreter and was engaged in rather hush-hush work. What happened remained a mystery; it was inexplicable but it leaked out despite efforts to hush it up on the part of our communist friends. The only person who dared create a loud scene about it was Milly. It was obvious that our Spanish colleagues were miserable and quite helpless to do anything about it. Robles was arrested as a spy by the secret police and, after a short time, executed. This happened just before Dos Passos came to Spain, though he may have been still in prison when Dos Passos arrived. Humphrey, who had met Robles, said he could not understand it though, in a civil war, you never know for certain about anyone's loyalty.

After his father's death, Coco was crushed and wretched, so ashamed he never spoke of it. He gave up his future at that point. He resigned from the Communist Youth. He had been destined for the diplomatic service. He was very intelligent and was learning Russian with a view to going to Russia.

During the time he remained in Valencia, he devoted himself to being the man of the family and taking care of his mother and little sister. His mother was ill, he said, and I believe hardly left the house. He sometimes begged me for cigarettes for her. Miggie sometimes came to the office at lunch-time, or in the evening, to fetch Coco, and they would take a few peanuts and apples and go for a picnic on the beach together. They were devoted to one another. I once heard Coco scolding Miggie for having gone to the Wodka café with another girl, and forbidding her to do it again. On another occasion, when they both spent an evening with an English member of the Brigade, the Englishman told me afterwards that in the cinema Coco had placed himself between the soldier and Miggie to prevent any impropriety. She was a very pretty girl and looked older than she was, though the Englishman only thought of them as two delightful children, much to be pitied.

After Miggie had left for America as Spanish delegate, Coco, at sixteen, volunteered for the militia. He went to the front and disappeared for ever.

Chapter 15
Progress

At last a day came when Jan was well enough to come to the flat in the Calle de las Comedias. A friend in the Brigade had offered his car. It came late. The driver was German-speaking and I directed him with difficulty. Jan was lying on his bed dressed in a brown corduroy suit which he had got from the hospital stores. The jacket was bloused at the back with elastic and much too short. The trousers were also gathered with elastic at the ankles which made them awkward to pull over his bad leg. I had brought a canvas shoe for his good foot. He said he had been ready a long time and thought I was never coming.

The Polish miners with their huge, flat faces, hands and feet, and outstanding ears were, for them, in a state of great animation. Unable to communicate in any language known to us they gabbled away gutturally. Between them they carried Jan down, sitting on their hands with his arms around their necks. A nurse and I followed carrying the crutches. The few men left in the ward shouted their congratulations. The driver helped him into the car which cost him some groans. The sentries waved and Jan waved back and told the driver to go carefully. I pointed out the river Turia that we crossed and some public gardens that we passed. He was amused by the giant cardboard eyes and ears on the street lamps, an eye on one and an ear on the next garishly coloured. 'The eyes and ears of the enemy are watching and listening,' I explained.

When we reached the flat, we ran into an obstacle that I had overlooked. In the hall of the building there were several marble steps before one reached the lift. With the help of the driver, we managed to get up them. I was afraid our day was going to do him harm as he was completely exhausted already. I got him on to my bed and gave him a glass of sherry and undid the elastic bandage which was too tight as his leg had swollen. I sat with him until he began to revive and then gave him some newspapers and told Teresa to look in now and again to see he was all right as, although it was Sunday, I had to go to the office.

When I returned, he was feeling better and said he could sit up for lunch and would like to go into the dining room for a change of scene. As he hobbled across the hall one of the cats ran away scared of the strange crutches stumping over the floor.

The dining room was the nicest part of the flat. It was on the corner of the building and had big curved bow windows looking down two streets. We could not use it at night as we could not darken these windows, which only had venetian blinds. The canary hung in one of them. Jan sat in the window in a big armchair with his foot up on a cushion on another chair with one of the cats purring on his knee.

Visitación fussed over him because he was young and blond. She had made *arroz*. This paella is a classic Valencian dish. She sighed at the lack of rich ingredients, only peas and pimentos and a little meat, but it was much better than the same old stew that was served every day at the hospital.

The boys were sympathetic and considerate. We had some of that white wine in a slender bottle, rather like hock, with wire netting on the outside. Jan was tired and slept in the afternoon. We gave him an early supper. Someone had given me a tin of herring roes but there was no tin opener. The maids struggled with it and finally attacked it with a chopper and extracted the mangled contents.

After Jan had been out once, he got on fast. Once or twice a week I managed to take him out. There were only three taxis in Valencia so, sometimes, I took a *victoria* – these were dilapidated carriages with very ancient horses and drivers. We sometimes went out for a drive in the afternoon. Since the carriages were open at the sides, the crutches tended to fall out. We would roll slowly down the Alameda, becoming entangled with groups of recruits drilling, and once we saw the British diplomats, with their red-bronzed faces, taking a brisk constitutional.

When we returned to the hospital, the Polish miners usually appeared to help him but if they were out he had to sit on the stairs until I could find someone to carry him. The Spaniards were small men and staggered under his weight up the two flights. At the flat, a French-speaking man, a neighbour, used to help him up the steps. After a time he was able to go down steps but not up and marble stairs are so dangerously slippery.

All the cab drivers got to know us. They usually stopped in the Plaza Castelar but sometimes I had to go as far as the station to find one and occasionally had to fall back on a rattling peasant cart. These vehicles had a canvas hood so they looked like small covered wagons.

One Sunday morning, as I was driving through the Plaza, I was hailed by a couple of soldiers. One was the pig-faced Frenchman, *el borracho*.

'Ton ami est bien?' he shouted. *'Toujours il fait le dessin.'* He made the motion of pencil over paper. *'Nous allons au mitin.'*[115]

'Oui, je vais a l'hôpital maintenant, salut,'[116] and we shook our fists amicably at one another.

There were several air raids at this time, mostly over Sagunto, which was a centre for making munitions. Jan felt their reverberations badly for the hospital was a mile or so along the road to Sagunto. All the men who could move used to rush out into the open. One raid on the centre of the town, in which the town hall was burned out, took place in the small hours when Jan was sleeping at the flat. The room shook and a bomb hit the Plaza Tetuán, which was only a block away. We did not get up but I closed the shutters as I have a horror of broken glass.

One Sunday morning, I saw the enemy planes from the roof, flying in and out of the clouds, and the white faces of groups on the street corners watching. This time they bombed the port. There was a Wagner concert on that morning and those inside were not aware of the raid at all.

I used to go on to the roof to sunbathe before going to the office. I often wished Jan could have got up there. My room was narrow and dark and he suffered from a lack of fresh air. Up on the roof he would have had a sense of freedom. However, the stairway was steep and awkward and he never managed to see that view.

Just next to our house a building had been pulled down leaving an open space. Opposite, and much lower, was the back of a poor tenement. On each floor the tenants had their irregular little bit of roof, some hardly more than extended awning, with plants in pots, a table and a couple of chairs, a scrap of awning, a place for the children to play, or to keep a few fowls, a place to hang out the washing or to have a meal.

Beyond this building was a small backwater of a square where there were a few market stalls selling fruit and green vegetables. Here I saw the flags hanging out over Communist headquarters, Republic striped red, yellow and purple – the purple a very poor quality dye, faded pink in the strong sun – and the scarlet with the white hammer and sickle, drooping side by side.

I was on a level with the top of the plain façade of a yellow stone church with the date 1772 under a sundial. Further off was a medley of grey roofs, shining in the sun, and above them all the strange old tower affectionately called 'Miguel el Grande' by the maids. In the distance were the blue hills.

Our birthdays fell around the same date and we celebrated them together. I bought a rich cake with sugared fruit and nuts on it. In the afternoon, Jan wanted to go to sit in a real café. *The Ideal Rooms* were opposite. The café was crowded but people made room for us near the door. In Barcelona, there were wide boulevards and pavement cafés with bright coloured chairs in the French style, but in Valencia open air cafés were almost completely lacking. *The Ideal Rooms* were sombre with brown-panelled walls and long seats running round them. Jan had an exotic fancy for whisky, which was still easy to obtain at a price.

I found the most irritating of all the inconveniences of those days was *no hay cambio* (there is no change). The peasants were hoarding silver and every kind of coin. There was inflation. There were notes printed for small sums, many of them only good for the district in which they were printed. The cafés issued *vales*, printed discs, sometimes with a knife and fork represented on them, which were only good for use in the same café. Even the tram conductors hoarded copper. It became almost impossible to pay for things. Rather than give change sellers would say, 'Pay me another day,' and often one never paid. When I left Barcelona for the last time, I owed the hotel bill. The manager told me to pay when I came back but I did not return for many years.

If I were in a carriage or taxi with Jan, it was dreadfully

awkward to wait and argue as he was so easily tired. One day he had a fancy to go to the cinema as he had not been since he was wounded. We stopped in the Plaza Castelar, always flooded with aimless, slow-moving crowds, and he was on the pavement, hanging there on his crutches, when I discovered I had no change to pay the driver. I forgot my Spanish; I lost my temper. I went to the booking office to try to get change but the girl looked blank and obstinately repeated '*no hay cambio.*' The afternoon was sultry; Jan was being jostled by people. At length, the driver went off on a promise of payment another day and I told the girl to give us the tickets for a note and keep the change. She was stupidly conscientious. 'Oh no, I couldn't do that. Wait until some more people come for tickets – they may offer small change.' Already a group of prospective customers had formed, all waiting for change; some were before me. People had collected idly to listen to the row. 'I know,' said the girl at last, 'give me the note and I'll give you the change when you come out.'

The Actualidades was the only comfortable cinema in Valencia, with blue plush seats, and with relief I got Jan into the stalls and we settled down in the welcoming darkness. The cinema was ventilated in some peculiar manner which cooled the stale air and combined it with disinfectant and scent which was then wafted back. The show was all *Popeye the Sailor* but Jan had not been in a cinema for five months so any programme pleased him. I knew all the films by heart as it was impossible to import new ones. One of the films was *The King of the Mardi Gras* in which the big man, with bass voice and black beard, has a mouse tattooed on his chest which, when he swells himself out, develops into an elephant. After following about six spinach-inspired triumphs Jan was tired of sitting up so we left.

Once Jan could get about on crutches and was able to remain sitting upright for longer periods, he began to lose patience. His ambition had been limited to getting up and going outside. He was tired of being an invalid. He wanted to be really well again. He had a nostalgia for peace and the comforts of a normal life. He would no longer hear of convalescence at a Spanish resort, though the Catalan coast was still moderately safe. He wanted to rest in France; a holiday by the sea, on the Riviera. He also needed much more physiotherapy than he could get in Spain.

I began to put the machinery in motion for obtaining his honourable discharge from the Brigade as he seemed permanently disabled. The policy then was not to allow any member of the Brigade to leave Spain on any pretext – all were to stay for the duration – except, of course, political bigwigs who could go home with but a scratch and speak at meetings.

The Brigade had an office in town for their *Service Sanitaire* and I began to haunt the ante-room. Dr Maupas was the *responsable*. He was usually in Albacete but I caught him every now and then. My aim was to coax him to the Pasionaria to examine Jan and write him a discharge. The doctor was a plump, short, sleek Frenchman, always well shaved and tightly buttoned into a dark, double-breasted civilian suit. He was always busy telephoning and dictating telegrams to France for medical supplies. I found him one morning in an explosive state of indignation over a long telegram from the American hospital. '*C'est fantastique,*' he gesticulated hopelessly. 'They ask for this and that – all the most modern and expensive appliances. Of course, Dr Scott knows his business. Naturally he needs all these things – but what does he think I am, the Rockefeller Foundation?'

Dr Maupas shrugged his high shoulders, which creased the back of his too fitted coat, and sighed. 'But this order, it is as long as your arm, and this is a question of money. These Americans don't realise that anti-fascists are not gold mines. Well, I'll send the order, in a moderated form, and hope for the best. They'll get the aspirins and gauze at least,' and he settled down to dictation.

'Now,' he said briskly, standing up, 'what do you want? What did you come about?'

I started to explain the case.

'Nerve severed, you say? Been operated on? They made a graft?' Then as I stumbled on. '*Il n'est pas paralysé alors?* – he's not paralysed, then?', this with a heartless nonchalance which quite took me aback.

'*Il a eu de la chance* – he was lucky. Well, give me the name of the hospital. I'll write him a letter saying that in my opinion he is not fit for active service again. This is the best I can do, I'm afraid. It still means he'll have to go before a medical board. And those medical boards in Albacete – well, I warn you. They have orders not to let anyone through their net. But the letter may help.'

'You mean he still has to go to Albacete and go through the board? He's hardly fit to go up there.'

'Then he isn't fit to leave Spain is all I can say.'

I was very dejected after this conversation but I took the letter to Jan and he put it away in a safe place. There was nothing for it but to wait and hope something would turn up. The waiting was easier for me than for Jan. I was busy working; he still had to spend the greater part of each day recumbent. He was sufficiently better to envy the healthy, and long to do the things he had not strength for. I would have liked to devote more time to amusing him but could not escape from the office.

One evening, I arrived home unusually early and it struck me how long the evenings must be to him and how he could not hope to sleep early as he had so little air and no exercise. I collected a bundle of English newspapers and hurried to the hospital. It was dreary there, stuffy with most of the shutters closed, most of the men out, the rest noisy, the lights dim and yet unshaded and glaring.

When I left, the big gate was shut for the night and I had to creep past the sentry through a small door in it and it was too late for a tram. It was bright moonlight. The streets were deserted; the houses shuttered and barred. A few dogs howled as I went by. I walked home along the white streets, the tram lines shining. I stopped to rest when I reached the river and leaned on the parapet. Summer was coming and the river was drying up; it ran thinly in two or three channels between mudbanks. Vegetable patches were cultivated on the banks. The black shadows were strange and theatrical.

* * * * *

Outside the windows of our office were balconies, so when we heard a band we would go out and look up and down the street.

Sometimes, the band preceded militia on their way to the railway station – watched now in silence and hardly cheered, as they had been in the early days. Generally, the bands accompanied funerals.

Whenever an important man was killed at the front his body was brought back. It lay in state in the appropriate trade union or political headquarters and then was paraded through the town, the coffin covered with a flag, republican or plain red, and the procession behind, mostly men, bearing wreaths so large it took three or four of them to carry one. There were plenty of flowers in Valencia.

Somehow these grand funerals were a consolation to people.

'Did you see me today?' asked an old Canadian brigader of me one evening. 'I happened to be hanging about communist headquarters and got roped in as a pall-bearer. He was a heavy man. I felt very awkward – not dressed for it as you might say. And I didn't know what to do with my cap. I thought of resting it on the coffin but then it might have been noticed or might have fallen off. You know I keep thinking about that funeral. They said at headquarters, 'Come on, it's for the morale we do it,' but I think of all the good fellows who have died at the front and no fancy burials for them. It doesn't seem right or democratic to me that this chap should have all this fuss made over him just because he had the rank of colonel. They're taking his body back to France by air, so they say. I keep thinking and I'm not easy in my mind about it.

Internationals never got leave but the Canadian had come to Valencia for a few days to see about parts for a broken machine-gun. He was with another man, a gentle English intellectual with a dreamy face. The Englishman was really a pacifist, driven to Spain by the frequent combination of idealism and unhappy domestic affairs.

'You know,' said Jack, the Canadian, when the other man had gone off on some errand, 'that chap is too good for a soldier. Why, you know he's a clever chap, writes poetry and plays the flute – it's often a fine distraction for us when we are marching. He needs looking after. Has no idea of taking care of himself. I admire him. What paper do you write for, lady?'

'The *Christian Science Monitor*.'

'Well now, shake hands on that. It's a fine paper – the only one we ever got in prison that had any foreign news in it.'

'You've been in prison?'

'Sure, been in trouble. Strikes, that kind of thing. I'm from Vancouver. Ever been there?'

'No.'

'It's a great country.' He began to tell me about it. He told me about the salmon and how they swim up river to lay their eggs.

'Once I had a job at a factory near a river. I saw the salmon heavy with eggs, falling exhausted because they couldn't make it. I was sorry for the creatures. I spent all day lifting them over the falls and putting them in the water on the other side. And believe me they were heavy, those fish. They seemed as heavy as the coffin today. When I got back to the factory the foreman asked where I had been and I told him I had been lifting female salmon over the falls – but of course he didn't believe me, and said I must have been drunk. But that's the kind of chap I am, always have a soft spot for the females. That poet now, he seems like a woman in a way, kind of helpless.' He nodded towards the Englishman, who was coming back.

'I suppose now the weather is getting warm, lice are inevitable,' said the poet, scratching as he sat down at the table. 'I'm sure I bathe whenever I get the chance.'

'I never have lice,' said Jack. 'Go stripped to the waist when it's hot. That is the secret of it; don't wear a shirt.'

The poet sighed. 'It's because they don't boil the clothes, just beat them out in cold water on stones. One doesn't get one's own shirt back from the wash, but just any old shirt. And the eggs are still alive in the seams even when the shirt looks clean. One can't see the eggs, that's the whole trouble. I can't go without a shirt, I get such blazing sunburn.'

Evidently one of our visiting journalists had been watching funerals too. Constancia brought me a typewritten piece that she could not quite make out and asked me to type it as she doubted if it would pass the censor.

'There are many funerals,' I read, 'with masses of wreaths. These are sometimes shaped like a star, sometimes in a hammer and sickle but never, never, the sign of the cross . . . I see here all the signs of revolution including a formidable bureaucracy.'

I laughed. 'That means us,' I said to Constancia. 'You must have wound him up in red tape and he's annoyed about it.'

But she was on her dignity and very angry.

'He should have seen the bureaucracy in Spain before the war, when the government was in Madrid. We only have the shadow of that now. I shan't let it go through.'

'I should if I were you. In any case, he will publish what he likes when he gets out of Spain and I shouldn't give colour to assertions that people are impeded by official restrictions here.'

In the afternoon we heard a band playing *The Internationale* and *Hijo del pueblo*, but not the Republican anthem. There was a sizeable concourse of the humbler people. A platform had been erected and someone got up and made a speech amid *vivas*.

'What's up?' I asked Aurora.

'They are renaming the street, Calle Largo Caballero.'

'Whatever for? Caballero is out of office – in fact he's out in France.'

'He is always intriguing to get back again, the old fox. This is a demonstration to show how many supporters he has.'

'Anarchists,' said Coco, as *Hijo del pueblo* struck up again.

A plaque with the new name was affixed to the street but people persisted in using the old one, just as they went on calling the Plaza de la República the Plaza Tetuán.

The politically minded members of the staff used to have meetings once a week in conjunction with some of the Propaganda Ministry. We used to discuss our work, and suggestions were made for its improvement and various problems were raised. The meetings were held at lunch time as it was impossible to assemble people who lived far away in the dark evenings.

It was a duty to go, if one understood Spanish. Though we achieved no positive results, at least everyone could have his say and they kept up our enthusiasm. One discussion was on the endeavour to unionise us all. This was a thorny subject as there were two rival unions, UGT and CNT. Those in favour of the moderate socialist union, UGT, were in a majority but the CNT advocates were noisier and, at one meeting, one of them brandished a revolver and we broke up in disorder.

We were asked to go into the fields and help the peasants on Sundays. We seldom had a whole Sunday off and the local crop, rice, required expert handling.

One of the staff was arrested as a spy and we had to decide whether efforts should be made to obtain his release. Constancia tactfully took charge of this. She was later under a temporary political cloud herself. She said we could not find out the facts and, even if the man were innocent, we could not do anything as he was in the hands of the police.

A man who was called up for the army wanted exemption.

'What! He wants exemption because he wears spectacles,' cried a small boy. '*Hay muchos en las milicias con gafas.*'[117]

These were the strangest meetings I have ever attended. There was complete equality between office boys and heads of departments. We listened politely to whoever spoke. It was the somnolent siesta hour, in the warm, sleepy afternoons, in a shaded room with one or two flies buzzing. The women in black, agitating their fans, looking like Goya portraits. The earthenware *porrón* with its narrow spout stood in the middle of the floor, and the speaker took an occasional swig of water. One of our members was a little messenger boy, who said he was twelve but looked eight, and wore his hair pomaded down. When I remarked that he was very small he said, 'When the war is over, I will grow,' as if he were too busy just then. The most frequent speaker was the doorkeeper, an old man from Málaga, who would roll up his shirt sleeves and hold forth in a combination of southern eloquence, Andaluz accent and toothlessness which was hard to follow. He chastised us all for slackness with his fiery words. 'We must work intensely to win the war,' he would cry, thumping the table.

His work consisted of dozing in the hall all day so he had more energy than some of us to spare for meetings.

* * * * *

We were becoming frustrated over Jan's progress and

294

prospect of leaving Spain when the Merrimans turned up. Bob's wound was almost healed and he would soon be going back to the front so they had got a few days' leave. He had been training recruits for some time and Marion had been working in an office in Albacete. They came with a good Ford and a Russian driver. We had dinner together at the Victoria after the waiters had made a bit of fuss, as the hotel refused to serve meals to non-residents even if invited by a resident, in this case Milly, who still lived there.

Bob was very brown and was wearing the biggest revolver I have ever seen and Marion, though a tall girl, looked frail and small by comparison, as he was very tall. She wore a checked cotton frock and a blue scarf tied round her head, which made her look obviously foreign.

There was no room to be had for them. I tried the *Casa de Cultura* as it seemed too bad that they should not have a proper room together. I told them that Bob was a professor of economics from California University, but they were full up. In the end, Marion had to sleep with Milly, and Bob slept at the *Socorro Rojo*, a sort of red YMCA. They made not the least complaint about this arrangement and begged us not to trouble about them. During the night, Marion told Milly that she had a presentiment that Bob would be killed and she desperately wanted to have a baby so that she would have something left to her. She was not lucky in this respect. Other American volunteers, who came from time to time, told Milly that it was considered very unfair for Bob to have his wife in Spain when the rest of them could not.

'Of course, they all adore her. They think she is a swell girl, how could they not?' said Milly. 'But I guess Bob thinks it isn't right either and will send her back to America soon.'

In time, he did send her back, not for her safety, but because he did not want to be happier than his men. She spoke at meetings and did very well, I believe.

They had decided to spend the next day at Las Arenas and we were to go with them. Before we could start, I had to buy Jan a shirt. Bob wanted one too and also a holster for his revolver. We chased all over town but Bob was such a large size that we could not find anything to fit him.

295

I gave directions to Bob which he translated into Russian for the driver. We could not talk to this man but he looked very scornful and knowing the whole time. He was a heavy, round shouldered man with a shaven head, little, blue, gimlet eyes and a nose like a duck's beak. Bob explained to us that the Russian disapproved of our gaiety and idleness. It was against his conscience to drive anyone to the beach. He had not been carefully selected from a number of mechanics to go to Spain merely to drive a crowd of laughing jackanapes off on a jaunt; but he had been allotted to Bob and had to do as he was told. His attitude cast rather a damper over our spirits and we were glad when he proposed returning to town and fetching us later.

Though the weather was fine it was not warm enough for bathing, but we all lay on the sand in the sun. Jan was very fond of the sea.

When we were all on the beach, Bob presented Marion with a cardboard box he had been carrying. It contained an embroidered Spanish shawl of yellow silk, a very handsome thing. They both stood up and he wrapped it round her to see how it looked and the fringe fluttered in the wind. Marion flung her arms round him. It was the anniversary of their wedding day. They had been married five years. They were so spontaneous, happy and fond of one another, and looked so young and handsome that I felt very sentimental.

There were rows of restaurants along the beach. One entered from the back and in front were terraces looking out to sea. We went into one through the kitchen where there was a very rich and savoury smell. It was crowded and difficult to find a table. It was full of fat Valencians, gobbling and sweating in their shirt sleeves. We felt momentarily angry when we saw the cars parked outside and the bourgeois inside. The waiters were very offhand but, after an age, we were served with a great paella with prawns, sizzling in its vast cartwheel of an iron dish.

We went back and lay on the sand. Out to sea stood one of the foreign warships of the 'Control'. Approaching the port was fairy-like, white-sailed cargo ship, probably carrying beans.

'It shouldn't be like that,' murmured Bob.

'What shouldn't be?'

'Oh, the sun and the blue sky and the green waves, and then that sailing ship to top it off. It is too beautiful. It makes one love life too much.'

As he spoke, he ran his fingers through the sand. Marion lay on her back, her bare arms under her head, her eyes closed, a contented smile on her face. Jan had hobbled to where a photographer was taking a picture of two fat sisters identically clad in white satin. His light hair was ruffled by the breeze, his fine, thin profile outlined against the sea. His short corduroy jacket rode up at the back as he hunched forward on his crutches.

'Have a picture taken,' I called. 'Let's have one taken together.'

'No, not with these,' he touched the crutches.

'Don't you and Marion want one,' I asked Bob, 'to remember this day by?'

'I'll remember it all right,' he said. 'It will be hard enough to leave it all as it is.'

We were harassed on the way home by the poker-faced driver and by an argument at a petrol pump. Bob had a chit from the War Office allowing more petrol than the car would hold. He wanted the garage to mark it with the number of gallons he had received and give it back so that he could use the rest another time. The garage man insisted on keeping it. So there were extra gallons left on the chit which the crafty man could sell to some private customer who had no right to an allowance at all. Bob's sense of justice was upset by this transaction, nor did he want to go back to the War Office so soon for another chit as it meant waiting for hours in a queue. His Spanish was weak and I tried to help but, at last, with a gesture of weariness and discouragement, he told me to desist.

'It doesn't matter. It's no use trying to enjoy oneself in wartime. It isn't right, and too difficult besides. Let the man be. It's time we were getting back. It's no use kidding oneself.'

Bob offered to take Jan to Albacete in the car with them the next day. This was a godsend. In the evening, Teresa washed and ironed a shirt for him to take with him and ran down to the hospital with it. She liked to do this as it amused her to see the hospital and gossip with the girls there. Meanwhile, I went to the International Office and procured a return pass (*hoja de ruta).*

Jan folded it with the letter from Dr Maupas. I was very anxious about his going, fearful that he would be detained in Albacete. Bob said they would drive quickly and get him straight to bed in a hospital.

The next morning, I saw the car from the balcony of the office and ran down to the Calle de la Paz. It was parked against the curb; one of the party doing a last minute bit of shopping. Marion came back with a pot of honey which she showed me, very pleased with the pretty pot. 'I shall take it home with me and use it as a flower vase.'

Jan and his crutches were ensconced in front. They all had cheerful grins fixed on their faces as people do when they do not know what the future has in store for them.

It was my last sight of the Merrimans. Bob distinguished himself in the taking of Belchite. After the Aragón offensive, he was missing. His body was never found. No one had seen him die. Enquiries were made through the American military attaché, Colonel Fuqua, a petition was sent from Californian professors, but his name was in no list of prisoners.

* * * * *

After Jan had left, I had a fit of depression and began to imagine all sorts of unlucky things happening as the days passed and I heard nothing. I was quite glad to see Manolo, who turned up on business from Barcelona and suggested taking me to a play.

'I've heard there's one about the Dreyfus case; I've always wanted to know the rights of the story,' he said.

The play was by a Spanish author; it was a melodrama and the actors put plenty of vigour into it and the audience was enthusiastic. We sat in the front row of the stalls. The stage was small and the scenery scanty. Rents and patches in the painted canvas and greasepaint dripping from the actors' faces were visible from where we sat. There were two back-drops: a drawing-room with a marble staircase and potted palms, and a church with stained glass windows. Doors shook and walls wobbled as the actors made passionate exits and entrances.

One the chief characters was a stout and lugubrious woman with bright yellow hair who caused Dreyfus' downfall out of pique over an unrequited passion and then was devoured by remorse and took to impenetrable widow's weeds. She was aided and abetted by an astute villain, her Jesuit confessor, and when she threatened to reveal her share in the plot he commissioned a young priest to push her out of the window of a nunnery where she was in retreat. She was fished out of the Seine by Dreyfus' son and this put the final touch on her penitence.

There was plenty of incident as someone shot himself on the stage in what was supposed to be the hall of the court during the re-trial of the case. There was also an irruption of 'the people' into Émile Zola's study, armed with sticks and staves, in which all the stage hands came on and acted so realistically that I really feared for poor Zola. Suddenly, he pulled off the beret of the ring-leader. Behold a tonsured head – the Jesuit again! Egging on the mob to violence. How the audience did hiss and shout! They made such an uproar that the Jesuitical speeches could not be heard. The army officers in their gold braid came in for only a minor share of the hissing.

One midday I was so restless that I walked to the Victoria with Milly and was walking back again when suddenly I saw Jan on his crutches on the pavement smiling at me. I ran to him.

'However did you get here?'

'On the tram. I meant to go to your flat but they put me off too soon.'

We went into the Café Popular. It was a big, empty café with coloured tiles in designs of ladies, fruits and flowers, a very loud radio, and a very large, slow fan, like an aeroplane propeller, on the ceiling.

'I tried to ring up from the hospital but, as there was no answer and I had heard there had just been a bad air raid I was afraid something might have happened to you.'

'That was a mile or so away at the port. Do you think you could get as far as the flat? It's five minutes from here.'

'Sure. I'll try.'

'Is it all right?' I asked when we reached home.

'Absolutely. I was very lucky; I ran into a friend up there and got a lift back in a car. And I have letters to people here and in Barcelona to say – well, I don't know what exactly, because they are in French, but it is all fixed up and I can go.'

The letters were identical. They said Jan had been an exemplary soldier and asked that he should receive any help he might require, in the way of medical attention or money for his journey.

After that there was not much more to be done. I had an interview with Rubio. He spoke before I did.

'Now, now,' shaking his finger. 'Don't tell me you want to leave us. I absolutely refuse to spare you. You may go on condition that you give me your word to come back.'

He wrote me a safe-conduct for leaving and returning to Spain within a month. I did return, but not until three months later.

I did not feel too bad about quitting just then. I was still naïve enough to believe that propaganda was effective and that my job was useful to the cause. I know now that issues of war and peace and commerce are manipulated by a very few people without regard for public opinion and very little for governments. War is made first and patriotism whipped up afterwards. Decisions are made, then a publicity campaign to reconcile the public to them. Now I am cynical enough to see the futility of protest. However, I thought our work was important then.

I was less reluctant to leave because the war seemed to be going fairly well and the situation stable. I did not see that the Spanish Republic was sinking under the weight of the refugees and the problem of feeding so many people. There was little sustaining food to be had. Most of the wheat was grown on the other side of Spain. We had a little rice and, in Catalunya, some potatoes. The fishermen were afraid to go out because of mines. As the Republic shrank in territory, it increased in population, and was much greater than on the other side. Every town and village was swarming with people, women and children, old people, gypsies, all the poorest of the poor, all helpless and without possessions. The Government was bourgeois but it was a people's republic and it was morally bound to help every one of these underdogs who had fled for fear of the fascists, and the authorities struggled gamely with their mounting humanitarian obligations.

Air raids were increasing and the Valencians shut their shops early, at seven, and the young people would run out into the *Huerta*, in a kind of hysterical gaiety, for safety. It was a time for flirtations, for which as a rule Spaniards had little opportunity.

'Tonight is full moon – *bombardeo* (air raid) – meet me in the *Huerta*,' was the formula.

Journeys were great undertakings in those days and required many preparations, almost like the early voyages of exploration. I went with Jan to the main *Hospital Militar* for a medical discharge from the Spanish authorities. It was a big building beside the river, round the usual patio, and so crowded, chaotic and dirty that I was glad he had never been a patient there.

A man from the Brigade office, a French Jewish student, got the use of a car for the afternoon and took Jan out to buy him a civilian suit. This was a thin, grey, papery outfit, always creased and out of shape. He looked strange, mild and gentlemanly in it.

I began to negotiate for a sleeper to Barcelona. I did not know of any cars going that way and by train the journey took all night. I went to the Brigade. The officer in charge was a Balkan type who spoke bad French.

'Nobody goes on a sleeper. I give you first class ticket; that's what we give wounded.'

'First and third are all the same for crowding. He probably wouldn't even get a seat and anyway couldn't sit up all night.'

'There are no sleepers,' he said, in the manner of one who is always being pressed to grant impossible demands and has developed a technique of obstruction. Two sick, or malingering, soldiers were sitting on the stairs smoking and listening, but without interest.

'There is one wagon-lit on every train because officials go on them. I will get places on it.'

'He can't be well enough to travel at all. Still, have it your own way. I'll make out the *salvo-conducto* and you sort yourselves out as best you can.'

I got Constancia to book us a sleeper from the office and then rang up Albacete about the money. I got bogged down in the usual babel of languages so I had to get Jan upstairs to the office and put through another call for him. Jan made contact with a German.

'All right,' said the man in Albacete. 'If that swine in Valencia won't give you the money get it reimbursed in Barcelona. I will send instructions there. *Salud*. Good luck.'

I was busy until the last moment. Two nights before we left, Almería was shelled by the *Deutschland*. It was a reprisal for a raid on Ibiza. This aroused a good deal of horror in Spain, for Almería was an unprotected, flimsy little town and the casualties were dreadful. The wretched inhabitants, many of them already refugees from Málaga, streamed out on foot, by the light of the fires in the town, moving on again towards Murcia.

Many correspondents hastened down there and, on my last night in Valencia, I was at the office until after midnight answering the phone and taking messages from them to put through the censor. It was very hot with the shutters closed. The room was full of journalists waiting for calls. Some had supper sent over from hotels and the long table was littered with typewriters and bottles of white wine in buckets of ice.

As fast as I had transcribed one call there would come another. 'This is X agency. I am sitting on the pavement amid a scene of desolation . . .' A pause. We had been cut off. Then we would be reconnected.

'Well, all right. Some other fellows are waiting to use the phone. Use your own judgement about it. It's a horror story anyway. Make it up. Get it in as fast as you can. Ask for a double-rate call to Paris and try to beat the others to it. So long. One can't hear on this line anyway. All the lights have gone. I'm in the Governor's office with a candle-end – say that.'

The whole of the last day I spent running around. Milly gave me her pair of white shoes as I had none; I used to wear sandals or canvas shoes. I bought a bottle of brandy for the journey. I wanted Jan to rest as much as he could but he was very nervous lying on my bed all day. We had little luggage. The maids were doing the last bits of ironing. I had to wear my suit but it was so hot I only put a scarf instead of a blouse under it. We tried to eat something. The maids carried the luggage down to the hall.

The Brigade had arranged to send a car because, after dark, it was not possible to hire any conveyance. The car did not come and it was getting late. I ran through the black streets to the Brigade office. There was a light upstairs and two Italians having supper with the stenographer.

'What's happened to the car? You promised it.'

'If it isn't in the garage below then it is gone.'

'Heavens, the driver must have lost the way.'

I hurried back; it was pitch dark. There were two or three different routes from the Plaza Tetuán to the Calle de las Comedias and I did not know what the car looked like.

As I turned into our street, I saw a car fumbling along the kerb. The driver shouted something in German.

'Here, here,' I yelled, indicating the door.

Jan had come down with the maids and was peering round the big door which was only open a crack because of the blackout. The driver was in a khaki uniform with a beret. He was very young and blond, with round apple cheeks, cheery and calm.

The station was teeming with would-be, struggling travellers and very dark. The driver, pushing good-humouredly ahead with the bags, managed to make way for us. I called out repeatedly '*un herido*' (a wounded man) to make the human knots disperse. The train was extremely long and the sleeper at the far end. I thought we should never reach it. It was kept locked to prevent it being rushed by the crowds, who made angry murmurs and a half-hearted attempt to follow us as we prepared to mount. There were high steps. The driver seized Jan under one arm and the bags under the other and forced his way up. It was breathlessly hot. The young German shouted, '*Salud! Rot Front!*' He raised his first to his beret, then his fresh, rosy face and sturdy figure disappeared into the crowd.

Chapter 16
Valencia—Barcelona—Paris

It must have been another hour before the train pulled out. In the meantime, the ever-increasing crowd milled about the platform and climbed up on to the coaches and down again in vain efforts to find some corner for themselves and their belongings. Latecomers arrived, breathless. This was the only train for Barcelona; there was now only one a day. I saw a bell marked 'attendant' and I rang it. I was astonished that this produced a little, bald old man in a navy-blue braided uniform.

'Have you any refreshments?' I asked him.

'Beer and mineral water,' he replied.

This was surprising as there had been no beer in Valencia for some time. The attendant spoke a smattering of French and English, was a very *antes* sort of man, and would obviously do anything for a tip. He lifted a flap to form a table, brought bottled beer and glasses and apologised because he had no ice and could offer no food. The lukewarm beer frothed over the lip of the bottle on to the varnished mahogany. He then arranged our shabby luggage in the most convenient manner. It felt strange to be in a privileged position. The blinds, pulled down to prevent any show of light, hid our felicity from the mob outside but it made the compartment horribly hot and stuffy during the long wait at the station.

At last the train got underway and moved out from under the echoing station roof. With the lights off, it was possible to open the window allowing moonlight and the scent of orange groves to pour in. The train crawled. Frequently, with a horrid grinding of unoiled wheels and brakes, it stopped and seemed to have given up. Sometimes there were trees so near that branches brushed against the windows. The coal was very poor and the engine snorted occasional puffs of evil-smelling black smoke in through the window. It was very warm and there was no wind; we did not move fast enough to create any, although later the night dew did freshen the air a little. The sky became overcast and lightning flickered along the horizon.

It was still early when we rumbled into the big, empty station. Barcelona appeared a metropolis compared to Valencia, and there was so much traffic I was frequently nearly run over. Everything looked grey, dreary, northern. We were back in a place were there were taxis and porters.

We drove to the old *pensión* where I had stayed before. The hunchbacked doorkeeper recognised me and helped us into the lift. The bleach-blonde maid fell on my neck.

'You said you would only be gone a few days, but it's six months! The things you left here are all safe.'

'Where's Montserrat?'

'She got married. I'll tell the *señora* you're here. Would you like some coffee? You'd like a bath I expect, but we have no fuel to heat the water nowadys – bad times.'

It was wonderful to be offered coffee; to hear an apology that the bath water was cold. I went out to the kitchen to talk to the *señora*. She launched into complaints. One maid had left, got a job in a munitions factory, ungrateful slut, they were all the same. The cost of living was soaring and she had had to raise the price of *pensión*. Food was scarce; for bread one had to stand in a queue. She herself, in person, had to stand in a queue; they would not give it to the girl. In Barcelona then there were no shortages that I could see except of bread and milk. The shops still had ham and other groceries.

Neither of us had any clothes for wet weather. My white shoes were already splashed with mud, but in the afternoon we went out to the Brigade office to get Jan's final discharge papers and a visa to leave Spain. When Jan hobbled into the office a big, fat Frenchman, in shirt-sleeves, who was sitting at a desk, jumped up in surprise and gave us chairs.

There was a number of other men to be attended to. First two elderly Scots:

'We want some money, we haven't a penny, nothing for smokes or anything,' they said, both speaking at once and looking with envy at the Frenchman's cigarettes.

'I haven't got any money,' said the Frenchman, winking in our direction. 'Where do you come from? I can't do anything for you.

You come here every day.'

'We told you about it already.' They looked at one another and then, after a lot of deep delving into pockets, produced a very dirty piece of paper folded over and over to a very small size. The Frenchman laid his cigarette on the desk and leisurely unfolded the paper, which was torn at the edges.

'This says you are both discharged and that you received the following sum at Albacete.'

'That's right,' they nodded.

'Well, you got free railway tickets. That money should have taken you to Perpignan. How long have you been in Barcelona? You haven't been staying in the barracks.'

'We have the last few days. We didn't know the money was to last further than here.'

'According to the date on this, you must have been here a week.'

The two Scots looked ruefully at one another. They had obviously drunk up the money.

'I'll make you out a *vale* for tickets to the frontier. You don't get any more cash until I have further orders. You can live in barracks.'

'What's the use of that? We can't go any further without francs. What's the good of us hanging about *Port Bow*? We might as well hang around here.'

They retired, muttering about *Port Bow*.

The next man was a German. His face had been horribly disfigured.

'I want a glass eye,' he said, standing over the desk.

'I'm not a doctor or a hospital. I can't supply you with that.'

'I'm not going back to France with this face. I've lost half my teeth too but I don't mind about that. I'm not going to face my wife without a glass eye. You must give me the money to buy one.'

'I'm not authorised to do that. I have no funds at my disposal to buy artificial limbs and things like that. The Spanish Government should supply them. But come back tomorrow and I'll enquire about it, though,' he said with a grimace. 'The Spanish comrades are not very comradely in this city.'

The German saluted and went out.

'What about us?' came a hoarse voice from the door where several Americans were seated on the steps.

'Just arrived?' asked the Frenchman pleasantly. 'How did you come?' (As if to say, by rail or road, and did you have a pleasant trip?)

'I came over the mountains,' croaked the man, 'and got this pretty case of laryngitis from sleeping outdoors – but I guess, at that, I did better than my two pals here. They *swam* ashore.'

'Ah,' said the Frenchman, with sympathetic interest. 'Then you must have been on the *Ciudad de Barcelona* and have no papers, I suppose.' Then, in an aside to us, 'It was a bad business. This ship was sunk just off the coast. Hundreds of volunteers on board were drowned. Too bad to lose their lives before they even had a chance to fight. Fishing boats picked up a few.'

'I know the boat,' I said. 'It was a white passenger ship. It used to be on the Palma service.'

'Well boys,' said the Frenchman, rubbing his hands cheerfully. 'Take this note downstairs. You'll get a meal and beds and uniforms. Take a rest. Better have some wine to warm you up.'

When we were alone, Jan produced the receipt for the wagon-lit and the letter from Albacete and asked about the money. The Frenchman demurred but at last, with a heavy sigh, he opened his desk drawer and counted it out. He also, with a secretive look, produced a packet of Woodbines which he offered us. We smoked them lingeringly as if they had been Abdullas.

Then we asked about the passport situation. In Albacete, Jan had been given a British passport in case he could use it. It belonged to a man, also fair, but much bigger than Jan. Jan had known and liked the man and the passport depressed him because he thought the man must be dead. In fact, he was alive and well but his passport had been collected, along with many others, in Albacete, and we did not know this.

The Frenchman studied the passport photo and looked at Jan. '*Il a maigri quoi?*'[118] he said, sucking in his cheeks. Finally he agreed that the passport was not usable.

'The people in this town are quite hopeless at faking visas, passports and such things. I wouldn't trust them to fake the simplest stamp; they'd be sure to bungle it. You'll have to try to get some sort of Catalan passport. You can't walk over the mountains; you have to try to get into France legally. It's not easy to cross the frontier now. You need Catalan exit visas. They are very sticky about them since the May troubles. Awfully suspicious of foreigners. What is the point of detaining spies and crooks here? I don't know.'

'I thought the Central Government had taken charge of the police here.'

'So they have. But it's all chaotic at present. All the passport officials have been sacked and no new ones appointed. The remaining Catalans have been putting a spoke in the wheel as much as they can out of pique at having things taken out of their hands. Go ahead. Don't let me discourage you. Go to the passport office and try your luck. I'll ring them up and tell them you're coming. But I have men here who have been waiting ten days already for their exit visas and who complain of being insulted besides by the *Guardias de Asalto* that are only fit for rummaging people's luggage and directing traffic.'

He put through a telephone call and I heard him expostulating, '*Voyez-vous – ces manières. Ça fait un effet déplorable sur la morale des voluntaires.*'[119]

'Well,' he said to us. 'Go over there and try.'

'Do you think we'll get into France?'

'It depends on the sort of officials you run into. You try it by Cerbère. Then if that fails you try again by Bourg. I'm afraid I can't suggest anything else, Madame.'

Jan was grimly tired but insisted on going on to the passport office. We waited for a long time on a stone bench on the deserted boulevard before a taxi passed; no café was in sight.

The car was diverted from the usual route, Calle Córsica, which was cordoned off. 'A policeman was just shot in that street,' said the driver casually, turning his head.

We pushed our way through the crowd into the passport office and upstairs to the foreigners' department. There was a queue being roughly kept in order by policemen with rifles and revolvers. The queue was noisy and protesting, entirely composed of disabled men of the Brigade, most of them French.

The man in front of us turned round and it was the same American in square spectacles that I had run into twice previously. He held out his hand.

'How's the knee?'

'Forgotten about it, had two or three wounds since then. Got a bullet still sitting in my lung now.'

'Going home?'

'We're hoping,' he said, indicating the queue. 'You must come and have a beer with me and my friend.' He presented a black man. 'There's a small joint round the corner. We are getting to know this neighbourhood,' he said resignedly. 'We could have a good time here, in a way. The town's wide open, dance halls and everything. We ride everywhere in taxi cabs. I have plenty of dough: captain's pay.' He tapped his breast pocket. 'But I hate to see a town like this in war time. It isn't right and the Catalans make me wild. Look at that.' He pointed to a notice on the closed door before which we all waited. It said: 'Office hours 2 - 6, Monday to Friday.' 'Well, it's between two and six on a Wednesday, ain't it? I've been here every afternoon this week. So have all these other poor devils. Some of them ought to be in hospital, not standing in line. The office has never once been open.'

Two Frenchmen were shaking the double door. One heaved his shoulder against it. It was locked. I went out on the gallery and walked round to the window and looked in. The office was neat and tidy; quite empty.

'You're wasting your time,' I said. 'There's nobody in.'

'You're telling me. We wait in hope somebody'll turn up. And if he does, it looks like the boys would tear him limb from limb. And this isn't all. You need four lousy Catalan stamps on your passport. The rest come from a different office. That's open but they won't fix you up until you've been through this one. Well, boys, let's call it a day.'

We called it a day and went home.

All the time we were in Barcelona it was rainy and cold. Every day we went to one or other of the passport offices and sometimes to the Brigade office as well.

I note, for people caught up in wars, that trams are invaluable and in Spain were finally the only way of getting about. Private cars, taxis and buses were all suppressed because of the petrol shortage. Local trains to the suburbs, running on coal, were cut almost completely. A bicycle was valuable until it needed new tyres. In Valencia, horse drawn vehicles were extremely useful and the only thing for carting luggage about. Barcelona was too modern; it had scrapped the horse long ago and it was so much bigger than Valencia that one could not cover the distances on foot.

To Jan, Barcelona seemed very much the same as pre-war. To me, it had changed very much for the worse in six months. When I was there earlier the anarchists were in control. Everyone was in a state of euphoria that was too good to last. People were gay, everything was free, everyone believed that Utopia was just around the corner, a marvellous future, a new life beginning. This atmosphere was exhilarating. Now the signs of revolution had disappeared but the most sinister signs of war had emerged – the *'especuladores'* (speculators), *'acaparadores'* (hoarders) and *'emboscados'* (shirkers) and, of course, the black market. There was a poster of the agricultural products, setting out innocently for the market, led by the egg and the almond hand-in-hand, while behind the trees lurked the speculators, knife in hand, and the big bad wolf of the black market.

There were plenty of jokes in the papers: a line of elegant young men, 'Is that a recruiting station?'

'No, it's the queue for brilliantine.'

There was the story of the Austrian prince who came to Barcelona and insisted on being a blood donor. His blood was found to be blue and the doctors filled their fountain pens with it.

Another story: 'We've formed a Party to end all Parties. It's called "The Enough Party". We need a headquarters but all the biggest and best buildings seem to have been requisitioned by other Parties. But we have our eyes on a very suitable place, at present totally unoccupied. It's the cathedral. Unfortunately, to date, we have been unable to obtain the keys.'

The streets of Barcelona were as gay and colourful as ever. In one square was a model of a boat, the Konsomol, sunk halfway into the pavement. In the Plaza Catalunya was a cardboard Tree of Guernika, part of a pro-Euzkadi campaign. There were some shoddy booths and stalls with lottery tickets and cheap, tawdry toys for sale. Somehow, things in Barcelona always looked like a commercial exhibition. The posters were fine; I bought one which was to warn picnickers against setting fire to the woods.

Very few wounded were about and Jan was regarded with astonishment and asked about the war as if it had nothing to do with Catalunya. Cafés and restaurants were crowded with young men of military age and smart girls. We sometimes managed to get across the street to a café restaurant called the Munich. Barcelona was very expensive. There was no milk but one could buy plates of whipped cream called *espuma de leche*. I bought a plate and then was ashamed and gave it to a ragged refugee child.

Once we arrived in Barcelona, Jan was determined, despite his handicap, to take charge of his own life again. He had always been active and independent and he found his physical weakness and need for help terribly galling. I am a clumsy and inept nurse. We were both irritable and the unnecessary difficulties put in our way were exasperating. He had suffered so long and patiently but was now becoming bitter. He made extraordinary efforts to get around and arrange things for himself but most of the time I had to accompany him as he could not manage steps unaided, and the language of the Brigade was French. I was much more fluent in French if anything complicated had to be explained. The *responsable* in charge was usually French and usually working class without much education, whose English or German consisted of a few comradely phrases.

At long last our papers were in order and we went to the Brigade to get *vales* for railway tickets. We also enquired about further funds.

'We never give out more than enough to reach Perpignan,' said the Frenchman. 'You see for yourself how it is. A lot of the men would only blow the money and be stranded. I'll give you a letter to an anti-fascist committee in Perpignan.'

I did not like the sound of this. Perpignan was noted as a centre for runaway Spaniards and fascist spies, being near the border. Our papers were not quite regular and we did not want to risk being sent back. In a big city like Paris, with friends, we would be safe. For Jan to land in a French prison, even temporarily, might seriously retard his recovery. He would have to decide what to do at the frontier. We could pay the fare to Paris and then try to obtain a refund.

We had pesetas to burn. One was not allowed to take any out of the country and they were almost worthless anywhere else. So we went shopping. Jan bought a pair of shoes, one of which we left behind as it seemed so unlikely he would ever get it on his bad foot. He regretted not having the pair later. He bought a tie, and a pair of socks to keep him warm and to cover the bandage on his bad foot to make it less noticeable and to make him look respectable to pass the frontier. I bought a pair of Swiss watches and some gramophone records. There was a book fair on that week and I bought some pretty, illustrated, children's books in Catalan for my little niece.

Finally, I went to an office in Montjuich to buy the railway tickets to Cerbère. It was a long way. The office was in what had been one of the exhibition buildings on the right, up some steps leading to the park. I asked for first class tickets. 'We don't put on first class coaches any more. I'll give you second class.'

He handed me a slip and it was only when I was back at the *pensión* that I discovered that it was only made out for one person. Tickets were often made out for two on the same piece of paper. To wait in a queue at the station was out of the question for Jan, apart from the risk of missing the train. I was very tired and nervous and I am afraid that I grumbled a bit. We had run our pesetas so low that we only had just enough to get away with. I had to go all the way back to Montjuich on the tram for the second ticket. When I returned, it was dusk and supper time. I was completely exhausted and wet through. We had to pack and make ready for a very early start; the only train to the frontier left at seven in the morning.

Jan refused supper. I tried to persuade him, becoming progressively crosser, as I wanted him to feel strong for the next day's ordeal. He persisted in his refusal but asked for wine. I fetched the bottle of red from the dining room table and placed it beside the bed. I sat in solitude in the little, dark dining room. I had not much appetite either, feeling as if I were getting a cold.

The croquettes were smaller than ever and their contents more mysterious. To spin out the mixture the *señora* had made them very sloppy.

I went back to the bedroom. Jan had drunk the wine and was lying quite silent. At first I thought he was asleep. I was afraid he was going to be ill as his manner seemed strange. I switched the light on; he asked me to turn it off in a stifled voice.

'What is it?' I asked. 'Are you angry or offended with me? I'm sorry I was so cross this afternoon but I was so tired and it was almost too much having to make two trips to Montjuich.'

At that moment I felt an immense burden on my shoulders. I was afraid he would break down from fatigue on the journey. At last he said, 'No, it isn't your fault, it's nothing to do with you.'

He had been drinking but was not drunk. He was just feeling terribly melancholy. He was thinking about his friends who had died, perhaps in vain. After he fell asleep, he repeated their names. I set to, as quietly as I could, to pack the bags.

We got on the train somehow. Like all trains in Spain it was almost impossible to get aboard at the start of the journey and yet by the end of it the train would be empty. This was because people flocked out to the villages to collect food. It stopped at every station and the passengers were hearty, lusty people who pushed and shoved. We secured seats but without space for Jan to put his foot up; for part of the journey, I held it on my knee. The journey dragged on for about six hours, Jan becoming ever more pale and drawn. By the time we had been through two rigorous customs posts and passport examinations, with much standing about, Jan was on the point of collapse and I was only able to keep going by a supreme effort of will. The express did not leave until the evening so we took a room at the station hotel in Cerbère so that he could rest for a few hours.

When I went to buy our tickets, the man at the booking office said, 'Why not get forty per cent off for the Exposition, if you are going to Paris?' I accepted this suggestion gratefully; if we were supposed to be tourists so much the better.

When the train pulled in, I secured a sleeper as Jan had to lie down. We boarded the train, the attendant, with an eye for a big tip, fussing round and being very helpful. At dusk we came to

Perpignan. The platform was alive with suspicious-looking characters and I was very glad we had decided not to break the journey there.

* * * * *

Jan had to stay for a time with friends in Paris while waiting for his papers to be arranged so that he would be allowed to return to England. As before, he spent most of his time lying on a sofa. His friends and I bought him luxuries and spoiled him but he was not well enough to enjoy things. I should have felt elated that he had escaped safely but I felt very deflated. I still bore a load of anxiety. I did not know if he would ever walk again. I thought he might be crippled for life. He felt the heartlessness of strangers towards his disability. He was alarmed by the solicitude of his friends who seemed to be accepting it as permanent.

He was very melancholy, despairing. In Spanish, the same word, *esperar*, is used for 'wait' and 'hope'. He had done so much waiting. A man cannot be left alone in bed for months thinking and be the same as he was before. Jan had done something which a few people thought heroic, to which many Spaniards were indifferent, and which had to be hidden, like a crime, in the country to which he returned.

There were hundreds of people who would give money to go to meetings for the Republican cause at home, dozens who would pop over to sample the privations in Spain and write of their experiences sincerely or simply for 'copy', to one who would make a personal sacrifice.

I went to the Spanish Pavilion at the Exposition. It was small and plain compared to most of the others. In the middle was a fountain of mercury from the mines of Almadén, and on one wall Picasso's painting: Guernica.

'Do you think you could get out on the balcony?' asked our hostess one evening. 'The Exposition fireworks are so pretty.'

Jan hobbled out. He watched showers of rockets and heard the distant explosions. 'It's just like a bombardment,' he said.

Afterword by Charlotte Kurzke

A note on the text

Some years after the death of my parents, Kate Mangan and Jan Kurzke, I found myself in possession of two separate manuscripts of their memoirs. I was always given to understand that the intention was to publish them both as one book but the way they were written made this very difficult, and I had no clues as to how the various sections had been intended to work together.

My mother's manuscript was fairly straightforward, covering as it does the first year of the war. The only complication was her use of pseudonyms throughout, although she pencilled in a few names much later. At the time, almost all the foreign communist agents had pseudonyms, sometimes several, but she invented her own which has made identification very difficult.

Her primary reason for going to Spain was to discover what had happened to Jan. This presented a real obstacle to uniting the two stories since Jan never mentions her at all apart from one oblique reference to picking up a pretty girl in Madrid.

I think the only explanation for this dichotomy lies in the nature of their relationship and their very different characters. Jan had left Kate behind and his only concern was with the conflict and his role in it. In a sense, I suspect, he resented her efforts on his behalf; the fact that he was not so completely alone amongst the horrors as his comrades. Their shared experience and pain was what bound them together afterwards but he was not prepared to concede her a role in his life as a soldier. Jan was an observer of life, fiercely independent, introspective and unwilling to commit himself to anyone at that time. He would never have put his feelings on paper and, eventually, was unable to express his feelings at all.

I did my best to fit the various sections together for my parents' sake. They found so much of life a disappointment. Reluctantly, I reached the conclusion that the two manuscripts were too far apart to be reunited, and to go ahead with the publication of Kate's as a standalone memoir. The story is so good and well-written and the issues are still relevant even if the Spanish Civil War itself seems a small and distant event.[120]

It has to be remembered that this war was a crucial confrontation between the Right and the Left. It was also the testing ground for a whole range of weapons and machines of war and, for the first time, civilian populations were attacked from the air. The astonishing thing is the obdurate courage shown by those populations in the face of this horror which, it was assumed, would demoralise them instantly.

Biographical Notes - Jan Kurzke

Jan was born Hans Robert Kurzke in Hamburg in 1905. His mother was Danish and his father was from Silesia, a Wehrmacht officer who was a very harsh and brutal parent. There were five children. The two oldest boys were drowned during the First World War and one, at least, is buried at Dover. The family was very poor and Jan left school at fourteen to work in the docks where he used to steal coffee, among other things. At sixteen, he won a scholarship to art school in Hamburg and set about educating himself. In 1927 he moved to Berlin. He became a Marxist and took part in street fights with the Nazis. He was obliged to leave Germany precipitately, aided by Gustaf Grundgens, in February 1931, sailing from Hamburg bound for Cape Town on the SS Ussukuma. He travelled part of the way along the coast of Africa before working his way back northwards to Europe.

He spent six months in Barcelona before he set out on his trek around southern Spain. By the autumn of 1934 he was in Mallorca where he met the English people who brought him to London, where he met my mother Kate. He did not like England and had no intention of staying there.

He and Kate spent the winter of 1935-36 in Spain and went to Portugal during the summer of 1936.

Once they were both back in England after their time in the Spanish war, they remained together and began work on their manuscripts. One great drawback to living in England was that

Jan was prohibited from taking paid employment and this stricture remained until the middle of 1941. Jan had his exhibition of drawings and paintings at the Delius Giese Gallery. On the whole, his work was not particularly well received although his drawings and water-colours were admired.

During the Spanish war, he drew constantly: comrades in arms, comrades in hospital and any scenes visible from windows. It is tragic that all this work seems to have been lost.

When the Second World War broke out, Jan and Kate were on Guernsey. They returned to England where Jan immediately tried to join up. He was rejected, not because of his leg but because of faults in his hearing and eyesight which had not prevented him from being an artist and a crack-shot. He was interned on the Isle of Man from June 1940 to July 1941. This really marked the beginning of the end of his relationship with Kate.

After he returned from the Isle of Man, Jan worked during the day in a horrible factory where skins were processed and tried to paint at night by the light of double summer time.

In 1942, he got a job painting scenery at the Arts Theatre where he met a young actress, Gillian Adams, whom he married in 1945.

After the war, he did a variety of work including painting portraits of children, cleaning and restoring private collections of pictures and also cleaning and restoring church art and decorations for the Church Commission, but somehow he contrived to fall out with everyone who could help him.

He was a man who changed greatly over the years. He was always reserved and disliked emotional scenes. He liked cleanliness and order. He was self-sufficient; there was no household task he could not perform. As a young man, he was talented, courageous, amusing, charming, irresistible to women and very susceptible to them. They all remained devoted to him and he remained very fond of them until he married.

He never naturalised so he could not have travelled even if he had wished to. He did keep up with a few very old friends. In his latter years he was very isolated. He did not paint any more. At the end, he refused to go out socially at all. He tried to close the doors on every past experience and suffered greatly as a result.

It must be said that it was his wife Gillian who kept him in touch with his children and who tried to welcome relatives and friends who wished to make contact with him.

He committed suicide in December 1981.

Biographical Notes - Kate Mangan (née Foster)

Katharine Prideaux Foster was born in Sedgley, Staffordshire, in 1904. Her father was a solicitor who took a keen interest in politics. Her mother was a very cultured lady and a gifted artist. The family lived a comfortable middle-class life with servants and governesses until the two daughters were old enough for secondary education. Kate was considered delicate and attended a day school while her elder sister was sent to Cheltenham Ladies' College. Kate was very introverted and solitary; she was referred to as 'the troglodyte.' She did have one bosom friend who lived close by but otherwise preferred to spend as much time as possible with her father, though her parents were often away. She did not get on very well with her elder sister who was much closer to their mother.

When she was fourteen, her father killed himself, leaving considerable financial problems. Kate was sent to relatives and took to her bed for six months. When she returned to the family, it was to a flat in London and St Paul's Girls' School. Her mother had disposed of almost everything. Kate never recovered from the shock of all this.

After matriculating, she went to the Slade Art School. She then spent time in Paris where she worked as a mannequin for a dress house run by White Russians. She worked for Chanel in London at one point.

In 1924, she met Sherry Mangan in Paris. He was an Irish American scholar, poet, writer and, later, Trotskyist revolutionary. They wrote to each other frequently. Kate travelled a great deal in southern Europe and to the United States. Neither his parents nor her mother approved of their relationship but they were married in 1931. The marriage was very unhappy for a variety of reasons including their extreme poverty. They spent the winter of 1933-34 in Mexico in the hope of patching things up, but later in 1934 Kate returned to England for a while.

She met Jan during the winter of 1934 and was divorced in 1935 which was another experience she never really recovered from. She remained fond of Sherry and in contact with him until his death in 1961.

It is difficult for me to understand why my mother failed to capitalise on her early promise and advantages. I think she suffered from her association with a writer and then a painter. Sherry urged her to stick to painting and to abandon her attempts at writing. Jan told her to give up painting and stick to writing. He also advised her to marry a rich man.

Intellectually, she kept up with modern trends until very near the end of her life, but in other respects she was very much a person of her time and found adjusting to the new order difficult. She depended on her old friends to remind her of who she was. She was emotionally chaotic; always seeking a security she never found, a curious mixture of practical and impractical, helplessness and determination, conventional and unconventional. In spite of being so much admired, courted and indulged, at some deep level she lacked confidence, a belief in her own worth.

In spite of being untrained for any work, she found jobs and did them well. It took her longer to master domestic skills. She could not open a tin until she was over forty. She could not ride a bicycle; she could not keep a car on the road, even in Texas. As a girl in Paris, her idea of catering was to line up a dozen hard-boiled eggs on a windowsill in case invitations to lunch or dinner should fail. However, she was an intrepid traveller; usually going the cheapest way, unfazed by lack of sanitation, fleas, bedbugs, or any other discomfort. She would walk for miles lugging an assortment of disintegrating baggage and supplies.

I think it would be true to say that Kate was never more alive, more capable, more purposeful, more truly in touch with the real world than during the year she spent in Spain.

Charlotte Kurzke.

Appendix 1: A Note on Certain Key Comintern Agents Involved with the Republic's Press Office in Spain by Dr Boris Volodarsky

1. Selke

Rudolf (Rodolfo) Selke, born in 1902 in Odessa, brother of Angela Selke. From 1921 to 1928 he was a member of the KPD (Kommunistiche Partei Deutschlands – Communist Party of Germany) but then joined its opposition branch, the KPD(O). He married Sita Thalheimer, the daughter of August Thalheimer. Selke did some academic research on the planned economy in the USSR at the Frankfurt Institute for Social Research (*Frankfurter Institut für Sozialforschung*). He is known as a translator of Soviet literature, including works by Gorky, Tretiakov, Ehrenburg, Liebermann, & Gladkov. His translations were published by Malik Verlag in Berlin, where he became acquainted with, among others, Maria Osten and Upton Sinclair.

In 1934, Selke moved to Ibiza where he ran a bar together with his sister, Angela.

In August 1936, he joined the militia unit headed up by Colonel Julio Mangada Rosenörn that became known as the *Columna Mangada*, based in the Sierra de Guadarrama near Madrid. He later served with *the Batallón Asturias número 1 'Aida Lafuente'*.

Because the PSOE did not accept foreigners, he tried (without success) to join the PCE and later worked in the Press Censorship section of the Information Department of the Foreign Ministry under Julio Álvarez del Vayo.

Due to his friendship (actually acquaintance) with Paul and Clara Thaelmann, the KPD security service (*KPD-Abwehr*) suspected that Selke was a Trotskyist, but thanks to Mikhail Koltsov, whom Selke knew through Maria Osten, he managed to avoid arrest and was simply removed from his post as a censor.

In spring 1938, he published a long article about the biggest naval battle of the Spanish Civil War, the Battle of Cabo de Palos, (5-6 March) in the popular weekly *Die Neue Weltbühne* (NWB, originally published in Berlin but, by that time, based in Prague and Vienna).

In 1939, Selke moved to France and was interned in Gurs. During the same year he managed to emigrate to Mexico where he worked as a translator, notably of Rudolf Rocker's biography of the German anarchist and historian Max Nettlau (*Max Nettlau: Leben und Werk des Historikers vergessener sozialer Bewegungen*). He also contributed articles to the Spanish exiles' newspaper, *Free World*.

In 1951, Selke returned to Europe where he became a correspondent of *Die Zeit*, writing articles about Ehrenburg for whom he had occasionally served as an interpreter in Albacete. In the 1960s, he was employed as an interpreter by the International Labour Organisation (ILO) in Geneva.

2. George Raft look-alike

Almost certainly Hubert von Ranke (aliases Mathias Bresser, Moritz Bresser, Henri-Georges Frank, Hubert Martin, Ludwig Bayer, and in Spain also Moritz Beier). Born on 24 September 1902 in Munich, died on 31 March 1978 in Munich.

Von Ranke was one of the top leaders of the *KPD-Abwehr* and *AM-Apparat*. In May 1936, he travelled undercover to Spain and instructed Alfred Herz to organise a secret German Information Bureau, reporting on all German communists resident in Catalunya. Von Ranke arrived in Barcelona in July 1936 as part of the KPD-Abwehr. After a short time at the front he was appointed as head of the *Servicio Extranjero* of the PSUC, based in the Hotel Colón, while his civil law wife Seppl Campalans was employed as his secretary, also working as a censor. Herz initially worked for him together with Werner Hermlin and Szaja Kindermann, before later forming his own group known as the *Servicio Alfredo Herz*. (Its official name was the *Servicio de la Defensa del Partido y de la República* and it had been formed as a branch of the *Servicio Especial Antifascista del Partido*, led by

Joaquín Olaso, head of the personnel department of the Central Committee of the PSUC and the 'eye of Moscow', who had worked together with Ernö Gerö.)

When Kate Mangan remembered 'synthetic blonde, highly painted secretaries' she was undoubtedly speaking about multiple female secretaries and stenographers who had worked for von Ranke, including young Margit Kurcz, the wife of Alexander Maas; Erzsébet Fazekas (Comr. Gelbert), the wife of Ernö Gerö ('Pedro'); Thea Friedemann, the wife of Haydu Friedemann; Minne (Wilhelmine) Artzt, first the wife of Robert Artzt but by the time she started working for von Ranke she had married Hannes Neubeck, who had been seriously wounded and was in hospital in Barcelona. There were also several 'blonde' Polish secretaries working at the department. In his letter to Franz Dahlem of 3 February 1937 (held in the RGASPI archives), von Ranke also mentions stenographer Adda (also known as Ada and Adde) Stehr, whom they long wanted to fire but didn't because 'she is a friend of Rudolf Selke from the Foreign Ministry'.

Adde Stehr was born in Nuremberg in February 1906, worked for the Central Committee of the KPD and moved to Spain in 1936. Like Selke, she lived in Ibiza and then in Barcelona working in the Propaganda and Agitation Department of the PSUC.[121]

3. Kellt

The individual whom Kate refers to as Kellt was almost certainly Szaja (aka Szaya) Kinderman(n), whose real name was Joseph Winkler. Szaja was one of Hubert von Ranke's closest collaborators. After the formation of the PSUC on 23 July 1936, its Central Committee decided to form a semi-secret foreign department (like the OMS/Comintern) to control and investigate foreigners coming to Catalunya. One of its sections was a service called *Servicio especial de extranjeros* also known simply as *Servicio especial*, founded in September 1936 and headed by Kindermann, who had settled in Barcelona long before. Together with the German Hans Beimler and Italian Armando Fedeli,

Kindermann formed a commission that oversaw foreigner cadres. Fedeli headed the *Servicio especial* after Kindermann left for Valencia.

In Valencia, using the alias 'Jorge' he 'lived very quietly', placed in charge of interrogations and investigations of the Trotskyists and 5th columnists based in the Convento de Santa Úrsula in Plaça de Santa Úrsula, 2. Kindermann worked in close contact with Orlov, Eitingon and Karl Kleinjung.

After the war, Kindermann served in the Polish communist Ministry for Public Security in Warsaw, better known as UB and later SB, under his real name Józef Winkler. He retired (as colonel, Head of Section III, Department VII) in April 1954.

Organisation Names and Abbreviations

Acción Popular – right-wing Catholic conservative party, later to become the *Confederación Española de Derechas Autónomas (CEDA)*.

CEDA – *Confederación Española de Derechas Autónomas* was founded in 1933, a successor to the *Acción Popular* party, representing right-wing Catholic conservatism. It was led by José María Gil Robles who styled himself as *'el Jefe'* – the equivalent of *Il Duce* and *Führer*.

CNT – *Confederación Nacional de Trabajadores*, the National Workers' Confederation, an association of anarcho-syndicalist trade unions. Closely associated with the FAI. Traditionally strong in Catalunya.

Comunión Tradicionalista – Carlist party.

Esquerra Republicana – Catalan pro-independence party established in 1931.

Estat Català – Catalan pro-independence party established in 1922.

Falange Española – a fascist political party founded in 1933 by José Antonio Primo de Rivera, son of the former dictator General Miguel Primo de Rivera. The following year, the party merged with *the Juntas de Ofensiva Nacional-Socialista*, led by Ramiro Ledesma, and was renamed *Falange Española de las JONS*. In 1937, Franco forced a further merger with the Carlist *Comunión Tradicionalista*, banning all other political parties.

FAI – *Federación Anarquista Ibérica* was founded in 1927. Closely associated with the CNT.

JONS – *Juntas de Ofensiva Nacional Sindicalista* – Fascist party founded in 1931 and merged with *Falange Española* in 1934.

JSU – *Juventudes Socialistas Unificadas* (Unified Socialist Youth) – combining Socialist and Communist youth movements.

PCE – *Partido Comunista Español* (Spanish Communist Party).

POUM – *Partido Obrero de Unificación Marxist* (Workers' Marxist Unification Party).

PSOE – Partido Socialista Obrero Español (Spanish Socialist Workers' Party).

PSUC – Partit Socialista Unificat de Catalunya (Unified Socialist Party of Catalunya). Like the PCE, the PSUC was affiliated to the Comintern.

Renovación Española was the political wing of *Acción Española*, a propaganda organisation founded within days of Alfonso XIII's departure in April 1931 with a view to undermining the Republic and creating the conditions for his return. Its members belonged to an umbrella organization of the right called *Acción Nacional*. When their extremism caused problems for the more gradualist groups, it split, in February 1933, into the *Confederación Española de Derechas Autónomas* and *Renovación Española*.

UGT – Unión General de Trabajadores (Workers' General Union) founded in 1888. It was (and is) affiliated to the PSOE. Traditionally stronger in Madrid, the Basque country and Asturias.

Notes

[1] William (Bill) McGuire (1917-2009): US writer, editor and scholar at Princeton University. He visited Kate and met Jan in the mid-1960s and tried unsuccessfully to find a publisher for their memoir of the Spanish Civil War. In the 1990s, with Bernard Knox, he tried again, also without success, using a new typescript produced by Charlotte Kurzke under the working title *The Good Comrade.*

[2] Cristina (Tina) was the daughter of Kate's sister Greville, whose ex-husband (Manolo Texidor) lived in Barcelona.

[3] General Francisco Franco (1892-1975): Leader of Spain's African Army. When he reached Spain in early August, a division was established between himself as southern commander of the rebel forces and General Mola as northern commander. He later assumed supreme military and political command of Spain, imposing a dictatorship until his death in 1975.

[4] General Mola (1887-1937): northern commander of the rebel army. He was killed in June 1937 when his plane crashed into a mountain, leaving Franco as supreme commander of the rebel forces.

[5] General Queipo de Llano (1875-1951): one of the core rebel officers and an ardent exponent of violent repression and revenge, earning him the sobriquet 'the butcher of Seville'. Sidelined by Franco after 1938.

[6] In the early days of the insurgency Franco flew from the Canary Islands to Morocco to take command of the rebel forces, largely comprising Morrocan mercenaries and the Spanish Foreign Legion (the latter known as *El Tercio*).

[7] *Thunder Over Mexico,* directed by Sergei Eisenstein in 1933, tells the story of an estate-worker whose life is threatened after he confronts a guest of his corrupt landowner over the rape of a girl.

[8] General Millán Astray (1879-1954): founder of the Spanish Foreign Legion, famous for his catch-phrase *'Viva la muerte (Long Live Death)'.* He was mutilated in Morocco, losing an arm and an eye. He played a leading role in the insurgency.

[9] The International Brigades were formed in September 1936 to provide

a structure for the thousands of foreigners volunteering to fight in support of the Republic.

[10] A Non-Intervention Agreement was signed in August 1936 by 27 European States, including Britain, France, Germany, Italy and the Soviet Union, as well as the United States and Canada. Signatories agreed not to intervene in the Spanish civil war. The Agreement was supposedly monitored by a Non-Intervention Committee.

[11] CNT-FAI: see p.325 (Organisation Names and Abbreviations).

[12] Manuel "Manolo" Texidor Catasus (1901-1970), who had been married to Kate's sister, Greville. He died in Abingdon, England. (Source: Oliver Slay i Texidor).

[13] The 'great man' was almost certainly Hubert von Ranke (aliases Mathias Bresser, Moritz Bresser, Henri-Georges Frank, Hubert Martin, Ludwig Bayer, and in Spain also Moritz Beier). See appendix 1.

[14] George Raft was a US actor notable for his second-lead roles in 1930s gangster movies, such as *Scarface* and *Dancers in the Dark*.

[15] PSUC: see p.326 (Organisation Names and Abbreviations).

[16] The Thaelmann Battalion was formed as part of the International Brigades and comprised mainly Germans, Austrians, Swiss and Scandinavians, with a dozen or so British volunteers. For a first-hand description of their contribution to the defence of Madrid see *Boadilla* by Esmond Romilly (Winston Churchill's nephew), London 1937 / The Clapton Press, 2018.

[17] The description matches John Cornford. See note 42.

[18] This might be William Forrest (1902-1989), correspondent for the *Daily Express* and, later, the *News Chronicle*, who had driven over to Spain with Slater in his white Rolls-Royce – see *We Saw Spain Die* p.61.

[19] Humphrey (Hugh) Slater (1906-1958): English writer and painter. He covered the early part of the war in Spain as a journalist, later signing up with the International Brigades.

[20] André Masson (1896-1987): French painter and scuptor. He was

living in Spain at the outbreak of the civil war, in 1936.

[21] Paulina Ódena García (1911-1936): Spanish communist activist who shot herself in the head rather than be captured when her chauffeur took a wrong turn and her car was surrounded Nationalist troops.

[22] The 'cloak and suit man' has not been identified.

[23] See p.325 (Organisation Names and Abbreviations).

[24] *Atarazanas Reales de Barcelona*: Barcelona Royal Shipyard and barracks.

[25] Juan March (1880-1962): multi-millionaire landowner, banker and bootlegger – granted a monopoly over tobacco in Morocco by the dictator General Primo de Rivera in the 1920s. He was said to have bankrolled the 1936 rebellion.

[26] Caracoles was (and still is) arguably one of the most elegant restaurants in Barcelona, named after its signature dish: snails.

[27] A lampoon in Catalán: *La Reina vol corona? Corona li darem, que vingui a Barcelona i el coll li tallarem! = So the Queen wants a crown? We'll give her a crown! Let her come to Barcelona and we'll cut her neck!*

[28] José Diaz (1895-1942): trade unionist and General Secretary of the PCE (Communist Party of Spain) from 1932-1939.

[29] See p.325 (Organisation Names and Abbreviations).

[30] Werner Droescher and Greville Texidor née Foster (1902-1964). Kate called them 'two old friends, Fritz and Lise' in her manuscript to disguise their identities. They later married. Greville was Kate's elder sister. At various times in her life she was a member of the Bloomsbury set, chorus girl in Paris, anarchist militia-woman, heroin addict, inmate at Holloway prison and novelist. She committed suicide in 1964. For more details of her extraordinary life see *All the Juicy Pastures: Greville Texidor and New Zealand*, by Margot Schwass, Victoria University Press, 2020.

[31] Tom Wintringham (1898-1949): member of the Communist Party of

Great Britain. Originally went to Spain as a journalist, working for the *Daily Worker*, and then joined the International Brigades, ending up as commander of the British Battalion. Wounded at Jarama, he ended up with typhoid and was nursed back to health by Kitty Bowler and Patience Darton. He later became a driving force behind the Home Guard. He died of a heart attack in 1949. See *The Last English Revolutionary: Tom Wintringham 1898-1949* by Hugh Purcell and Phyll Smith, Sussex Academic Press (2nd edition), 2012.

[32] *Siete domingos rojos (Seven Red Sundays)* was a novel by Ramón J. Sender published in 1931. A translation into English by Sir Peter Chalmers Mitchell was published in 1938.

[33] *Los Aguiluchos de las Corts (The Las Corts Eaglets)*. Las Corts (now more commonly referred to in Catalán, as Les Corts) is a neighbourhood of Barcelona.

[34] Zachary was almost certainly the Bulgarian, Zachari Simeon Zachariev (1904-1987), for a long time known under his Russian name Volkan Semyonovich Goranov (alias 'Halil Ekrem'). Zachariev was a military commander and pilot, serving in the Red Army from 1929 to 1944. Kate asserts that he went to Albacete and had great influence there. This is entirely feasible, because pilots were the legendary elite of the Soviet army and there were two training bases for bombers not far away in the region of Murcia. (Note based on information from Dr Boris Volodarsky.)

[35] Buenaventura Durruti (1886-1936): charismatic militant within the FAI and CNT, he became a key leader in the CNT-FAI's armed resistance to the military rising of July 1936. Died from a bullet wound in November 1936 while leading the anarchist militia in defence of Madrid: it is not known whether from an enemy sniper or friendly fire.

[36] *No pasarán* = They shall not pass.

[37] Ilse & Karl —not identified.

[38] It has not been possible to identify 'the Mad Hatter'.

[39] "The Austrian woman" was Ilsa Barea.

[40] See Appendix 1 for more information on Selke's identity.

[41] Edgar Quinet (1803-1875): French historian.

[42] The youth with the fresh face was Donald Gabriel Hutchison, born in 1915. He was wounded in the wrist at the Battle of Boadilla, serving in the Thaelmann Battalion alongside Esmond Romilly, and was discovered by Kate languishing in the San Carlos hospital in Madrid. Source: Dr. Katharine Campbell, IBMT Newsletter 35, 2-2013.

[43] The poet John Cornford (1915-1936) was among the first British volunteers to arrive in Spain to fight against the rebels, first with the POUM militia at Huesca and later with the International Brigades. He survived the Battle of Boadilla in December 1936, only to be killed in action a few days later at Lopera, near Córdoba.

[44] Walter Reuter (1906-2005): German photographer. He worked on the same newspaper as Jan in Berlin in the early 1930s. They met up again in 1934, both refugees in Spain, when Walter was travelling with his wife, Sulamith Siliava, and a young German girl named Margarethe Zembal (nicknamed "Putz"). After spending some time in a French concentration camp in 1939, he escaped to Morocco with his family, was captured by the French and sent to a Labour camp, and finally escaped again and emigrated with his family to Mexico (Source: *Walter Reuter, el fotógrafo alemán que retrató México*. El Mundo, March 27, 2005).

[45] Sir Arthur Leslie Plummer (1901-1963): known to his friends as Dick, at that time an up-and-coming executive at the *Daily Express*. He later went on to greater things as Chairman of the British Overseas Company during the Tanganyika groundnut scandal of the late 1940s. He resigned and stood as the Labour Party candidate for Deptford in the 1951 general election, winning a comfortable majority.

[46] Hans Beimler (1895-1936): member of the Reichstag and the German Communist Party.

[47] In her original manuscript Kate changes the Pozners' name to Dupois, in order to protect their identity. Mrs Pozner was an ex-girlfried of Jan's from his days in Berlin. (Source: Charlotte Kurzke.)

[48] English Penny: wartime sobriquet for Penny Phelps (1909-2011), who went to Spain as a volunteer nurse in January 1937. She was briefly made a lieutenant in the Garibaldi XV International Brigade, until the

demilitarisation of women. She was seriously wounded in a bomb blast in 1938 and evacuated back to England, where she met her future husband, Dr Michael Feiwel, during her convalescence.

[49] Peggy – unidentified

[50] Kitty Bowler (1908-1966): Tom Wintringham's American girlfriend, who was later expelled from Spain. Kate refers to her in the original text as Louise Mallory, to protect her identity.

[51] In all likelihood she means Frederick Griffin (1880-1946): Irish-born Canadian reporter for the *Toronto Star Weekly*. (Source: Charlotte Kurzke.)

[52] Juan García Oliver (1901-1980): CNT-FAI militant. Appointed Minister of Justice by Largo Caballero. Exiled in 1939; died in Mexico.

[53] The Swedish nurse was Inge Cohn-Stark. (Source: Charlotte Kurzke.)

[54] *En Castilla la Vieja siempre una miseria* = There's always been poverty in Old Castille.

[55] Liston Oak (1895-1970): American left-wing journalist, appointed as Director of Publicity for the Republican government in Spain. Origially sympathetic to the Soviet cause, he became disillusioned with Stalinist policies and what he considered their detrimental effect on the loyalist war effort. He returned to the US in 1938.

[56] Milly Bennet (1897-1960): professional pseudonym for Mildred Bremler, an American journalist born in California. While in Spain, she met and married her third husband, Hans Amlie, with whom she returned to the US in 1938. Kate calls her 'Poppy Smith' in her manuscript to protect her identity.

[57] Kellt was almost certainly Szaja (aka Szaya) Kinderman(n), whose real name was Joseph Winkler. See Appendix 1 for more information.

[58] Luis Rubio Hidalgo, Chief Censor at the Republican Government's Foreign Press and Propaganda Office.

[59] Francisco 'Coco' Robles Villegas (1920- ?) worked for the Republican Press Bureau and later joined the militia. His father, José Robles Pazos

was arrested in early 1937 by counter-espionage agents and executed in April. He is often described as an interpreter for the Russian authorities in Spain. This is unlikely since the Russians had their own highly trained and vetted translators. It is more likely that Robles was a liaison officer between the head of Soviet intelligence in Spain, General Vladimir Gorev and the Republican General Staff. José's demise came about as a result of his contacts with his brother Ramón, an important member of the Francoist fifth column. Perhaps wrongly, but understandably, José was suspected of passing secrets to Ramón. Coco survived the war but was captured by Franco's troops and sent to a concentration camp. He was released in 1944 and allowed to join his mother and sister in Mexico. For more details, see Paul Preston, *We Saw Spain Die. Foreign Correspondents in the Spanish Civil War* (London: Constable, 2008) pp.72-108; and *The Spanish Holocaust. Inquisition and Extermination in Twentieth Century Spain* (London; HarperCollins, 2012) pp.393-396; and also, Ignacio Martínez Pisón, *Enterrar a los muertos* (Madrid, Seix Barral, 2005).

[60] Manuel Azaña (1880-1940): Prime Minister of the Second Spanish Republic from 1931-1933 and 1936, and President of the Republic from 1936-1939. Died in exile in France.

[61] Edward Knoblaugh (1904-1976): an American journalist and propagandist for Franco. The book referred to was *Correspondent in Spain* published by Sheed and Ward, 1937. Kate Mangan refers to him as 'Hank' in her manuscript to disguise his identify. Other correspondents nicknamed him 'Doaks'.

[62] Francisco Largo Caballero (1869-1946): leader of the PSOE and UGT. Replaced José Giral as Prime Minister on 4th September 1936 and remained in office until 17th May 1937.

[63] 'Oscar Telge' was a *nom de guerre* used by Tsvetan Angelov Kristanov (1898-1972), a Bulgarian communist, who was head of the International Brigades' medical services.

[64] 'Texas' was a pseudonym for Harold Edward Dahl (1909-1956), an American mercenary pilot, known to everyone as 'Whitey'. He was shot down over enemy territory in June 1937, and was captured and sentenced to death. He was released in 1940. For more details, see *Some Still Live* by F. G. Tinker Jnr, Funk & Wagnalls, 1938 & The Clapton

Press, 2019.

[65] Professor Franz Borkenau (1900-1957): Austrian sociologist. Visited Spain in October 1936 and stayed for two months, returning in January 1937, when he was arrested as a spy. He wrote about his experiences in Spain in *The Spanish Cockpit: An Eye-Witness Account of the Political and Social Conflicts of the Spanish Civil War,* Faber & Faber, 1937.

[66] W.H. Auden (1907-1973): British-American poet. He went to Spain in 1937 and stayed for seven weeks.

[67] Constancia de la Mora (1906-1950): censor in the Republican Foreign Press Bureau, eventually replacing Luis Rubio Hidalgo as its head. Her grandfather was Antonio Maura, Prime Minister of Spain at the head of five different governments, between 1903 and 1921. After a disastrous first marriage into the Bolín family, she was the first woman to obtain a divorce under the Spanish Republic. Her second marriage was to Ignacio Hidalgo de Cisneros, head of the Republican air force. She died in exile in Mexico. Her autobiography, *In Place of Spendour*, was published in 1940.

[68] André Marty (1886-1956): member of the French Communist Party and French National Assembly for over 30 years (with interruptions to fight in the Spanish civil war and World War II). He was political commissar of the International Brigades from 1936 until 1938, known by some as 'the butcher of Albacete'.

[69] Claud Cockburn, aka Frank Pitcairn (1904-1981): member of the Communist Party and correspondent for the *Daily Worker*. His memoir *Reporter in Spain* was published by Lawrence & Wishart in October 1936. The comments on his character were incorporated into the main text from a footnote by Kate.

[70] *Voulez-vous donner quelque chose por la couronne. Un camarade dans la salle sept vient de mourir* = Would you like to give something towards a wreath? One of the comrades in Ward 7 has just died.

[71] George Seldes (1890-1995): American journalist, Spanish correspondent for the *New York Post* during the civil war, accompanied by his wife Helen. Kate refers to them as 'Isidore and Sarah' to conceal their identities. (Note based on information from Charlotte Kurzke.)

[72] The reference has nothing to do with knife crime; Albacete was, and remains, famous for the quality of the knives produced there.

[73] The 'Canadian boy' was Hazen Sise (1906-1974).

[74] Dr Norman Bethune (1890-1949): Canadian doctor. He set up a mobile blood transfusion unit in Spain. Later went to China, where he died of blood poisoning in 1949. See *Norman Bethune in Spain: Commitment, Crisis and Conspiracy*, by David Lethbridge, Sussex Academic Press/Cañada Blanch Centre, 2008.

[75] Robert Hale Merriman (1908-1938): US volunteer. Joined the Abraham Lincoln battalion in 1937 and was appointed as Battalion Commander. Bob was hit in the shoulder by a bullet during the Battle of Jarama in February 1937. He recovered and returned to the front line. He was missing presumed killed during the battalion's retreat from Belchite in April 1938. Marion Merriman, Bob's wife, also joined the battalion in early 1937 and returned to the US in November 1937. As well as being widowed in Spain she was also raped by another brigader, but never told her husband lest it affect his morale. See *American Commander in Spain*, Marion Merriman and Warren Lerude, Univerity of Nevada Press, 1986.

[76] Basil Murray (1902-1937): British journalist and correspondent in Valencia for the International News Service, lampooned in Evelyn Waugh's 1932 novel *Black Mischief*. Caught pneumonia and died on the British hospital ship *SS Maine* as he was being evacuated to Marseilles. Claud Cockburn claimed that Murray was actually bitten to death by his pet monkey as he lay in a drunken stupor in his hotel room in Valencia; Sefton Delmer in *Trail Sinister* suggested a rather more sordid relationship with the animal.

[77] *Boinas rojas*: another name for the Requetés, the Carlist militia. This originally referred to the members of the *Tercer Batallón de Navarra* who fought on the side of Carlos de Borbón during the First Carlist War, from 1833 to 1840. Their uniform included a red beret. In 1936, their regent was Francisco Javier de Borbón-Parma.

[78] Gerda Grepp (1907-1940) was a Norwegian journalist; Arthur Koestler (1905-1983) was a Hungarian journalist, working for the *News Chronicle*. They visited Málaga shortly before it was taken by Italian

troops. Grepp narrowly escaped but Koestler (who Franco's propaganda chief, Luis Bolín, had vowed to 'shoot like a dog') sought refuge with Sir Peter Chalmers Mitchell (1864-1945), former Secretary of the Zoological Society of London. They were both arrested and imprisoned under threat of execution, but were eventually released. See *My House in Málaga* by Sir Peter Chalmers Mitchell (Faber & Faber, 1938 / The Clapton Press, 2019).

[79] Lawrence Fernsworth (1908-1987): American journalist, reporting from Valencia for *The Times* of London and the *New York Times*.

[80] Griffin Barry (1884-1957): American writer and journalist who had an affair and two children with Dora Russell. While in Spain, he was working for Reuters. Their daughter Harriet Ward produced a book about his life: *A Man of Small Importance: My Father Griffin Barry*, Dormouse Books, 2003, in which she drew on Kate's memoir regarding his time in Spain.

[81] Robert Capa (1913-1954), born Endre Ernő Friedmann. Outstanding war photographer, eventually killed when he stepped on a land mine in Vietnam.

[82] Gerda Taro (1910-1937), born Gerta Pohorylle. She was Robert Capa's partner and a talented war photographer in her own right. She was crushed by a tank during the Republican army retreat after the Battle of Brunete, in June 1937. Kate later wrote: 'The poor girl is now dead. She was killed accidentally by a tank which swept her off the running-board of a car. They tried to save her with a blood transfusion but it was the wrong kind of blood and she died of shock. Perhaps it was as well as she was much too pretty and gay to live as a cripple. Capa was in Bilbao at the time. Other photographers told me he was the most daring of all in taking pictures at the front. Gerda was daring too but she had not the sense to know when she could afford to be and, when he was not there to take care of her, she came to her end.'

[83] *Il a de chance le bougre, d'avoir sa femme ici!* = He's a lucky bugger, having his wife here!

[84] The horrors of the Málaga exodus are described in detail in *The Crime on the Road Malaga-Almeria*, by Dr Norman Bethune (n.p.: Publicaciones Iberia, 1937) and *Behind the Battle* by T.C. Worsley

(London, Robert Hale, 1939). Worsley had flown to Spain with Stephen Spender in 1937 to investigate the sinking of the Russian ship *Komsomol* and stayed on to work with Bethune's blood transfusion unit.

[85] *Je vais danser avec ta femme, le quatorze juillet* = I'm going to dance with your wife on the 14th July.

[86] *Tu n'est pas jaloux, hein? Ah, c'est parce que tu sais que ce n'est pas vrai – seulement une plaisanterie* = You're not jealous are you? Just so you know, it's not true, it was only a joke.

[87] As detailed by Paul Preston in *We Saw Spain Die*, *The Times* had a plethora of correspondents in Spain during the war: Lawrence Fernsworth, based in the Loyalist zone; James Holburn, who covered the Basque campaign from the Nationalist camp until replaced by Kim Philby in May 1937. W.F. Stirling also briefly represented *The Times* in the Nationalist zone and complained about Franco's chief propagandist, Luis Bolín. George Steer spent 6 months in the Nationalist zone in 1936 before being expelled, and returned to Spain in early 1937 as Special Envoy with the Republican forces in Bilbao.

[88] Kajsa Hellin Rothman. Born in Karlstad in 1903. Virginia Cowles, an American journalist she worked for as an interpreter, described her as 'a Swedish girl who dressed in men's clothes and wore her hair in a Greta Garbo bob. She had held jobs all over Europe ranging from governess to tourist guide, and had finally wound up in Barcelona as a marathon dancer. On the twelfth day of the dance, war broke out and she went to the front as a nurse. She spoke seven languages fluently and her talents finally had been employed by the Press Bureau, who appointed her as a semi-official interpreter for the foreign journalists.' (Source: *Looking for Trouble* by Virginia Cowles, Faber & Faber, 1941, p.32)

[89] *Aquí Kajsa, sabes, la sueca, alta, rubia!* = Kajsa here, you know, the tall, blonde Swedish girl!

[90] Sullivan, British Consul, 'had previously held posts in Chicago and Marseilles.' There is no record of him in the *FCO's British Diplomats Directory*. Not to be confused with Sullivan, the 'rather stupid American photographer' (p.141). Both unidentified.

[91] Stephen Spender (1909-1995): English poet. Joined the Communist Party in 1936 and went to Spain several times in 1937, endeavouring to

obtain the release of his former lover, Tony Hyndman, who was held in a Republican prison on a charge of desertion from the International Brigades. Hyndman was eventually released.

[92] Patience Darton (1911-1996): British nurse who arrived in Spain as a volunteer in February 1937. For more details see her biography, *For Us It Was Heaven: The Passion, Grief and Fortitude of Patience Darton from the Spanish Civil War to Mao's China*, by Angela Jackson, Sussex Academic Press/Cañada Blanch Centre, 2012.

[93] 'Geraldine O'Brien': identified as Mary Mulliner by Paul Preston (*We Saw Spain Die*). He also quotes Claud Cockburn as saying 'had she the words 'I am a Nazi spy' printed on her hat, that could hardly have made her position clearer than it was.'

[94] *Parce que je suis anti-fasciste* = Because I'm an anti-fascist.

[95] *Parce que je suis anti-fasciste et mon mari est blessé de la Brigade* = Because I'm an anti-fascist and my husband was wounded [fighting for] the International Brigade.

[96] *Oh ça ira, ça ira, les aristocrats seront pendus* = Oh, it'll be fine, it'll be fine, the aristocrats will be hung. Popular *sans culotte* song from the French Revolution.

[97] *Oh, assez de Polonais, je m'en fous du Polonais* = Oh, enough about Poles. I'm sick to death of Poles.

[98] Alkeos Angelopoulos (1907-1990): Greek journalist; had previously covered the Italo-Ethiopian War (1935-1936). Later worked for the Encyclopaedia Britannica and the Disney Corporation.

[99] *Mussolini's Roman Empire* by G.T. Garratt, Penguin Books, 1938.

[100] Kate later wrote: 'After I left Spain, I was able to send Quiroga a Dutch cheese. In the spring of 1939 I saw him in Paris in a club for refugees. Paris was then full of Spanish refugees, most of them trying to obtain visas for somewhere else. They had been interned in south-eastern France but France was so full of foreigners at that time, many of them living there illegally, that it was impossible to keep track of them all. Numbers of them escaped from the camps; one told me how he had travelled from Perpignan hidden behind a right-wing French

newspaper. Long afterwards, there was a large colony of them in what used to be French Catalonia; there were many there in 1947.'

[101] Norman Thomas: (1884-1968): 'an American socialist.' *Annotation by Kate Mangan.*

[102] William Gallagher (1881-1965): Scottish trade unionist and communist Member of Parliament.

[103] Ernest Hemingway (1899-1961): US journalist and novelist, particularly famous for his novel *For Whom the Bell Tolls* (1940).

[104] Sidney Franklin (1903-1977): born in Brooklyn, New York. He fought bulls in Mexico and Spain in the late 1920s and early 1930s. (Note based on information from Charlotte Kurzke.)

[105] Martha Gellhorn (1908-1998): American novelist, travel writer and war correspondent; married to Ernest Hemingway from 1940 to 1945.

[106] Otto Katz (1895-1952): born in Jistebnice, Bohemia. He was a Soviet agent, also using the alias André Simone. Kate later wrote. 'Otto had so many narrow escapes, was so really tough underneath the charm, was such an opportunist and seemed to have nine lives, that I was astounded at his fate after 1945. He returned to Prague; he was arrested; produced an abject confession and was executed.' According to Sefton Delmer, 'Simon, alias Otto Katz, the sardonic German Communist director of [the Spanish News Service] had been a member of Münzenberg's propaganda team in Paris. He was liquidated in a purge that followed the Communist takeover of Czechoslovakia in 1948.' (*Trail Sinister* by Sefton Delmer, Secker & Warburg, 1961, p.338).

[107] Duchess of Atholl: Katharine 'Kitty' Stewart-Murray (1874-1960): Scottish Unionist MP, visited Spain in 1937 together with Eleanor Rathbone and Ellen Wilkinson, following which she wrote *Searchlight on Spain*, published as a Penguin Special in 1938.

[108] Eleanor Rathbone (1872-1946): British MP (independent). Visited Spain as a member of a parliamentary delegation in 1937 and set up the Committee on Refugees to assist Spanish evacuees. Her book *War Can Be Averted* was published in 1938.

[109] Ellen Wilkinson (1891-1947): Labour MP for Jarrow and played a key

role in organising the 1936 march. Made several visits to the front line in Republican Spain during the civil war.

[110] Lillian Hellman (1905-1984): American screenwriter and dramatist. Stayed in Spain for a few weeks in 1937 and later clashed with Martha Gellhorn over the recollections in her memoirs. Blacklisted by the House Committee on Un-American Activities.

[111] Louis Fischer (1896-1970): American journalist covering the war for *The Nation*. Later joined the International Brigades. His autobiography, *Men and Politics*, was published in 1940.

[112] Egon Kisch (1885-1948): Austrian/Czechoslovak journalist and member of the Austrian Communist Party.

[113] Ilya Ehrenburg (1891-1967): Russian revolutionary writer and activist. His first novel, *The Extraordinary Adventures of Julio Jurenito and his Disciples* was published in 1928, with an English translation by Usick Vanzler following in 1930.

[114] John Dos Passos (1896-1970): American novelist. Travelled to Spain with Ernest Hemingway in 1937, but fell out over what he claimed was a cover-up of the execution of José Robles as an alleged traitor. Robles was his Spanish translator and father of 'Coco Robles', who worked in the Republican Press Office.

[115] *Ton ami est bien? Toujours il fait le dessin. Nous allons au mitin.* = Is your friend OK? He's always drawing. We're going to the rally.

[116] *Oui, je vais a l'hôpital maintenant, salut.* = Yes, I'm going to the hospital now. *Salud.*

[117] *Hay muchos en las milicias con gafas.* = Lots of people in the militias wear glasses.

[118] *Il a maigri quoi?* = He's lost a lot of weight, wouldn't you say?

[119] *Voyez-vous – ces manières. Ça fait un effet déplorable sur la morale des voluntaires.* = Listen, you should watch your manners. That sort of thing has a terrible effect on the volunteers' morale.

[120] A combined version of the two manuscripts is held at the

International Institute of Social History (IISH) in Amsterdam, under the title *The Good Comrade*. In that version, sections of the two manuscripts are intercalated, and the final chapter is an amalgam of both final chapters. For this publication, Kate's original final chapter has been reinstated. The IISH manuscript, although previously unpublished, has been drawn on extensively by historians of modern Spain, including Soledad Fox, Angela Jackson, Richard Baxell, and Paul Preston.

[121] *Death of Alexander Orlov* by Boris Volodarsky, Oxford University Press, 2015, pp.250-251.

Also available from The Clapton Press:

FIRING A SHOT FOR FREEDOM: THE MEMOIRS OF FRIDA STEWART with a Foreword and Afterword by Angela Jackson
Frida Stewart campaigned tirelessly to raise funds for the Republican cause. She drove an ambulance to Murcia, worked in a hospital and visited the front in Madrid. During the Second World War she was arrested by the Gestapo in Paris and escaped from her internment camp with help from the French Resistance, returning to London where she worked with General de Gaulle.

BRITISH WOMEN AND THE SPANISH CIVIL WAR by Angela Jackson – 2020 Edition
Angela Jackson's classic examination of the interaction between British women and the war in Spain, through their own oral and written narratives. Revised and updated for this new edition.

BOADILLA by Esmond Romilly
The nephew that Winston Churchill disowned describes his experiences fighting with the International Brigade to defend the Spanish Republic. Written on his honeymoon in France after he eloped with Jessica Mitford.

MY HOUSE IN MALAGA by Sir Peter Chalmers Mitchell
While most ex-pats fled to Gibraltar in 1936, Sir Peter stayed on to protect his house and servants from the rebels. He ended up in prison for sheltering Arthur Koestler from Franco's rabid head of propaganda, who had threatened to 'shoot him like a dog'.

SPANISH PORTRAIT by Elizabeth Lake
A brutally honest, semi-autobiographical novel set in San Sebastián and Madrid between 1934 and 1936, portraying a frantic love affair against a background of confusion and apprehension as Spain drifted inexorably towards civil war.

SOME STILL LIVE by F.G. Tinker Jr.
Frank Tinker was a US pilot who signed up with the Republican forces because he didn't like Mussolini. He was also attracted by the prospect of adventure and a generous pay cheque. This is an account of his experiences in Spain.

CPSIA information can be obtained
at www.ICGtesting.com
Printed in the USA
BVHW061043240321
603332BV00002B/151

9 781913 693039